Financial Institutions and Services

An Introduction to the World of Banking Investing, and Insurance

M L Rimorak

Trient Press
3375 S Rainbow Blvd
#81710, SMB 13135
Las Vegas,NV 89180

Ordering Information:
Quantity sales. Special discounts are available on quantity purchases by corporations, associations, and others. For details, contact the publisher at the address above.
Orders by U.S. trade bookstores and wholesalers. Please contact Trient Press: Tel: (775) 996-3844; or visit www.trientpress.com.

Printed in the United States of America

Publisher's Cataloging-in-Publication data
Armstrong, Tracey
A title of a book : Financial Institutions and Services: An Introduction to the World of Banking, Investing, and Insurance
ISBN
Paper Back   979-8-88990-080-1
Ebook   979-8-88990-081-8
Hardcover   979-8-88990-079-5

Financial Institutions and Services

Introduction

Financial institutions play a vital role in the economy, providing services that help individuals, businesses, and governments manage their finances. Banks, credit unions, investment banks, brokerage firms, financial planners, and insurance companies all fall under the umbrella of financial institutions, and understanding how these institutions operate is essential for anyone who wants to make informed financial decisions.

The purpose of this book, Financial Institutions and Services: An Introduction to the World of Banking, Investing, and Insurance, is to provide a comprehensive overview of the various types of financial institutions, the products and services they offer, and the regulatory framework that governs their activities. This book is intended for students entering a first or second-year college course in finance, as well as anyone who wants to gain a better understanding of the financial industry.

The book is organized into seven chapters, each of which focuses on a specific type of financial institution. Chapter I provides an overview of financial institutions, their importance in the economy, and the types of services they offer. The subsequent chapters provide an in-depth analysis of each type of financial institution, including commercial banks, credit unions, investment banks, brokerage firms and financial planners, and insurance companies.

Throughout the book, we will explore the various products and services offered by each type of financial institution, including deposit accounts, loans, credit cards, investment products, and insurance policies. We will also examine the role of regulation in the financial industry, including the various laws and regulations that govern financial institutions, the regulatory agencies responsible for enforcing these laws, and the impact of regulatory changes on the industry.

To ensure a thorough understanding of the material, we will use examples from a variety of fields, including psychology and cognitive science, to help explain complex scientific concepts in a clear and accessible way. We will also present counter-arguments and dissenting opinions in a balanced and objective way, providing students with a nuanced understanding of the financial industry and the challenges it faces.

In addition to the seven chapters, the book will include a conclusion that summarizes the key points covered in the book and emphasizes the importance of financial institutions in the economy. We will also provide a glossary of key terms and concepts to help students master the vocabulary of the financial industry.

Overall, Financial Institutions and Services: An Introduction to the World of Banking, Investing, and Insurance is a comprehensive guide to the financial industry that provides students with the knowledge and skills they need to make informed financial decisions. We hope that this book will serve as a valuable resource for students, educators, and anyone who wants to gain a deeper understanding of the financial world.

Definition of Financial Institutions

Financial institutions are organizations that provide financial products and services to individuals, businesses, and governments. These institutions play a critical role in the economy, helping to allocate capital and manage financial risk. Financial institutions come in many forms, ranging from large commercial banks to small credit unions, and each type of institution has its own unique set of products and services.

In this section, we will provide a more detailed definition of financial institutions, including the types of services they offer and the regulatory framework that governs their activities.

Types of Financial Institutions:

As mentioned earlier, there are many different types of financial institutions, each of which offers a unique set of products and services. The following are some of the most common types of financial institutions:

Commercial Banks: Commercial banks are the most well-known type of financial institution. These banks offer a range of financial products and services, including checking and savings accounts, loans, and credit cards. They also serve as intermediaries between savers and borrowers, taking in deposits from customers and lending that money out to individuals and businesses.

Credit Unions: Credit unions are similar to banks, but they are owned and operated by their members. Credit unions typically offer lower fees and interest rates than banks, and they often focus on providing services to a specific group of people, such as employees of a particular company or members of a specific community.

Investment Banks: Investment banks specialize in providing financial services to large corporations and governments. These services can include underwriting new securities, providing advice on mergers and acquisitions, and managing large investment portfolios.

Brokerage Firms and Financial Planners: Brokerage firms and financial planners provide investment advice and services to individuals and businesses. They can help clients manage their investment portfolios, make investment decisions, and plan for retirement.

Insurance Companies: Insurance companies provide a range of insurance products, including life insurance, health insurance, and property insurance. These companies help individuals and businesses manage financial risk by providing financial protection in the event of an unexpected event, such as a natural disaster or a medical emergency.

Regulatory Framework:

Financial institutions are heavily regulated to ensure that they operate in a safe and sound manner and to protect consumers. The regulatory framework for financial institutions is complex and includes a variety of laws and regulations at both the federal and state level.

At the federal level, the primary regulatory agencies include the Federal Reserve System, the Office of the Comptroller of the Currency, and the Federal Deposit Insurance Corporation. These agencies are responsible for supervising and regulating banks and other financial institutions to ensure that they operate in a safe and sound manner.

In addition to federal regulations, financial institutions are also subject to state-level regulations. Each state has its own regulatory agency responsible for overseeing financial institutions operating within its borders.

Definition of cryptocurrency

Cryptocurrency is a type of digital currency that uses cryptography to secure transactions and to control the creation of new units. Cryptocurrencies are decentralized and operate independently of a central bank or government. They are stored on a distributed ledger called a blockchain, which records all transactions and ensures the integrity of the currency. Cryptocurrencies have gained widespread attention in recent years due to their potential as an alternative to traditional currencies, their potential as an investment, and their use in various types of online transactions.

History of Cryptocurrency

The history of cryptocurrency can be traced back to the late 1990s when the concept of digital currencies was first introduced. However, it was not until the release of Bitcoin in 2009 that the world saw the first fully functioning cryptocurrency. Bitcoin was created by an unknown person or group of people under the pseudonym Satoshi Nakamoto, and it was designed as a peer-to-peer electronic cash system that would allow people to send and receive payments without the need for a centralized authority.

Since then, thousands of other cryptocurrencies have been created, each with its own unique features and characteristics. Some of the most popular cryptocurrencies include Ethereum, Ripple, Litecoin, and Bitcoin Cash. As of 2021, the total market capitalization of cryptocurrencies was around $1.5 trillion, and there were more than 9,000 different cryptocurrencies in circulation.

How Cryptocurrency Works

Cryptocurrency is based on blockchain technology, which is a decentralized ledger that records all transactions in a secure and transparent manner. Each block in the blockchain contains a list of transactions, and once a block is added to the chain, it cannot be altered or deleted. This makes the blockchain a reliable and tamper-proof system for recording transactions.

When a user wants to send cryptocurrency to someone else, they create a transaction that is verified by other users on the network. Once the transaction is verified, it is added to the blockchain, and the recipient can then access the funds.

Mining Cryptocurrency

In order to create new units of cryptocurrency, a process called mining is used. Mining involves using powerful computers to solve complex mathematical equations, which help to validate transactions and add new blocks to the blockchain. As a reward for this work, miners are paid in the cryptocurrency they are mining.

The amount of cryptocurrency that can be mined is usually fixed, which means that the supply is limited. This is one of the key features of cryptocurrency, as it helps to prevent inflation and ensures that the currency is not subject to the same economic pressures as traditional currencies.

Uses of Cryptocurrency

Cryptocurrency has a wide range of uses, from being used as a means of payment to being used as an investment. Some of the most common uses of cryptocurrency include:

Payment: Cryptocurrency can be used to pay for goods and services online, and it can be sent and received anywhere in the world. Because it is decentralized and operates independently of a central bank, it can be used to avoid traditional banking fees and regulations.

Investment: Many people view cryptocurrency as a potential investment, as its value can fluctuate widely over time. Some investors buy and hold cryptocurrency in the hope that its value will increase, while others trade it actively in order to profit from short-term price movements.

Fundraising: Some companies and organizations use cryptocurrency as a means of raising funds. They may create their own cryptocurrency and sell it to investors in exchange for traditional currency, which can then be used to finance projects or operations.

Asset transfer: Cryptocurrency can be used to transfer assets, such as real estate or stocks, without the need for a middleman or a central authority. This can help to reduce costs and streamline the transfer process.

Criticism of Cryptocurrency

Despite its many potential benefits, cryptocurrency has also faced criticism from some quarters.

Criticism of cryptocurrency has been widespread and varied, with concerns ranging from its lack of regulation to its potential for criminal activity. Some of the main criticisms of cryptocurrency include:

Volatility: One of the most common criticisms of cryptocurrency is its volatility. Cryptocurrencies are known for their wild fluctuations in value, with prices sometimes rising or falling by as much as 20% or more in a single day. This can make it difficult for investors to predict how much their investments will be worth in the future, and can make it risky for businesses to accept cryptocurrencies as payment.

Lack of regulation: Another major criticism of cryptocurrency is the lack of regulation. Unlike traditional currencies, which are subject to strict government oversight and regulation, cryptocurrencies are not backed by any government or financial institution. This can make them more susceptible to fraud and other criminal activity, as well as making it difficult for investors to know whether or not they can trust the companies or exchanges that deal in cryptocurrencies.

Security concerns: Cryptocurrency is often touted as being more secure than traditional forms of currency, but it has also faced criticism for its own security vulnerabilities. Because cryptocurrencies are stored on decentralized networks and are often traded anonymously, they can be more vulnerable to hacking and other forms of cybercrime. This has led to several high-profile cases of cryptocurrency theft, including the Mt. Gox exchange hack in 2014, which saw over 850,000 bitcoins stolen.

Environmental concerns: Another criticism of cryptocurrency is its impact on the environment. Cryptocurrency mining requires large amounts of energy, and some estimates suggest that the amount of energy used by the Bitcoin network alone is equivalent to the energy consumption of a small country. This has led to concerns about the environmental impact of cryptocurrency mining, particularly in regions where energy is generated from fossil fuels.

Lack of widespread adoption: Despite the growing popularity of cryptocurrency, it still faces challenges when it comes to widespread adoption. Many businesses and individuals are hesitant to embrace cryptocurrencies due to their volatility, lack of regulation, and other concerns. This can make it difficult for cryptocurrency to become a widely accepted form of payment or investment.

Association with criminal activity: Finally, cryptocurrency has faced criticism for its association with criminal activity. Because cryptocurrencies can be traded anonymously and are not subject to government oversight, they have been used in a number of illegal activities, including money laundering, drug trafficking, and terrorism financing. This has led some governments to crack down on cryptocurrency exchanges and other forms of cryptocurrency trading.

Overall, while cryptocurrency has the potential to revolutionize the way we think about money and finance, it also faces a number of significant challenges and criticisms. Whether or not cryptocurrency will be able to overcome these challenges and become a widely accepted form of currency remains to be seen.

Importance of cryptocurrency in modern society

Cryptocurrency, a digital or virtual currency that is secured by cryptography and operates independently of a central bank, has gained significant attention in recent years. While its volatility and regulatory concerns have been widely debated, there is no denying the importance of cryptocurrency in modern society. In this section, we will explore the different ways in which cryptocurrency is important in modern society.

Decentralization of finance:
The traditional financial system is centralized, meaning that it is controlled by a few major players such as banks and governments. This centralization has led to a lack of transparency and trust, as well as high transaction fees and slow processing times. Cryptocurrency, on the other hand, operates on a decentralized system, where transactions are verified and recorded on a public ledger called the blockchain. This decentralization has several benefits, including:

Increased transparency: Transactions are recorded on a public ledger, allowing anyone to view them.
Greater security: Transactions are secured through complex cryptographic algorithms, making them virtually impossible to hack or alter.
Lower transaction fees: Transactions can be conducted directly between individuals, eliminating the need for intermediaries and reducing transaction fees.
Financial inclusion:
Cryptocurrency has the potential to increase financial inclusion, particularly for those who are underserved by the traditional financial system. According to a report by the World Bank, there are approximately 1.7 billion adults worldwide who do not have access to a bank account. Cryptocurrency can provide these individuals with a means of conducting financial transactions without the need for a traditional bank account. This can include:

Remittances: Cryptocurrency can be used to send money across borders quickly and inexpensively.

Microtransactions: Cryptocurrency can enable small transactions that would not be cost-effective using traditional payment methods.

Alternative financing: Cryptocurrency can provide a means of financing for small businesses and startups that may not be able to access traditional financing.

Empowerment of individuals:

Cryptocurrency empowers individuals by giving them greater control over their finances. With traditional financial systems, individuals are often at the mercy of banks and governments, which can restrict access to funds or freeze accounts. Cryptocurrency, on the other hand, provides individuals with greater financial autonomy by:

Allowing individuals to control their own funds: With cryptocurrency, individuals are in complete control of their funds and do not need to rely on intermediaries.

Providing a means of conducting transactions anonymously: Cryptocurrency can provide greater privacy for individuals, allowing them to conduct transactions without revealing personal information.

Facilitating peer-to-peer transactions: Cryptocurrency allows individuals to conduct transactions directly with one another, without the need for intermediaries.

Innovation:

Cryptocurrency has spurred innovation in the financial industry, driving the development of new technologies and business models. This innovation includes:

Blockchain technology: The blockchain technology that underpins cryptocurrency has many potential applications beyond finance, including supply chain management, voting systems, and more.

Cryptocurrency exchanges: The rise of cryptocurrency has led to the development of new types of financial institutions, such as cryptocurrency exchanges, which provide a means of buying and selling cryptocurrency.

Decentralized applications: Decentralized applications, or dApps, are applications that operate on a blockchain and do not require a central authority to function. These dApps have the potential to revolutionize many industries, from healthcare to real estate.

International trade:

Cryptocurrency has the potential to facilitate international trade by eliminating barriers such as currency conversion and high transaction fees. Cryptocurrency can be used as a means of payment for goods and services, making it an attractive option for businesses engaged in international trade. Additionally, cryptocurrency can facilitate cross-border transactions, enabling individuals to conduct business with one another regardless of geographic location.

Conclusion:

Cryptocurrency has become an increasingly important part of modern society, offering many benefits such as increased financial freedom, security, and accessibility. While there are certainly challenges and criticisms facing the world of cryptocurrency, its potential for positive impact cannot be ignored.

As the technology and adoption of cryptocurrency continues to evolve, it is likely that its importance in modern society will only continue to grow. From providing financial access to the unbanked, to enabling global commerce and decentralized applications, cryptocurrency has the potential to revolutionize the way we interact with money and information.

It is important for individuals, businesses, and governments to carefully consider the potential benefits and risks of cryptocurrency, and to approach its use and regulation in a thoughtful and informed manner.

Overall, while cryptocurrency may still be in its early stages, its impact on modern society is already significant and will likely continue to shape the future of finance and technology for years to come.

Conclusion:

In conclusion, financial institutions play a critical role in the economy by providing a range of financial products and services to individuals, businesses, and governments. These institutions come in many forms, from large commercial banks to small credit unions, and each type of institution has its own unique set of products and services.

Financial institutions are heavily regulated to ensure that they operate in a safe and sound manner and to protect consumers. The regulatory framework for financial institutions is complex and includes a variety of laws and regulations at both the federal and state level. It is essential that students entering the world of finance have a solid understanding of financial institutions and the regulatory framework that governs their activities.

Importance of Financial Institutions in the economy

Financial institutions play a vital role in any modern economy. They provide essential financial services to individuals, businesses, and governments. The importance of financial institutions in the economy cannot be overstated. This section will discuss the significance of financial institutions in the economy and how they help promote economic growth.

The Role of Financial Institutions in Economic Development:

Financial institutions serve as intermediaries between savers and investors. They facilitate the flow of funds from savers to borrowers and provide a range of financial services. The availability of financial services is crucial for economic development. Financial institutions provide capital to businesses, enabling them to invest in new projects, expand their operations, and create jobs. Financial institutions also provide financial services to households, such as loans for education, housing, and personal consumption. The availability of credit is essential for households to make significant purchases and investments.

Promotion of Economic Growth:

Financial institutions play a crucial role in promoting economic growth. They provide the necessary funding for businesses to invest in new projects and expand their operations. By doing so, financial institutions help create jobs and increase productivity, which leads to economic growth. Furthermore, financial institutions provide the necessary capital for research and development, which is essential for innovation and technological advancement. These developments lead to new products and services, which further stimulate economic growth.

The Importance of Financial Stability:

Financial institutions also play a vital role in maintaining financial stability in the economy. They are responsible for managing financial risks, such as credit and market risks. In doing so, they help prevent financial crises that could have severe consequences for the economy. Financial institutions also provide financial services to governments, such as managing public debt, which helps maintain fiscal stability.

Financial Inclusion:

Financial institutions play a crucial role in promoting financial inclusion. They provide access to financial services to individuals and businesses that might not otherwise have access to them. Financial inclusion is essential for promoting economic growth and reducing poverty. By providing access to financial services, financial institutions enable individuals and businesses to save, invest, and access credit, which can improve their financial well-being.

Conclusion:

Financial institutions are essential to any modern economy. They provide a range of financial services to individuals, businesses, and governments. The availability of financial services is crucial for economic development, promoting economic growth, maintaining financial stability, and promoting financial inclusion.

CHAPTER 1 : ANCIENT BANKING AND COMMERCE

Banking and commerce are some of the oldest professions in human history. The exchange of goods and services has been a crucial part of human civilization since the earliest times, and the development of banking has been instrumental in facilitating this exchange. The origins of banking and commerce can be traced back to ancient civilizations such as Mesopotamia, Egypt, Greece, and Rome, where the first banking systems and financial instruments were developed.

This section will provide a brief overview of the history of banking and commerce, starting from their ancient origins and leading up to modern times. We will explore the various forms of banking and commerce that have emerged over time, the key developments that have shaped their evolution, and the impact they have had on society and the economy.

Ancient Mesopotamia and Egypt

The origins of banking and commerce can be traced back to ancient Mesopotamia, which was located in the region now known as Iraq. The Mesopotamians developed a system of grain banks around 2000 BCE, which allowed farmers to store their crops in a centralized location and obtain credit against their future harvests. This was one of the earliest forms of banking, and it helped to facilitate trade and commerce in the region.

In ancient Egypt, the pharaohs developed a system of taxation and record-keeping that relied on the use of papyrus scrolls. This system of accounting helped to facilitate trade and commerce, and it laid the foundation for the development of more sophisticated financial instruments such as bills of exchange and promissory notes.

Ancient Greece and Rome

The ancient Greeks and Romans also played a significant role in the development of banking and commerce. In Greece, the temple of Apollo at Delphi served as a central repository for coins and other valuables, and it facilitated trade and commerce between the various Greek city-states. The

Greeks also developed the concept of the trireme, which was a type of warship that could also be used for trade and commerce.

In Rome, the development of banking and commerce was closely tied to the expansion of the Roman Empire. The Romans developed a system of public banking, which allowed them to finance their military campaigns and public works projects. They also developed a sophisticated system of trade and commerce that relied on the use of coinage and bills of exchange.

Medieval Europe

The Middle Ages saw the emergence of a new form of banking and commerce in Europe. During this time, feudal lords and monarchs began to borrow money from wealthy merchants and bankers in order to finance their wars and other endeavors. This led to the development of private banking and the emergence of the first merchant banks, which were established to facilitate international trade and commerce.

The merchant banks of medieval Europe were instrumental in the development of bills of exchange, which were used to facilitate trade between different regions and countries. These bills of exchange were the precursor to modern-day checks, and they helped to facilitate the exchange of goods and services across borders.

Industrial Revolution

The Industrial Revolution in the 18th and 19th centuries brought about significant changes in banking and commerce. The growth of industry and commerce led to an increase in demand for credit and capital, which led to the development of new financial instruments such as stocks, bonds, and futures contracts.

The growth of banking and commerce during the Industrial Revolution also led to the emergence of new financial institutions, such as investment banks and stock exchanges. These institutions played a crucial role in the growth of capitalism and the expansion of global trade and commerce.

Modern Times

In the 20th and 21st centuries, banking and commerce have continued to evolve and change in response to new technologies and changing economic conditions. The development of computers and the internet has led to the emergence of new forms of banking and commerce, such as online banking and e-commerce.

The global economy has also become increasingly interconnected, with international trade and investment growing rapidly over the past few decades. As a result, the role of banks and other financial institutions has become more important than ever before, as they facilitate the movement of capital and the financing of international trade.

However, the global financial system has also faced numerous challenges and crises in recent years. The 2008 financial crisis, for example, was a major shock to the global economy, causing significant disruptions in the banking and financial sectors. This crisis highlighted the need for increased regulation and oversight of the financial industry, as well as the importance of effective risk management and the need for more transparency in financial transactions.

In addition, the rise of new technologies and the emergence of digital currencies have created new challenges and opportunities for the banking and financial industry. Cryptocurrencies, for example, offer the potential for greater transparency and security in financial transactions, but also raise questions about regulation and oversight.

Despite these challenges, banking and commerce remain essential components of the global economy, playing a crucial role in facilitating trade, investment, and economic growth. As such, they will continue to evolve and adapt to new technologies and changing economic conditions, ensuring their ongoing relevance and importance in the modern world.

Bartering as the earliest form of trade

Bartering is the oldest known method of trade and commerce, dating back to prehistoric times. It was used by early humans as a means of obtaining goods and services they could not produce themselves, such as food, tools, and clothing. Bartering involves the exchange of goods or services for other goods or services, without the use of money. This practice was the precursor to the modern economic system of buying and selling goods and services for currency.

The Basics of Bartering

Bartering is a simple process that involves trading one good or service for another. In a bartering transaction, each party brings something of value to the table and both parties leave with something they need or want. For example, a farmer may barter some of their crops to a blacksmith in exchange for tools, or a carpenter may trade furniture they made for a cow from a nearby farm.

The Advantages of Bartering

Bartering has several advantages over more modern forms of trade and commerce. One of the most significant benefits of bartering is that it allows people to obtain goods and services without the use of currency. This means that individuals who do not have access to money can still obtain the items they need to survive. Additionally, bartering can be a more direct and personal form of trade, as it often involves face-to-face interactions and negotiations between individuals.

The Challenges of Bartering

Although bartering has its advantages, it also has several challenges that can make it difficult to use as a primary form of commerce. One of the biggest challenges of bartering is the issue of value. When two parties engage in a bartering transaction, it can be difficult to determine the value of the goods or services being exchanged. This can lead to disagreements or misunderstandings, which can hinder the success of the transaction. Additionally, bartering can be a time-consuming process, as it often requires negotiation and the physical exchange of goods or services.

The Role of Bartering in Modern Society

While bartering is not commonly used as a primary form of trade in modern society, it still plays a role in certain industries and communities. For example, in some rural areas, farmers and ranchers may engage in bartering to obtain the goods and services they need to operate their businesses. Additionally, some small businesses may barter their goods or services with other businesses as a way to save money on expenses or acquire resources they need.

The Future of Bartering

The future of bartering remains uncertain, as it is unlikely to become a primary form of commerce in modern society. However, as more people become interested in sustainable living and alternative forms of commerce, it is possible that bartering may experience a resurgence. Additionally, as technology continues to evolve, new forms of bartering may emerge that make the process easier and more efficient.

Conclusion

Bartering is the oldest known form of trade and commerce, dating back to prehistoric times. It involves the exchange of goods or services without the use of money, and has several advantages over modern forms of trade, such as the ability to obtain goods and services without currency. However, bartering also has several challenges, such as determining the value of goods and services, and can be a time-consuming process. While it is unlikely to become a primary form of commerce in modern society, it still plays a role in certain industries and communities, and may experience a resurgence as interest in sustainable living and alternative forms of commerce grows.

Emergence of currency

The use of currency as a medium of exchange is an essential aspect of modern economies. It allows for the exchange of goods and services across different regions and enables the accumulation of wealth. However, the concept of currency did not always exist, and it has evolved over time. This section will explore the emergence of currency and its role in economic development.

Barter to Currency:

Before currency, the earliest form of trade was bartering, where people exchanged goods and services directly. While bartering was a practical method of trade, it had limitations. For instance, the value of goods could not be easily measured, and it was challenging to find someone willing to exchange the desired goods or services.

As trade grew, people began to develop systems to address these limitations. One such system was commodity money, where goods with intrinsic value such as gold, silver, or salt were used as a medium of exchange. However, this system had its drawbacks, such as the challenge of storing and transporting valuable commodities.

Development of Currency:

To overcome the challenges of commodity money, societies began to develop currencies that had no intrinsic value but were backed by a central authority, such as a government or a religious institution. These currencies, made of precious metals or paper, were easier to transport and store, and their value was guaranteed by the backing authority.

The first known currency was created in Lydia, a kingdom in Asia Minor, around 600 BCE. Lydia's currency was made of electrum, a naturally occurring alloy of gold and silver. Other ancient civilizations such as China, India, and Rome also developed their own currencies.

As currency became more widespread, it helped to stimulate trade and economic growth. It allowed people to exchange goods and services more easily, facilitating commerce and enabling the accumulation of wealth.

Modern Currency:

Today, currency takes many different forms, including physical banknotes and coins, digital currencies such as Bitcoin, and even non-fungible tokens (NFTs). While the fundamental principles of currency remain the same, technological advancements and changing economic conditions have led to new forms of currency and new ways of using them.

The role of central banks and governments in managing currencies has also evolved over time. Many countries have adopted a system of fiat currency, where the value of the currency is not linked to any physical commodity but is based on the strength of the economy and the government's ability to maintain its value.

Conclusion:

Currency has played a vital role in the development of modern economies. From the early days of bartering to the creation of currencies backed by central authorities, the evolution of currency has enabled people to exchange goods and services more easily and facilitated economic growth. As technology continues to advance, new forms of currency are likely to emerge, shaping the future of trade and commerce.

Mesopotamian banking and accounting

Mesopotamia, located in present-day Iraq, is often considered the birthplace of modern civilization. The region was home to several powerful empires, including the Sumerians, Akkadians, Babylonians, and Assyrians, all of whom made significant contributions to the fields of banking and accounting.

Banking in Mesopotamia

The Mesopotamians are believed to have been the first civilization to use a form of banking. They developed an advanced system of credit, loans, and interest, which allowed them to conduct complex economic transactions.

One of the most important institutions in Mesopotamian banking was the temple. Temples served as both religious and economic centers, and their vast resources made them powerful players in the Mesopotamian economy. Temples acted as lenders, borrowers, and guarantors of loans, and they played a critical role in the development of credit.

The temple-based banking system was based on a system of debits and credits. Accounts were kept using clay tablets, which recorded transactions in cuneiform script. These tablets served as early accounting ledgers, and they have provided modern scholars with valuable insights into the workings of the Mesopotamian economy.

The temple-based banking system was also responsible for the development of the first forms of currency in Mesopotamia. Temples issued their own forms of currency, which could be used to pay for goods and services within the temple's sphere of influence.

Accounting in Mesopotamia

The Mesopotamians were also pioneers in the field of accounting. They developed an advanced system of record-keeping that allowed them to track complex economic transactions. The system was based on the use of clay tablets, which were inscribed with cuneiform script.

The Mesopotamians used a double-entry bookkeeping system, which was based on the principle of balancing debits and credits. This system allowed them to keep track of multiple transactions at once, and it was an important precursor to modern accounting practices.

The Mesopotamians also developed sophisticated methods of calculating interest and depreciation. They used mathematical formulas to calculate interest rates, and they had a clear understanding of the concept of compound interest. They also developed methods for calculating the depreciation of assets, which allowed them to accurately track the value of their holdings over time.

The Mesopotamians were also the first to develop a code of ethics for accountants. They recognized the importance of honesty and accuracy in accounting, and they punished those who violated these principles. This code of ethics was an important precursor to modern accounting standards.

Legacy of Mesopotamian Banking and Accounting

The legacy of Mesopotamian banking and accounting can still be seen in modern financial systems. Many of the practices and principles developed by the Mesopotamians, such as double-entry bookkeeping, interest calculations, and codes of ethics, are still in use today.

The Mesopotamians also made significant contributions to the development of trade and commerce. Their advanced banking and accounting systems allowed them to conduct complex economic transactions, which helped to drive economic growth and development.

Conclusion

The Mesopotamians were pioneers in the fields of banking and accounting. They developed sophisticated systems of credit, loans, and interest, which allowed them to conduct complex economic transactions. They also developed advanced methods of record-keeping and accounting, which were based on the use of clay tablets inscribed with cuneiform script.

The legacy of Mesopotamian banking and accounting can still be seen in modern financial systems. Many of the practices and principles developed by the Mesopotamians are still in use today, and their contributions to the development of trade and commerce were critical in shaping the modern world.

Roman banking and credit

The Romans were known for their impressive achievements in architecture, literature, art, and law, but they also made significant contributions to the world of banking and finance. Roman banking and credit were crucial to the growth and stability of the Roman economy, and their influence can still be seen in modern banking practices today.

This section will provide an in-depth analysis of Roman banking and credit. We will explore the history of Roman banking, the types of financial institutions that existed in ancient Rome, the role of credit in Roman society, and the impact of Roman banking and credit on the modern world.

History of Roman Banking:

Roman banking can be traced back to the 3rd century BCE when Rome was still a republic. At that time, the main function of banks was to exchange foreign currencies and to provide safe storage for wealthy citizens. The first Roman banks were privately owned and operated by wealthy individuals. However, as Rome grew into an empire, the government began to play a more active role in the banking industry.

Types of Financial Institutions:

There were several types of financial institutions that existed in ancient Rome. These included:

Argentarii: These were private bankers who conducted business in their own homes or shops. They offered a range of services, including exchanging currencies, providing loans, and storing money and valuables for their clients.

Mensarii: These were state bankers who were responsible for collecting taxes and other government revenues. They also lent money to the government and to private citizens.

Nummularii: These were money changers who exchanged small coins for larger denominations. They were often found in markets and were an essential part of the Roman economy.

Role of Credit:

Credit played a significant role in Roman society. The wealthy elite used credit to finance their businesses and to invest in real estate. The Roman government also used credit to finance public projects such as aqueducts and roads.

One of the most significant developments in Roman credit was the creation of the negotium traiectum, or negotiable instrument. This was a form of credit that could be traded between individuals and could be redeemed for cash at a later date. These instruments made it easier for individuals to conduct business and helped to promote economic growth.

Impact on Modern Banking:

The legacy of Roman banking and credit can still be seen in modern banking practices today. The concept of the negotiable instrument, for example, has evolved into the modern-day check. Additionally, many modern banking terms, such as "debit," "credit," and "balance," have their roots in Latin.

Conclusion:

Roman banking and credit were essential to the growth and stability of the Roman economy. The development of financial institutions, such as private and state banks, and the use of credit and negotiable instruments, helped to promote economic growth and to finance public projects. The influence of Roman banking and credit can still be seen in modern banking practices today.

CHAPTER 2: MEDIEVAL BANKING AND COMMERCE

The medieval period, spanning from the 5th to the 15th century, is often referred to as the "Dark Ages". However, this era witnessed significant developments in banking and commerce, which laid the foundation for modern financial systems. The feudal system, where lords granted lands to vassals in exchange for loyalty and military service, dominated medieval Europe. As a result, commerce and trade were localized, and there was no central authority regulating economic activity. In this section, we will explore the emergence of medieval banking and commerce, the role of the Church, and the development of trade fairs and banking institutions.

Emergence of Medieval Banking and Commerce

The feudal system was not conducive to commerce and trade, and the majority of economic activity was based on subsistence agriculture. However, with the growth of towns and cities, there was an increased demand for goods and services, which led to the emergence of a merchant class. These merchants engaged in long-distance trade, importing and exporting goods from different parts of Europe and the East. The expansion of trade routes, such as the Silk Road, also facilitated trade between Europe and Asia.

However, long-distance trade posed several challenges, such as the risk of piracy, theft, and currency exchange. Merchants needed a secure way to transport their goods and protect their wealth. This led to the development of medieval banking, where merchants deposited their wealth with trusted individuals or institutions, who issued letters of credit or bills of exchange. These financial instruments enabled merchants to transact business without carrying large amounts of cash, and they could be exchanged for goods or cash in different locations.

Role of the Church in Medieval Banking

The Church played a crucial role in medieval banking, as it was the only institution with the power and influence to regulate economic activity. The Church had strict rules against charging interest on loans, which was seen as a sin. However, it allowed for the concept of usury, which allowed for the charging of reasonable fees for the use of money.

The Church also encouraged the development of charitable institutions, such as hospitals, orphanages, and monasteries, which provided loans to the poor and needy. These institutions became the first banks in Europe, and they played a significant role in providing credit to merchants and facilitating economic activity.

Development of Trade Fairs and Banking Institutions

Trade fairs were an important feature of medieval commerce, where merchants from different regions gathered to trade their goods. These fairs were held at regular intervals and provided a platform for merchants to exchange goods and information. The fairs were also a place for banking activities, where merchants could deposit their wealth, exchange currencies, and obtain credit.

As trade expanded, so did the need for specialized banking institutions. The first commercial banks in Europe emerged in Italy in the 14th century, such as the Medici Bank and the Banco di San Giorgio. These banks provided loans to governments, financed long-distance trade, and facilitated currency exchange. They also developed the concept of double-entry bookkeeping, which enabled accurate record-keeping and financial reporting.

Conclusion

Medieval banking and commerce laid the foundation for modern financial systems, and the developments of this era still influence the way we conduct business today. The emergence of a merchant class, the role of the Church, the development of trade fairs, and the creation of banking institutions all played a significant role in shaping the economic landscape of medieval Europe. These developments allowed for increased economic activity, specialization, and innovation, paving the way for the growth of modern economies.

Development of paper money in China

Paper money is a form of currency made from paper or banknotes that are accepted as legal tender by a country's government. The development of paper money is an important milestone in the history of currency. China is often credited with inventing paper money, as it was the first country to use it on a large scale. This section will explore the development of paper money in China, from its origins to its widespread use.

Origins of paper money in China:

The use of paper money in China can be traced back to the Tang Dynasty (618-907 AD), when merchants would deposit their goods with government officials in exchange for a paper receipt. This receipt could then be used to redeem the goods at a later time. The use of these paper receipts was a more convenient alternative to carrying heavy amounts of copper coins, which were the predominant form of currency at the time.

During the Song Dynasty (960-1279 AD), the use of paper money became more widespread. The government began issuing paper money in the form of promissory notes, which were backed by the government's promise to pay in silver or gold. These notes were widely accepted and soon became the preferred form of currency.

The benefits of paper money:

The use of paper money brought several benefits to China's economy. First, it was more convenient than carrying around heavy coins. Second, it allowed for more efficient trade, as it was easier to transport paper money than coins. Third, it reduced the risk of theft, as paper money was less desirable to thieves than coins. Finally, it helped to unify China's economy, as paper money was accepted throughout the country.

The drawbacks of paper money:

Despite its benefits, paper money also had its drawbacks. Counterfeiting was a major problem, as counterfeiters could easily replicate the paper used to make the notes. This led to the government taking measures to prevent counterfeiting, such as using watermarks and other security features.

Another drawback was inflation. As the government could print more paper money than it had silver or gold to back it, the value of the paper money decreased over time. This led to inflation, which could be detrimental to the economy.

The spread of paper money:

Paper money eventually spread beyond China's borders. In the 13th century, the Mongol Empire began using paper money, which they called "chao." The use of paper money then spread to the Middle East and Europe. However, it was not until the 17th century that paper money became widely used in Europe, with the introduction of banknotes by the Bank of Stockholm in Sweden.

Conclusion:

The development of paper money in China was a significant milestone in the history of currency. It allowed for more efficient trade, reduced the risk of theft, and helped to unify China's economy. However, it also had its drawbacks, such as counterfeiting and inflation. Despite these drawbacks, the use of paper money eventually spread to other countries and became a widely accepted form of currency.

Medieval European banking and commerce

Medieval European banking and commerce refer to the economic activities that took place during the Middle Ages in Europe, specifically between the 5th and 15th centuries. This period was characterized by feudalism, the manorial system, and the growth of towns, which led to the development of trade and commerce. During this time, there was an increase in economic transactions, and this led to the need for financial institutions to facilitate these transactions. This section will explore the development of medieval European banking and commerce, the institutions that emerged, and the impact they had on the economy.

The Emergence of Medieval European Banking and Commerce

During the early Middle Ages, economic activity was mainly centered on the manor. However, the growth of towns led to the development of a merchant class, and this gave rise to a more complex economic system. The development of trade and commerce led to the need for financial institutions to facilitate transactions, and this gave rise to the emergence of medieval European banking.

The earliest banks in medieval Europe were developed in Italy during the 12th century. These banks were known as "merchant banks," and they provided financial services to the merchant class. The primary function of these banks was to provide loans to merchants who needed capital to finance their trade. The banks would also issue bills of exchange, which were used to facilitate international trade. These bills of exchange were similar to modern-day checks and were used to transfer funds from one location to another.

As trade and commerce continued to grow in medieval Europe, the need for financial institutions increased. By the 14th century, banking had spread throughout Europe, and new institutions had emerged to cater to the growing demand for financial services. These institutions included:

The Medici Bank: This bank was established in Florence, Italy, in the 14th century. It was one of the most prominent banks of its time and played a significant role in the development of the Italian Renaissance. The bank provided financial services to the Pope and various European monarchs, and it also financed major public worforcing insurance laws and regulations, licensing insurance companies and agents, approving insurance policies, and overseeing insurance company financial stability. The state insurance department also conducts examinations of insurance companies to ensure that theyare complying with state laws and regulations.

National Association of Insurance Commissioners (NAIC)

The National Association of Insurance Commissioners (NAIC) is a national organization of state insurance regulators that develops model laws and regul ations for insurance companies and provides a forum for state regulators to share information and coordinate their efforts. The NAIC also provides a central repository for insurance company financi al information, which is used by state regulators to monitor the financial health of insurance companies.

Federal Insurance Office (FIO)

The Federal Insurance Office (FIO) is a federal agency that monitors the insurance industry and provides advice to federal policymakers on insurance issues. The FIO is part of the U.S. Department of the Treasury and was created by the Dodd-Frank Wall Street Reform and Consumer Protection Act of 2010. The FIO's responsibilities include identifying issues and gaps in the regulation of insurance companies, monitoring the insurance industry's systemic risk, and representing the United States in international insurance matters.

Types of Insurance Regulation

Insurance regulation can be divided into several categories, including solvency regulation, market conduct regulation, and consumer protection regulation.

Sol vency Regulation

Solvency regulation is the process of ensuring that insurance companies have sufficient financial resources to meet their obligations to policyholders. Solvency regulation typically involves the following:

Minimum cap

Emergence of merchant banks

i tal and surplus requirements: Insurance companies must maintain a certain amount of capital and surplus to ensure that they can meet their financial obligations to policyholders.

Risk-based capital requirements: Insurance companies muviding specialized financial services to merchants, such as foreign exchange, credit, and investment advice. This section will explore the emergence of merchant banks in medieval Europe and their impact on the development of European commerce.

Origins of Merchant Banking:
Merchant banking emerged in Italy in the 13th century, with the development of banking centers in Florence, Genoa, and Venice. These cities had thriving merchant communities engaged in international trade, which required a sophisticated system of financial services to facilitate transactions. The merchant banks that emerged in these cities were typically family-run businesses, which relied on personal relationships with their clients to establish trust and loyalty.

The Rise of the Medici Family:
One of the most prominent merchant banking families was the Medici family of Florence, who rose to prominence in the 14th century. The Medici family established a network of banks throughout Europe, which provided credit, foreign exchange, and investment advice to merchants. The Medici family also played a significant role in the development of the Renaissance, sponsoring artists and scholars and commissioning works of art.

The Role of Merchant Banks in International Trade:
Merchant banks played a crucial role in facilitating international trade, which was the backbone of the medieval European economy. Merchant banks provided credit to merchants to finance their voyages, which were often risky and expensive. They also provided foreign exchange services, allowing merchants to exchange one currency for another at a fair rate. This was crucial

for international trade, as merchants needed to be able to pay for goods and services in the local currency.

The Emergence of Joint Stock Companies:
Merchant banks also played a significant role in the development of joint-stock companies, which emerged in the late 16th century. Joint-stock companies were a new form of business organization, which allowed investors to pool their resources and share the risks and profits of a venture. Merchant banks provided the financial services necessary to support joint-stock companies, such as underwriting, which involved guaranteeing the sale of shares in a company.

The Decline of Merchant Banking:
Merchant banking declined in the 17th and 18th centuries, as traditional banks began to offer the same services as merchant banks. Traditional banks, which were often larger and more established than merchant banks, were able to offer credit at lower interest rates, making it difficult for merchant banks to compete. The rise of colonialism and imperialism also played a role in the decline of merchant banking, as the focus of international trade shifted from Europe to the colonies.

Conclusion:
Merchant banking played a significant role in the development of European commerce, providing specialized financial services to merchants engaged in international trade. Merchant banks facilitated the growth of joint-stock companies, which were a new form of business organization that allowed investors to pool their resources and share the risks and profits of a venture. Although merchant banking declined in the 17th and 18th centuries, its legacy continued in the form of modern investment banking, which provides similar services to those offered by medieval merchant banks.

The Medici family and their influence on banking

The Medici family is one of the most well-known families in the history of banking. They were a powerful and wealthy family who dominated the economic and political scene in Florence during the 15th century. Their influence on the banking industry was significant, as they were the pioneers of modern banking practices, which laid the foundation for the banking system we know today. This section will delve into the history of the Medici family and their impact on the banking industry.

History of the Medici Family:

The Medici family was a wealthy banking family that originated from Florence, Italy. They started their banking business in the 13th century and quickly became one of the wealthiest and most influential families in Italy. The family was involved in various businesses, including wool trade, textile production, and banking.

The Medici family gained political power in the 15th century when Cosimo de' Medici became the unofficial ruler of Florence. Under his leadership, Florence flourished both economically and culturally. The Medici family continued to hold political power in Florence for several generations and produced four popes.

Impact on Banking:
The Medici family played a significant role in the development of modern banking practices. They were responsible for many innovations that changed the way banking was conducted during their time. Some of the key innovations that the Medici family introduced to banking include:

Double-Entry Bookkeeping: The Medici family was the first to use double-entry bookkeeping in their banking business. This system helped them keep track of their finances more accurately and efficiently.

Letters of Credit: The Medici family introduced the use of letters of credit, which allowed merchants to conduct business without carrying large amounts of cash. This system made international trade more efficient and secure.

Banking Networks: The Medici family established a network of banks throughout Europe, which made it easier for them to conduct business across borders.

Investment Banking: The Medici family was also involved in investment banking, which involved investing money in various businesses and ventures. This practice helped them diversify their wealth and grow their business empire.

The Medici family's innovations transformed the banking industry and laid the foundation for the modern banking system we know today.

Legacy:
The Medici family's influence on banking extended beyond their time. Their innovations and practices were adopted by other banking families and

became the standard for the banking industry. Today, their legacy lives on in the banking industry, as many of the practices they introduced are still in use.

The Medici family's influence was not limited to banking alone. They were also patrons of the arts and played a significant role in the Renaissance movement. The family commissioned many works of art from famous artists such as Leonardo da Vinci and Michelangelo, which helped promote art and culture in Italy.

Conclusion:
The Medici family's impact on banking and the economy was significant. They were pioneers of modern banking practices and helped lay the foundation for the banking system we know today. Their innovations transformed the banking industry and made it more efficient and secure. The Medici family's legacy lives on in the banking industry and continues to influence the way we conduct business today.

CHAPTER 3: MODERN BANKING AND COMMERCE

The modern banking and commerce system that we know today has a rich history that has been shaped by numerous factors, including technological advancements, economic and political changes, and the evolution of societal needs. In this section, we will explore the introduction of modern banking and commerce, the key events that shaped its evolution, and its impact on the world today.

The Emergence of Modern Banking and Commerce:

The development of modern banking and commerce can be traced back to the early days of civilization, when merchants and traders needed a reliable system to exchange goods and services. Over time, this system evolved into a more sophisticated form of commerce, with the introduction of coins, paper money, and other forms of currency.

The modern banking system emerged in the 15th century, with the establishment of banks in Italy and other European countries. These banks were initially established to provide financial services to wealthy individuals and merchants, but they soon expanded to serve the needs of the broader population. By the 18th century, modern banking had become an integral part of the European economy, with banks offering a wide range of financial services, including loans, deposits, and investment opportunities.

The Rise of Modern Commerce:

The emergence of modern commerce can be traced back to the Industrial Revolution of the 19th century. This period marked a significant shift in the way goods were produced and distributed, with the development of new technologies and manufacturing processes that enabled mass production.

The rise of modern commerce was also facilitated by the development of transportation infrastructure, including railroads, steamships, and highways, which made it easier and faster to transport goods over long distances. This, in turn, led to the growth of global trade and the expansion of international commerce.

The Introduction of Credit:

One of the key developments that shaped the evolution of modern banking and commerce was the introduction of credit. Credit allowed individuals and businesses to borrow money to finance their activities, which in turn fueled economic growth and innovation.

The use of credit became more widespread in the 19th century, with the introduction of new financial instruments such as bonds and stocks. These instruments allowed businesses to raise large amounts of capital to finance their operations, and they also provided investors with a way to invest in the growth of these businesses.

The Impact of Technology:

The impact of technology has been a major driver of the evolution of modern banking and commerce. The introduction of computers and other digital technologies in the 20th century revolutionized the way financial transactions were processed and managed, making them faster, more efficient, and more secure.

The development of the internet in the 1990s marked another major milestone in the evolution of modern banking and commerce. The internet provided a new platform for conducting financial transactions, and it also enabled the development of new financial services, such as online banking, e-commerce, and mobile payments.

The Future of Modern Banking and Commerce:

As we look to the future, it is clear that modern banking and commerce will continue to evolve, driven by technological advancements, changing consumer needs, and new economic and political realities. Some of the key trends that are likely to shape the future of modern banking and commerce include:

The Rise of Fintech:
Fintech, or financial technology, has emerged as a major disruptor in the banking and commerce industry in recent years. Fintech companies are

leveraging new technologies to develop innovative financial products and services that are challenging traditional banks and financial institutions.

The Growth of Digital Payments:
The rise of digital payments, including mobile payments and e-wallets, is also likely to continue in the coming years. These new payment methods offer greater convenience, speed, and security than traditional payment methods, and they are becoming increasingly popular among consumers.

The Impact of Big Data:
Big data is also likely to have a significant impact on the future of modern banking and commerce. With the growth of the internet and mobile devices, enormous amounts of data are being generated and collected every day. This data can be used by banks and other financial institutions to gain insights into customer behavior, preferences, and needs, which can help them provide more personalized products and services.

Big data can also help banks and financial institutions manage risk more effectively by analyzing large volumes of transaction data and identifying patterns that could indicate fraudulent activity. This can help prevent financial losses and protect both the bank and its customers.

Another area where big data can have a significant impact is in the development of new financial products and services. By analyzing large amounts of data, banks and other financial institutions can identify new market opportunities and design products that meet the evolving needs of customers. For example, data analysis can be used to create new credit scoring models that take into account non-traditional sources of information, such as social media activity or online shopping behavior.

Despite the many benefits of big data, there are also potential drawbacks to consider. One of the biggest challenges is ensuring the security and privacy of sensitive customer data. Banks and other financial institutions must take steps to protect customer data from cyber threats and data breaches, which can have serious financial and reputational consequences.

Moreover, the increasing reliance on data analytics and machine learning algorithms raises concerns about potential biases in decision-making. If data sets are incomplete or biased, algorithms can perpetuate or amplify these biases, leading to discriminatory outcomes. Banks and other financial institutions must be mindful of these risks and work to ensure that their algorithms are fair and transparent.

Overall, the impact of big data on modern banking and commerce is likely to be profound. By leveraging data analytics and machine learning algorithms, banks and financial institutions can gain new insights into customer behavior, manage risk more effectively, and develop new products and services that meet the evolving needs of customers. However, these benefits must be balanced against the need to protect customer data and ensure that algorithms are fair and transparent.

Conclusion

In conclusion, the introduction of modern banking and commerce has had a significant impact on the global economy and society as a whole. From the development of fractional reserve banking to the emergence of central banks and the rise of modern technology, the banking industry has undergone a series of transformations that have shaped the world we live in today.

Looking to the future, it is clear that technology will continue to play a critical role in the evolution of the banking and commerce industries. From blockchain to big data, new technologies are emerging that have the potential to transform the way we think about money and financial transactions.

However, it is important to remember that technology is not a panacea. As the banking industry continues to evolve, it is important to balance the benefits of technology with the need to protect customer data and ensure that financial institutions operate in a fair and transparent manner. By doing so, we can help to ensure that the banking and commerce industries continue to contribute to the growth and prosperity of our global economy for years to come.

The rise of the modern banking system

The modern banking system is a complex and multifaceted system that plays a crucial role in the global economy. It has evolved over centuries and undergone significant changes throughout history. In this section, we will explore the rise of the modern banking system and how it has developed into the sophisticated system we know today.

Origins of Modern Banking

The origins of modern banking can be traced back to the early Italian city-states during the Renaissance period. These city-states, such as Florence and

Venice, were centers of trade and commerce, and merchants needed a way to conduct transactions safely and efficiently.

One of the earliest forms of banking was the Medici Bank, which was founded in Florence in 1397 by Giovanni di Bicci de' Medici. The Medici Bank was instrumental in facilitating trade between Italy and other European countries and played a significant role in the development of the modern banking system.

The Rise of Fractional Reserve Banking

Fractional reserve banking is a system in which banks only hold a fraction of the money deposited by customers in reserve, with the rest of the funds being loaned out to other customers. This system allowed banks to earn interest on the loans they made, which was a significant source of income.

Fractional reserve banking became widespread in the 18th and 19th centuries and was an essential factor in the growth of the modern banking system. It allowed banks to expand their operations, make more loans, and earn more profits.

The Emergence of Central Banks

Central banks play a critical role in the modern banking system. They are responsible for managing the money supply, regulating the banking industry, and ensuring the stability of the financial system. The first central bank was the Bank of Sweden, which was established in 1668.

Central banks became more common in the 19th century, with the establishment of the Bank of England in 1694, the Federal Reserve in the United States in 1913, and the European Central Bank in 1998. These central banks played a crucial role in stabilizing the banking system, preventing financial crises, and promoting economic growth.

The Impact of Technology

The rise of technology has had a significant impact on the modern banking system. The introduction of electronic banking, online banking, and mobile banking has made it easier for customers to access their accounts and conduct transactions.

Technology has also made it easier for banks to manage their operations, reduce costs, and increase efficiency. The use of automated teller machines (ATMs) and other self-service technologies has reduced the need for bank tellers and other staff, allowing banks to operate more efficiently and with fewer employees.

The Future of Banking

The modern banking system is constantly evolving, and the future of banking is likely to be shaped by technological advances and changing consumer behavior. Some of the trends that are likely to shape the future of banking include:

Mobile banking and payments: As smartphones and other mobile devices become more widespread, mobile banking and payments are likely to become more common.

Fintech innovation: Fintech companies are using technology to disrupt the traditional banking industry, offering innovative products and services that challenge traditional banks.

Blockchain technology: Blockchain technology has the potential to revolutionize the banking industry by providing a secure, transparent, and decentralized way of conducting transactions.

Digital currencies: The rise of digital currencies, such as Bitcoin and Ethereum, has the potential to disrupt the traditional banking system by providing an alternative way of conducting transactions.

Conclusion

The rise of the modern banking system has been a long and complex process that has evolved over centuries. The development of fractional reserve banking, the emergence of central banks, and the impact of technology have all played a significant role in shaping the modern banking system.

As the banking industry continues to evolve, it is likely to be shaped by technological advancements and changing consumer behavior. The rise of digital banking and fintech startups has disrupted traditional banking models, offering customers new options for managing their finances.

In addition, regulatory changes and global economic trends will continue to influence the banking industry. The financial crisis of 2008 resulted in increased scrutiny of banks and stricter regulations, and it remains to be seen how future economic events will shape the industry.

Despite these challenges, the modern banking system remains a cornerstone of the global economy, providing essential services to individuals, businesses, and governments around the world.

As technology continues to shape the banking industry, it is likely that we will see new innovations and advancements in the years to come. However, it is important that these changes are balanced with responsible and ethical business practices, in order to ensure that the banking system remains a stable and reliable part of the global economy.

Overall, the rise of the modern banking system has been a complex and fascinating process, shaped by a range of historical, political, and economic factors. As we move into the future, it is important to continue studying and understanding this vital industry, in order to ensure its continued success and stability.

The Bank of England and the gold standard

The Bank of England played a significant role in the adoption and implementation of the gold standard in the 19th century. This monetary system, which tied the value of a country's currency to a fixed amount of gold, was seen as a way to stabilize exchange rates and promote international trade.

In this section, we will examine the history of the gold standard, the role of the Bank of England in its implementation, and the impact it had on the global economy.

The History of the Gold Standard

The concept of using gold as a form of currency can be traced back to ancient civilizations, where gold was used as a medium of exchange and a store of value. However, it was not until the 19th century that the gold standard as we know it today began to emerge.

The first country to adopt the gold standard was Great Britain in 1821. Under this system, the Bank of England would exchange paper money for gold at a fixed rate, and the value of the pound sterling was tied to a fixed amount of gold. Other countries, including the United States, Germany, and France, soon followed suit.

The gold standard remained the dominant monetary system until the outbreak of World War I, when many countries suspended their adherence to it to finance the war effort. Following the war, attempts were made to revive the gold standard, but these efforts were largely unsuccessful.

The Role of the Bank of England

The Bank of England played a crucial role in the implementation of the gold standard in Great Britain. As the central bank of the country, it was responsible for managing the supply of money and ensuring the stability of the currency.

Under the gold standard, the Bank of England was required to hold a certain amount of gold reserves to back the value of the pound sterling. If the bank printed too much money, the value of the pound would fall, and the bank would have to exchange more gold for each pound, depleting its reserves. Conversely, if the bank did not print enough money, the economy could suffer from deflation.

The Bank of England's role in the gold standard was not without controversy. Critics argued that the strict adherence to the gold standard limited the bank's ability to respond to economic crises, as it could not increase the money supply to stimulate the economy. Additionally, some argued that the gold standard contributed to the Great Depression of the 1930s, as countries were unable to print enough money to combat the economic downturn.

The Impact of the Gold Standard

The gold standard had a significant impact on the global economy in the 19th and early 20th centuries. Here are some of the key ways in which it affected the world:

Stability of Exchange Rates: By fixing the value of currencies to a fixed amount of gold, the gold standard provided stability in exchange rates between countries. This made international trade easier and more predictable, as businesses could rely on stable exchange rates.

Limited Government Intervention: The gold standard limited the ability of governments to intervene in the economy, as they could not print unlimited amounts of money. This helped to promote fiscal responsibility and limit inflation.

Increased Price Stability: Under the gold standard, inflation was generally limited, as the supply of money was tied to the supply of gold. This helped to stabilize prices and promote economic growth.

However, the gold standard also had its drawbacks. The fixed exchange rates could limit the ability of countries to respond to economic crises, and the limited money supply could contribute to deflation and economic downturns.

Conclusion

The gold standard was a significant monetary system that played a crucial role in the global economy in the 19th and early 20th centuries. The Bank of England was instrumental in its implementation and management, and the system had both benefits and drawbacks.

Today, the gold standard is no longer used as a monetary system by any country, and its relevance has diminished. However, it remains an important historical and economic concept that can provide insight into the development and evolution of modern monetary systems.

While the gold standard was a stable and relatively predictable monetary system, it had its limitations. The fixed exchange rate meant that countries had limited flexibility to adjust to economic shocks or changes in trade patterns, and it also limited the ability of central banks to respond to fluctuations in the economy.

In contrast, the flexible exchange rate system that has emerged in the post-gold standard era has allowed for greater flexibility and responsiveness to economic changes. However, it has also introduced new challenges, such as increased volatility in exchange rates and potential currency manipulation.

Ultimately, the role of the Bank of England in the gold standard era provides important insights into the evolution of modern central banking and monetary policy. The lessons learned from the successes and failures of the gold standard have informed the development of modern monetary systems and continue to shape the way we think about monetary policy today.

The emergence of credit cards

The use of credit cards has become ubiquitous in modern society. They are a convenient way to make purchases, and many people rely on them for everyday transactions. However, the history of credit cards is relatively recent, and their widespread adoption is a testament to their usefulness and innovation. In this section, we will explore the emergence of credit cards, their impact on society, and their future potential.

Early Forms of Credit

The concept of using credit has existed for centuries, with various forms of credit being used throughout history. For example, in ancient Babylon, merchants used clay tablets to record transactions and provide loans to their customers. In the Middle Ages, the Italian banking system introduced the concept of bills of exchange, which allowed for the transfer of funds between different countries.

The emergence of credit cards, however, was a more recent development that took place in the mid-20th century. In the 1940s, individual merchants began offering credit to their customers through charge accounts, which allowed them to purchase goods and services on credit and pay for them at a later date.

The Diners Club Card

The first modern credit card was the Diners Club card, which was introduced in 1950 by Frank McNamara, a businessman from New York. The Diners Club card was initially intended to be used only in restaurants, but it soon expanded to other merchants and became a popular way to make purchases.

The Diners Club card was a charge card, which meant that users had to pay their balance in full each month. The card was initially marketed to businessmen who traveled frequently and needed a convenient way to pay for meals and other expenses. It was an immediate success and paved the way for the development of other credit cards.

BankAmericard and Master Charge

In 1958, Bank of America introduced the BankAmericard, which was the first credit card to be issued by a bank. The BankAmericard was initially offered only to customers in California but quickly expanded to other states.

In response to the success of the BankAmericard, a group of banks formed the Interbank Card Association (ICA) in 1966, which later became MasterCard. The ICA developed the Master Charge card, which was similar to the BankAmericard but was issued by multiple banks instead of just one.

The Emergence of Credit Card Networks

The emergence of credit card networks was a significant development in the history of credit cards. Credit card networks are a group of banks that issue credit cards and process transactions for merchants.

The two largest credit card networks are Visa and MasterCard, which together account for more than 80% of all credit card transactions worldwide. These networks provide a convenient and efficient way for merchants to accept credit card payments and for consumers to use their credit cards.

The Impact of Credit Cards on Society

The widespread adoption of credit cards has had a significant impact on society, both positive and negative. Here are some of the key ways in which credit cards have influenced society:

Convenience: Credit cards provide a convenient way to make purchases, whether in person or online, without the need for cash or checks.

Increased spending: Credit cards have been linked to increased spending, as users tend to spend more when using credit cards than when using cash.

Debt: Credit cards can also lead to debt, as users who do not pay their balances in full each month may accumulate interest charges and fees.

Rewards: Many credit cards offer rewards programs, which provide users with incentives to use their cards, such as cashback or points that can be redeemed for merchandise or travel.

Fraud: Credit card fraud is a significant concern, as criminals can steal credit card information and use it to make unauthorized purchases.

The Future of Credit Cards

As technology continues to evolve, credit cards are likely to change as well.

The future of credit cards is an exciting prospect, with new innovations and technologies poised to transform the way we make purchases and manage our finances. Here are some potential developments to watch for in the coming years:

Mobile payments: Mobile payments have already gained popularity in recent years, with the rise of services like Apple Pay, Google Wallet, and Samsung Pay. These services allow consumers to pay for goods and services using their smartphones, rather than a physical credit card. As mobile payments become more widely accepted, we may see a decline in the use of physical credit cards.

Biometric authentication: Biometric authentication is becoming more common in a variety of settings, from unlocking our smartphones with facial recognition to using our fingerprints to access bank accounts. In the future, credit card companies may incorporate biometric authentication into their products, allowing customers to make purchases using a fingerprint or facial scan, rather than a PIN or signature.

Contactless cards: Contactless credit cards, which allow customers to make purchases by tapping their card against a payment terminal, have been available in some countries for several years. However, they have only recently started gaining traction in the United States. As consumers become more comfortable with this technology, contactless cards could become the norm.

Personalized rewards: Credit card companies have long offered rewards programs to incentivize customers to use their products. However, these programs have typically been one-size-fits-all. In the future, we may see credit card companies using data analytics and artificial intelligence to offer more personalized rewards to customers based on their individual spending habits and preferences.

Cryptocurrency integration: With the rise of cryptocurrencies like Bitcoin and Ethereum, some credit card companies have already started offering cards that allow customers to earn rewards in cryptocurrency. In the future, we may see credit card companies integrating cryptocurrency more fully into their products, allowing customers to make purchases using Bitcoin or other digital currencies.

Counterarguments and critiques of credit cards

While credit cards have many advantages, they are not without their drawbacks. Some critics argue that credit cards can contribute to financial instability and debt, while others have raised concerns about privacy and security.

Financial instability: One of the biggest criticisms of credit cards is that they can encourage consumers to spend beyond their means, leading to debt and financial instability. The ease of making purchases with a credit card can make it difficult for some consumers to keep track of their spending and stick to a budget.

Interest rates and fees: Credit card companies make money by charging interest on outstanding balances and fees for late payments, balance transfers, and cash advances. Some critics argue that these fees and rates are unfairly high, and can trap consumers in a cycle of debt.

Privacy and security: Credit card companies collect a vast amount of data on their customers' spending habits, which has raised concerns about privacy and data security. In addition, credit card fraud and identity theft are significant concerns, and consumers must be vigilant in protecting their personal information.

Conclusion

Credit cards have come a long way since their introduction in the mid-20th century, evolving from a simple convenience to a vital financial tool for millions of consumers worldwide. While there are certainly risks associated with credit cards, the benefits they offer in terms of convenience, rewards, and building credit make them a valuable tool for many people.

As technology continues to advance, credit cards are likely to continue evolving to meet the changing needs and expectations of consumers. From mobile payments to biometric authentication to cryptocurrency integration, the future of credit cards is an exciting prospect. However, it is important to remain aware of the risks and drawbacks associated with credit card use, and to use them responsibly to avoid financial instability and debt.

The development of online banking

The emergence of online banking has been a significant development in the financial industry. Online banking allows customers to perform various banking activities through the internet, such as checking account balances, paying bills, transferring funds, and even applying for loans. Online banking has brought about many changes to the banking industry, including increased convenience for customers, increased efficiency for banks, and a shift towards a more digital and mobile-focused banking experience.

History of Online Banking:

The origins of online banking can be traced back to the 1980s when banks began experimenting with the concept of providing customers with access to their accounts via computer terminals. However, it was not until the late 1990s that online banking became widely available to consumers.

In the early days of online banking, customers were limited to basic features such as checking account balances and transferring funds between accounts. However, as technology continued to evolve, so did the capabilities of online banking. Today, customers can perform a wide range of banking activities online, including applying for loans, opening new accounts, and even managing their investments.

Benefits of Online Banking:

Online banking has many benefits for both customers and banks. Some of the key benefits include:

Increased Convenience: Online banking allows customers to perform banking activities from anywhere with an internet connection, making it much more convenient than traditional banking methods.

Time-Saving: Online banking allows customers to perform banking activities quickly and efficiently, saving them time and effort.

Lower Fees: Online banking often has lower fees than traditional banking methods, as banks can save money on overhead costs by conducting transactions online.

Enhanced Security: Online banking utilizes advanced security measures such as encryption and two-factor authentication to protect customer information and prevent fraud.

Challenges of Online Banking:

Despite its many benefits, online banking also poses some challenges for both customers and banks. Some of the key challenges include:

Security Risks: Online banking poses security risks, as cybercriminals can attempt to steal sensitive information such as account numbers and passwords.

Technical Issues: Online banking can be subject to technical issues such as system failures or slow processing times, which can cause frustration for customers.

Lack of Personal Touch: Online banking can lack the personal touch of traditional banking methods, as customers may not have the opportunity to interact with bank employees face-to-face.

Accessibility Issues: Online banking may not be accessible to all customers, particularly those who do not have access to the internet or who are not comfortable using technology.

The Future of Online Banking:

As technology continues to evolve, so too will online banking. Some of the trends that are likely to shape the future of online banking include:

Mobile Banking: Mobile banking has already become a popular way for customers to perform banking activities, and this trend is likely to continue in the future.

Artificial Intelligence: Artificial intelligence can be used to improve the online banking experience, such as by providing personalized recommendations and assisting with financial planning.

Blockchain Technology: Blockchain technology can be used to improve the security of online banking transactions by providing a tamper-proof ledger of all transactions.

Integration with Other Services: Online banking may become more integrated with other services such as social media and e-commerce, allowing customers to perform a wide range of activities through a single platform.

Conclusion:

The development of online banking has brought about many changes to the banking industry, including increased convenience for customers, increased efficiency for banks, and a shift towards a more digital and mobile-focused banking experience. While online banking has many benefits, it also poses some challenges, such as security risks and technical issues. However, as technology continues to evolve, so too will online banking, and it is likely to become even more advanced and integrated with other services in the future.

CHAPTER 4: REGULATION OF BANKING AND COMMERCE

The regulation of banking and commerce is an important aspect of ensuring the stability and safety of the financial system. In the United States, the regulation of banks and other financial institutions is primarily the responsibility of the federal government, specifically the Federal Reserve System and other regulatory agencies. The regulation of commerce, on the other hand, is primarily the responsibility of the Department of Commerce and other federal agencies.

The regulation of banking and commerce has a long history in the United States, dating back to the early 19th century. Over the years, the regulatory environment has changed significantly in response to various economic and political factors. This section will examine the development of banking and commerce regulation in the United States, including key legislation and regulatory agencies, as well as their impact on the financial system and the broader economy.

Early Regulation of Banking and Commerce

In the early years of the United States, banking and commerce were largely unregulated. This led to a number of problems, including bank failures, fraudulent practices, and the emergence of a wide range of currencies. To address these issues, Congress passed the National Banking Act in 1863, which established a national banking system and provided for the regulation and supervision of banks.

The National Banking Act also created the Office of the Comptroller of the Currency (OCC), which is responsible for supervising and regulating all national banks. The OCC plays a critical role in ensuring the safety and soundness of the national banking system, as well as protecting the interests of bank customers.

In addition to the National Banking Act, a number of other regulatory measures were put in place to address various issues related to banking and commerce. For example, the Sherman Antitrust Act of 1890 was passed to prevent the formation of monopolies and promote competition in the marketplace. The Federal Reserve Act of 1913 established the Federal Reserve System, which is responsible for implementing monetary policy and ensuring the stability of the financial system.

The Great Depression and the New Deal

The Great Depression of the 1930s had a profound impact on the regulation of banking and commerce in the United States. The stock market crash of 1929 led to widespread bank failures and a severe economic downturn. In response, Congress passed a number of key pieces of legislation aimed at stabilizing the financial system and promoting economic recovery.

One of the most significant pieces of legislation passed during this period was the Glass-Steagall Act of 1933. This law separated commercial and investment banking activities and established the Federal Deposit Insurance Corporation (FDIC) to insure bank deposits. The Glass-Steagall Act remained in place until it was repealed in 1999.

The New Deal also brought about significant changes to the regulatory environment. President Franklin D. Roosevelt signed a number of laws aimed at regulating various industries, including banking and finance. These included the Securities Act of 1933, which required companies to provide full disclosure of financial information to investors, and the Securities Exchange Act of 1934, which established the Securities and Exchange Commission (SEC) to regulate the securities markets.

Post-World War II and the Rise of Globalization

Following World War II, the United States entered a period of economic expansion and global dominance. This era was marked by the emergence of multinational corporations, the rise of consumer culture, and the growth of financial markets. As a result, the regulatory environment became increasingly complex and fragmented.

During the 1950s and 1960s, the regulatory landscape continued to evolve. The Federal Reserve System was given additional powers to regulate the money supply, and the Bank Holding Company Act of 1956 was passed to regulate the activities of bank holding companies. The Equal Credit

Opportunity Act of 1974 was also passed to prohibit discrimination in lending practices.

In the 1980s and 1990s, the regulatory landscape for banking and commerce underwent significant changes as well.

Deregulation and Repeal of the Glass-Steagall Act

In the 1980s, there was a movement towards deregulation of the banking industry. This was partly a response to the high inflation and interest rates of the 1970s, which had made it difficult for banks to compete with other financial institutions. In 1980, the Depository Institutions Deregulation and Monetary Control Act was passed, which removed many of the restrictions on banks' ability to offer higher interest rates on deposits.

In 1999, the Gramm-Leach-Bliley Act (GLBA) was passed, which repealed certain provisions of the Glass-Steagall Act of 1933. The Glass-Steagall Act had separated commercial banking (taking deposits and making loans) from investment banking (underwriting securities and engaging in securities trading). The repeal of the Glass-Steagall Act allowed banks to engage in a wider range of activities, such as securities trading and investment banking.

The repeal of Glass-Steagall has been a topic of debate, with some arguing that it contributed to the financial crisis of 2008. Proponents of the repeal argue that it was necessary to allow banks to compete in a global economy.

Financial Services Modernization Act

The Financial Services Modernization Act, also known as the Gramm-Leach-Bliley Act, was passed in 1999. It removed many of the restrictions on banks, allowing them to offer a wider range of financial services, including insurance and securities. This led to the consolidation of the financial services industry, as banks acquired other financial institutions.

The passage of the Financial Services Modernization Act was controversial, with critics arguing that it would lead to the concentration of economic power in the hands of a few large institutions.

Consumer Protection and the Dodd-Frank Act

In response to the financial crisis of 2008, the Dodd-Frank Wall Street Reform and Consumer Protection Act was passed in 2010. The Dodd-Frank

Act was designed to reform the financial regulatory system and address some of the factors that contributed to the financial crisis.

One of the key provisions of the Dodd-Frank Act was the creation of the Consumer Financial Protection Bureau (CFPB), which is responsible for enforcing federal consumer financial laws and protecting consumers in the financial marketplace. The CFPB has the authority to regulate a wide range of financial products and services, including mortgages, credit cards, and student loans.

The Dodd-Frank Act also included provisions to increase transparency and accountability in the financial system, such as the requirement for certain financial institutions to provide annual reports on their risk management practices.

Impact of Regulation on Banking and Commerce

The regulation of banking and commerce has had a significant impact on the industry and the economy as a whole. Some of the key effects of regulation include:

Increased stability: The regulatory framework has helped to increase the stability of the banking system and reduce the risk of bank failures. Regulations such as capital requirements and stress testing have helped to ensure that banks have sufficient reserves to weather economic downturns.

Consumer protection: Regulations such as the Truth in Lending Act and the Fair Credit Reporting Act have helped to protect consumers from predatory lending practices and other forms of financial abuse.

Increased competition: Deregulation has helped to increase competition in the banking industry, as banks are able to offer a wider range of services and compete with other financial institutions.

Consolidation: The consolidation of the financial services industry has been a controversial aspect of deregulation, with some arguing that it has led to the concentration of economic power in the hands of a few large institutions.

The role of government in regulating banks and commerce
The role of government in regulating banks and commerce has been an essential component of modern economic systems. Governments have played a critical role in establishing regulatory frameworks that govern how banks

and other financial institutions operate. These regulations aim to promote fair competition, prevent market failures, and protect consumers from fraud and other forms of abuse. This article provides an in-depth analysis of the role of government in regulating banks and commerce, exploring the history, evolution, and current state of regulation.

History of Banking and Commerce Regulation

The history of banking and commerce regulation dates back to the early days of modern economic systems. In the United States, the first national bank was established in 1791, followed by the creation of the Federal Reserve System in 1913. These institutions were established to provide a stable and secure financial system that could support economic growth and development.

During the early years of banking and commerce regulation, the government's primary focus was on ensuring that banks and other financial institutions were financially sound and stable. The regulatory framework was designed to prevent bank runs and other forms of financial instability that could disrupt the economy.

Over time, the regulatory landscape evolved to include other concerns such as consumer protection, fair competition, and preventing market failures. The government's role in regulating banks and commerce continued to expand, with new laws and regulations being introduced to address emerging issues.

The Evolution of Banking and Commerce Regulation

The regulatory landscape for banking and commerce has continued to evolve over the years. This evolution has been driven by a range of factors, including technological advances, globalization, and changing market conditions.

One significant development in the evolution of banking and commerce regulation has been the increasing focus on consumer protection. Governments have introduced new laws and regulations to protect consumers from fraud and other forms of abuse. These regulations include requirements for financial institutions to provide clear and concise information to consumers about their products and services, as well as strict penalties for institutions that engage in abusive practices.

Another important trend in the evolution of banking and commerce regulation has been the increasing focus on preventing market failures. Governments have introduced regulations to ensure that financial institutions are adequately capitalized and have appropriate risk management systems in place. These regulations aim to prevent financial institutions from engaging in risky activities that could threaten financial stability and disrupt the economy.

The Role of Government in Regulating Banks and Commerce
The government plays a critical role in regulating banks and commerce. This role is based on several key principles:

Protecting Consumers: One of the primary roles of government in regulating banks and commerce is to protect consumers from fraud and other forms of abuse. This includes ensuring that financial institutions provide clear and concise information about their products and services, as well as strict penalties for institutions that engage in abusive practices.

Promoting Fair Competition: Another key role of government in regulating banks and commerce is to promote fair competition. This includes preventing monopolies and other forms of anti-competitive behavior that could harm consumers and limit innovation.

Ensuring Financial Stability: Governments also play a critical role in ensuring financial stability. This includes establishing regulations that require financial institutions to maintain adequate capital levels and risk management systems, as well as providing a lender of last resort to prevent financial crises.

Supporting Economic Growth and Development: Finally, governments play a critical role in supporting economic growth and development. This includes providing access to credit for businesses and individuals, as well as supporting the development of new industries and technologies.

Examples of Government Regulation of Banks and Commerce
There are numerous examples of government regulation of banks and commerce. Some of the most notable examples include:

The Dodd-Frank Wall Street Reform and Consumer Protection Act: This act, which was passed in response to the 2008 financial crisis, established a range of new regulations for financial institutions. These regulations include requirements for financial institutions to maintain adequate capital levels, as well as provisions for consumer protection and oversight of the financial industry. The Dodd-Frank Act also created new government agencies, such as the Consumer Financial Protection Bureau, to oversee financial institutions and protect consumers.

The Sarbanes-Oxley Act: This act, passed in 2002, was created in response to corporate accounting scandals such as Enron and WorldCom. The act established new requirements for public companies, such as the creation of an independent audit committee and increased financial disclosures. The goal of the Sarbanes-Oxley Act was to increase transparency and accountability in corporate financial reporting.

The Community Reinvestment Act: This act, passed in 1977, requires banks to serve the credit needs of the communities in which they operate, including low- and moderate-income neighborhoods. The act aims to prevent discrimination in lending practices and ensure that banks are providing credit to all segments of the population.

The Fair Credit Reporting Act: This act, passed in 1970, regulates the collection, dissemination, and use of consumer credit information. The act requires credit reporting agencies to ensure the accuracy and privacy of consumer credit information, and provides consumers with the right to access and correct their credit reports.

The Anti-Money Laundering Act: This act, passed in 2020, strengthens the government's ability to prevent and combat money laundering and terrorist financing. The act requires financial institutions to establish anti-money laundering programs, conduct customer due diligence, and report suspicious activities to the government.

Challenges and Criticisms of Government Regulation of Banks and Commerce

While government regulation of banks and commerce is generally seen as necessary to protect consumers and ensure the stability of the financial system, it is not without its challenges and criticisms. Some of the main challenges and criticisms include:

Regulatory capture: This occurs when the regulators tasked with overseeing the financial industry become too closely aligned with the industry they are supposed to be regulating. Regulatory capture can lead to a weakening of regulations and a lack of enforcement.

Compliance costs: The cost of complying with government regulations can be significant, especially for smaller banks and businesses. These costs can make it difficult for smaller institutions to compete with larger ones.

Unintended consequences: Government regulations can sometimes have unintended consequences, such as reducing access to credit for certain populations or creating barriers to entry for new businesses.

Political influence: The regulatory landscape can be influenced by political factors, such as changes in administration or shifts in political ideology. This can lead to changes in regulations that may not always be in the best interests of consumers or the financial system.

Conclusion

In conclusion, the role of government in regulating banks and commerce has evolved significantly over time. While the initial focus was on ensuring the safety and soundness of the financial system, this has expanded to include consumer protection, anti-discrimination measures, and oversight of the broader financial industry. Government regulation of banks and commerce is generally seen as necessary to protect consumers and ensure the stability of the financial system, but it is not without its challenges and criticisms. As the financial industry and regulatory landscape continue to evolve, it will be important for government regulators to strike a balance between protecting consumers and ensuring a competitive and innovative financial industry.

Bank failures and the Great Depression

The Great Depression was one of the most significant economic crises in American history. It had far-reaching effects on the country's financial system and led to the failure of numerous banks. In this section, we will explore the causes and consequences of bank failures during the Great Depression.

Overview of the Great Depression

The Great Depression was a period of severe economic downturn that began in 1929 and lasted until the late 1930s. The depression was triggered by the stock market crash of 1929, which resulted in a sharp decline in economic activity, mass unemployment, and widespread poverty. The Great Depression had far-reaching effects on the American economy, leading to significant changes in government policy, banking regulation, and the overall financial system.

Bank failures during the Great Depression

During the Great Depression, thousands of banks failed across the United States. The exact number of bank failures is difficult to determine, as many small banks were not officially recorded as failing. However, it is estimated that over 9,000 banks failed between 1930 and 1933, resulting in the loss of millions of dollars in deposits.

The causes of bank failures during the Great Depression were numerous and complex. Some of the main factors included:

Economic instability: The Great Depression was a period of significant economic instability, with mass unemployment, declining wages, and falling prices. This instability put pressure on the banking system, leading to a decline in deposits and an increase in loan defaults.

Speculation: Many banks engaged in speculative investments during the 1920s, which led to significant losses when the stock market crashed in 1929. These losses weakened the financial position of many banks, making them more vulnerable to failure.

Overexpansion: Some banks had expanded too rapidly during the 1920s, opening new branches and making risky loans. When economic conditions deteriorated in the 1930s, these banks were unable to sustain their operations and failed.

Panics and bank runs: The Great Depression was characterized by a series of panics and bank runs, where depositors rushed to withdraw their money from banks that they perceived to be in trouble. These runs put further pressure on the banking system, leading to more failures.

The consequences of bank failures during the Great Depression were severe. Many depositors lost their life savings, and the banking system was left in shambles. The failure of banks also had a ripple effect on the broader economy, leading to a decline in lending and investment and further exacerbating the economic downturn.

Government response to bank failures

The government responded to the crisis of bank failures during the Great Depression with a range of measures aimed at stabilizing the financial system and preventing further failures. Some of the key actions taken by the government included:

Bank holidays: In 1933, President Franklin D. Roosevelt declared a national bank holiday, which closed all banks in the country for four days. This holiday allowed the government to inspect the financial condition of banks and reopen only those that were deemed to be solvent.

Creation of the Federal Deposit Insurance Corporation (FDIC): The FDIC was established in 1933 to provide insurance for bank deposits. This insurance protected depositors from losing their savings in the event of a bank failure and helped restore confidence in the banking system.

Regulation of banking: The government passed a range of new regulations to prevent risky banking practices and promote stability in the financial system. These regulations included the Glass-Steagall Act of 1933, which separated commercial and investment banking activities, and the Securities Act of 1933, which required companies to disclose information about their financial position.

The government's response to the crisis of bank failures during the Great Depression was effective in stabilizing the financial system and preventing further failures. The measures taken by the government during this time set the stage for future banking regulation and the creation of institutions like the Federal Deposit Insurance Corporation (FDIC) that continue to protect the American financial system today.

The Glass-Steagall Act of 1933

One of the key pieces of legislation that was passed in response to the Great Depression was the Glass-Steagall Act of 1933. This act separated commercial and investment banking activities, with the aim of preventing banks from taking excessive risks with depositors' money. The act also established the FDIC, which guaranteed bank deposits up to $2,500, providing depositors with confidence in the safety of their money.

The Glass-Steagall Act remained in place for several decades, but was eventually repealed in 1999 with the passage of the Gramm-Leach-Bliley Act. This repeal was controversial, with some critics arguing that it contributed to the financial crisis of 2008.

Lessons Learned from the Great Depression

The Great Depression and the crisis of bank failures that accompanied it taught important lessons about the importance of banking regulation and the risks of unbridled speculation in financial markets. Some of the key lessons that were learned during this time include:

The importance of a stable financial system: The Great Depression demonstrated the devastating effects of a financial crisis on the economy and the importance of a stable financial system. In response to the crisis, the government implemented a range of measures to stabilize the system and prevent further failures.

The need for deposit insurance: The establishment of the FDIC provided depositors with confidence in the safety of their money and helped to prevent runs on banks.

The risks of excessive speculation: The speculative excesses of the 1920s, particularly in the stock market, contributed to the financial crisis and the failure of many banks. The crisis underscored the need for prudent risk management practices in financial institutions.

The role of government in regulating the financial system: The government's response to the crisis of bank failures during the Great Depression demonstrated the important role that government can play in regulating the financial system and ensuring its stability.

Conclusion

The Great Depression was a defining moment in American history, with significant implications for the financial system and the role of government in regulating banks and commerce. The crisis of bank failures that accompanied the Depression led to important reforms in banking regulation, including the establishment of the FDIC and the separation of commercial and investment banking activities.

The lessons learned from the Great Depression continue to be relevant today, as financial crises remain a significant risk to the global economy. The events of the 1930s serve as a reminder of the importance of prudent risk management practices in financial institutions and the critical role that government can play in ensuring the stability of the financial system.

The formation of the Federal Reserve System

The Federal Reserve System, often referred to as the "Fed," is the central banking system of the United States. It was created in 1913 to address a variety of economic and financial issues that had plagued the country for decades. This section will explore the formation of the Federal Reserve System, including the events leading up to its creation, the political and economic factors that shaped its design, and its early impact on the US economy.

The Need for a Central Bank

Throughout the 19th century, the United States experienced numerous financial panics and economic downturns. These crises were often triggered by banking failures, which led to widespread bank runs and a contraction of credit in the economy. In response, various proposals were put forth to create a central bank that could act as a lender of last resort during times of financial stress.

One of the earliest proposals for a central bank came in 1790, when Alexander Hamilton, the first Secretary of the Treasury, proposed the creation of a national bank. This proposal was controversial and ultimately rejected by Congress, which feared that a centralized banking system would concentrate too much power in the hands of the federal government.

In the years that followed, various other proposals for a central bank were put forth and debated, but none were successful. It wasn't until the early 20th century, after a series of financial crises and panics, that momentum began to build for the creation of a central bank.

The Aldrich Plan

In 1907, the United States experienced a severe financial crisis that highlighted the need for a more stable and secure banking system. In response, a group of prominent bankers and politicians convened at Jekyll Island, Georgia in 1910 to develop a plan for a central bank.

The resulting plan, known as the Aldrich Plan, proposed the creation of a central bank with a decentralized structure that would be governed by a board of directors composed of representatives from regional banks. The plan also called for the establishment of a national currency that would be backed by gold reserves.

The Aldrich Plan was met with significant opposition from many quarters, including farmers, small business owners, and progressive politicians, who argued that it would concentrate too much power in the hands of bankers and wealthy elites. The plan failed to gain traction in Congress, but it helped to stimulate debate and discussion about the need for a central bank.

The Federal Reserve Act

In 1913, after years of debate and political maneuvering, Congress passed the Federal Reserve Act, which established the Federal Reserve System as the central banking system of the United States. The Act was signed into law by President Woodrow Wilson on December 23, 1913.

The Federal Reserve System was designed to be a decentralized institution, with 12 regional banks located throughout the country. Each regional bank was to be governed by a board of directors composed of representatives from member banks in the region. The Federal Reserve Board, located in Washington, D.C., was responsible for overseeing the operations of the regional banks and setting monetary policy for the country as a whole.

The Federal Reserve System was given a number of important powers and responsibilities, including:

Acting as a lender of last resort to banks during times of financial stress
Regulating the money supply to promote economic stability and growth
Setting interest rates to influence economic activity
Regulating and supervising member banks to ensure their safety and soundness
The Impact of the Federal Reserve System

In its early years, the Federal Reserve System faced a number of challenges and controversies. Some critics argued that it was too centralized and powerful, while others argued that it was too decentralized and lacked the ability to coordinate monetary policy effectively.

Despite these challenges, the Federal Reserve System played a crucial role in stabilizing the US economy during the early 20th century. Its ability to act as a lender of last resort helped to prevent bank runs and financial panics, and its control over the money supply allowed it to respond to changing economic conditions and manage inflation.

One of the key impacts of the Federal Reserve System has been its role in promoting economic growth and stability. By controlling the money supply and interest rates, the Fed is able to influence economic activity and help maintain stable prices. This has been particularly important in times of economic downturns, such as during the Great Recession of 2008, when the Fed took aggressive action to inject liquidity into the financial system and lower interest rates.

Another impact of the Federal Reserve System has been its role in promoting financial stability. The Fed is responsible for supervising and regulating banks, and it has the authority to take action to prevent systemic risk and protect the stability of the financial system. This was demonstrated during the 2008 financial crisis, when the Fed played a key role in preventing the collapse of the banking system and stabilizing financial markets.

The Federal Reserve System has also had an impact on international finance and monetary policy. As the world's largest economy and the issuer of the world's reserve currency, the actions of the Fed have a significant impact on global financial markets. The Fed's monetary policy decisions can affect exchange rates, capital flows, and financial stability in other countries, and the Fed has been active in coordinating its policies with other central banks around the world.

Conclusion

The Federal Reserve System has played a critical role in shaping the US economy and financial system over the past century. Its establishment in 1913 was a response to the challenges of the era, including the need for a more stable and flexible monetary system. The Fed has faced numerous challenges and controversies over the years, but it has also been credited with promoting economic growth, stability, and financial system safety. Despite its successes, the Fed continues to face new challenges in the 21st century, including the impact of new technologies on the financial system and the changing role of central banks in a globalized world.

The Dodd-Frank Act and financial regulation today

The Dodd-Frank Wall Street Reform and Consumer Protection Act, commonly known as the Dodd-Frank Act, is a comprehensive piece of legislation that was signed into law in 2010. The act was passed in response to the 2008 financial crisis and was intended to address many of the issues that contributed to the crisis. The Dodd-Frank Act is one of the most significant pieces of financial regulation to be passed in recent history, and it has had a profound impact on the financial industry.

Overview of the Dodd-Frank Act

The Dodd-Frank Act is a complex piece of legislation that contains numerous provisions designed to regulate the financial industry. Some of the most significant provisions of the act include:

Creation of the Consumer Financial Protection Bureau: The Dodd-Frank Act created the Consumer Financial Protection Bureau (CFPB) to oversee and regulate financial products and services offered to consumers. The CFPB is responsible for enforcing regulations related to consumer protection, including mortgage lending, credit card practices, and payday lending.

Regulation of Systemically Important Financial Institutions: The Dodd-Frank Act also created new regulations for systemically important financial institutions (SIFIs), which are financial institutions that are deemed to be too big to fail. These regulations are designed to prevent SIFIs from engaging in risky behavior that could lead to another financial crisis.

Increase in Capital Requirements: The Dodd-Frank Act also increased the capital requirements for banks and other financial institutions. This is intended to ensure that financial institutions have enough capital to weather economic downturns and other shocks to the financial system.

Derivatives Regulation: The Dodd-Frank Act includes provisions to regulate the derivatives market, which was largely unregulated prior to the financial crisis. These provisions require that certain derivatives be traded on exchanges and cleared through central counterparties, and they also require that regulators have access to information about these transactions.

Volcker Rule: The Dodd-Frank Act also includes the Volcker Rule, which prohibits banks from engaging in proprietary trading and limits their ability to invest in hedge funds and private equity funds.

Impact of the Dodd-Frank Act

The Dodd-Frank Act has had a significant impact on the financial industry since it was passed in 2010. Some of the key impacts include:

Increased Oversight and Regulation: The Dodd-Frank Act has increased the level of oversight and regulation of the financial industry. This has resulted in increased compliance costs for financial institutions and has led to changes in the way that they conduct business.

Reduction in Risky Behavior: The Dodd-Frank Act has also reduced risky behavior in the financial industry by imposing new regulations on SIFIs and increasing capital requirements for banks and other financial institutions. This has made the financial system more stable and less susceptible to systemic risk.

Consumer Protection: The creation of the CFPB has also had a significant impact on consumer protection in the financial industry. The bureau has taken action against financial institutions that engage in predatory lending practices and has worked to ensure that consumers are not taken advantage of by financial institutions.

Derivatives Regulation: The regulations related to derivatives trading have also had an impact on the financial industry. By requiring certain derivatives to be traded on exchanges and cleared through central counterparties, regulators have increased transparency in the derivatives market and reduced the risk of another financial crisis.

Criticism of the Dodd-Frank Act

Despite its many benefits, the Dodd-Frank Act has also faced criticism from some quarters. Some of the main criticisms include:

Excessive Regulation: Some critics argue that the Dodd-Frank Act is overly burdensome and imposes excessive regulations on the financial industry. They argue that these regulations have stifled innovation and economic growth.

Too Big to Fail: Some critics argue that the Dodd-Frank Act has not gone far enough in addressing the issue of "too big to fail" banks. They argue that the act did not break up the largest banks or prevent them from becoming even larger, and that this leaves the financial system vulnerable to future crises.

Inadequate Consumer Protection: Some critics argue that the Dodd-Frank Act did not do enough to protect consumers from abusive and fraudulent practices by financial institutions. They argue that the act did not sufficiently empower regulatory agencies to take action against bad actors, and that consumers are still at risk of being taken advantage of by the financial industry.

Political Influence: Some critics argue that the Dodd-Frank Act is influenced by political interests and that it does not do enough to address the root causes of the financial crisis. They argue that the act does not adequately address issues such as income inequality and the concentration of wealth in the hands of a few powerful individuals and corporations.

Impact on Small Banks: Some critics argue that the Dodd-Frank Act has had a disproportionate impact on small banks and credit unions, which are unable to bear the costs of compliance with the act's regulations. They argue that this has led to a consolidation of the banking industry, with small banks being acquired by larger ones or going out of business altogether.

Challenges to Implementation: Finally, some critics argue that the Dodd-Frank Act has faced significant challenges in implementation, with regulatory agencies struggling to interpret and enforce its provisions. They argue that this has led to confusion and uncertainty in the financial industry, making it difficult for businesses to plan and invest for the future.

Despite these criticisms, many experts argue that the Dodd-Frank Act has been an important step forward in the regulation of the financial industry. It has helped to stabilize the financial system and prevent future crises, while also providing greater transparency and protection for consumers. However, there is still much work to be done to ensure that the financial industry operates in a safe and responsible manner, and that the benefits of the Dodd-Frank Act are realized by all members of society.

CHAPTER 5: EVOLUTION OF CRYPTOCURRENCY

Cryptocurrency is a digital or virtual currency that uses cryptography for security purposes. It is decentralized, meaning it operates independently of any central authority, such as a government or financial institution. Cryptocurrency has gained significant attention in recent years as a potential alternative to traditional currency and payment systems. The most well-known and valuable cryptocurrency is Bitcoin, but there are now thousands of different cryptocurrencies in circulation.

The concept of cryptocurrency is not new. In fact, the idea of digital cash dates back to the 1980s. However, it was not until the invention of Bitcoin in 2009 that cryptocurrency gained widespread attention and began to be taken seriously as a potential alternative to traditional currency.

This section will provide an overview of the evolution of cryptocurrency, from its earliest origins to its current state. It will examine the major milestones and developments that have shaped the cryptocurrency landscape, including the rise of Bitcoin, the emergence of alternative cryptocurrencies, and the challenges and opportunities facing the cryptocurrency industry today.

Origins of Cryptocurrency

The concept of digital cash can be traced back to the 1980s, when computer scientists were exploring ways to facilitate electronic transactions. One early example was David Chaum's concept of "eCash," which he proposed in a 1983 paper. Chaum's idea was to create a system of digital cash that would allow users to make anonymous and untraceable electronic payments.

Another important milestone in the development of cryptocurrency was the creation of "hashcash" in 1997. Hashcash was a proof-of-work system that was designed to prevent email spam and denial-of-service attacks. It involved the use of a computationally intensive puzzle that had to be solved in order to send an email or access a website.

The Birth of Bitcoin

The true birth of cryptocurrency can be traced back to 2008, when an unknown individual or group using the pseudonym "Satoshi Nakamoto" published a white paper entitled "Bitcoin: A Peer-to-Peer Electronic Cash System." The paper described a decentralized electronic cash system that would allow users to send and receive payments without the need for a central authority.

The key innovation of Bitcoin was the use of a distributed ledger called the "blockchain" to maintain a secure and transparent record of all transactions. The blockchain is a public ledger that is maintained by a network of computers around the world. Each computer in the network has a copy of the blockchain, and all transactions are verified and recorded in real time.

Bitcoin quickly gained a following among computer enthusiasts and libertarians who were interested in the idea of a decentralized currency that was not subject to government control or manipulation. In 2010, the first Bitcoin exchange was established, allowing users to buy and sell Bitcoins using traditional currencies.

The Rise of Alternative Cryptocurrencies

In the years following the introduction of Bitcoin, a number of alternative cryptocurrencies, or "altcoins," emerged. These cryptocurrencies were designed to address some of the perceived limitations of Bitcoin, such as slow transaction speeds and high fees.

One of the most successful alternative cryptocurrencies is Litecoin, which was created in 2011 by Charlie Lee, a former Google engineer. Litecoin is similar to Bitcoin, but it has a faster block time and a larger maximum supply. Other popular altcoins include Ethereum, Ripple, and Bitcoin Cash.

Challenges and Opportunities

Despite its many successes, the cryptocurrency industry faces a number of challenges and opportunities. Some of the key issues facing the industry include:

Regulation: Cryptocurrency is largely unregulated, which has led to concerns about money laundering, tax evasion, and other illegal activities. Governments around the world are grappling with how to regulate the cryptocurrency industry, and there is ongoing debate about whether and how to do so.

Volatility: Cryptocurrencies are highly volatile, with prices often fluctuating wildly in short periods of time. This volatility has made them attractive to investors seeking high returns, but it also makes them risky investments that can lead to significant losses.

Security: The decentralized nature of cryptocurrency means that there is no central authority to oversee transactions or protect investors in the event of theft or fraud. As a result, security is a major concern in the cryptocurrency industry, and there have been numerous high-profile hacks and thefts of cryptocurrency.

Adoption: While the number of people using cryptocurrency is growing, it is still a relatively niche technology. Adoption is hindered by a lack of awareness and understanding, as well as limited accessibility and usability for non-technical users.

Scalability: Cryptocurrencies such as Bitcoin have faced challenges with scalability, as the technology struggles to process large volumes of transactions quickly and efficiently. This has led to concerns about the viability of cryptocurrency as a mainstream payment system.

Opportunities

Despite these challenges, the cryptocurrency industry also presents numerous opportunities. Some of the key opportunities include:

Financial Inclusion: Cryptocurrency has the potential to provide financial services to individuals who are unbanked or underbanked. By allowing people to transact without the need for a bank account, cryptocurrency can help to promote financial inclusion and expand access to financial services.

Decentralization: The decentralized nature of cryptocurrency means that it is not subject to the same control as traditional financial systems. This can provide greater financial freedom and autonomy to users, and can help to prevent corruption and abuse of power.

Innovation: The cryptocurrency industry is a hotbed of innovation, with developers and entrepreneurs constantly working to create new and better technologies. This innovation has the potential to drive significant growth and create new opportunities for investors and users alike.

Globalization: Cryptocurrency is a global technology that can be used by anyone, anywhere in the world. This has the potential to break down barriers to international trade and create new opportunities for cross-border commerce.

Conclusion

The evolution of cryptocurrency has been a fascinating journey, marked by both successes and challenges. While the technology is still relatively new and faces numerous obstacles, it has already made a significant impact on the world of finance and has the potential to revolutionize the way we think about money and value.

As the cryptocurrency industry continues to grow and mature, it will be important to address the challenges it faces while also capitalizing on the opportunities it presents. This will require collaboration between developers, entrepreneurs, regulators, and users, as well as ongoing innovation and experimentation with new technologies and approaches.

Overall, the future of cryptocurrency is bright, and it will be exciting to see how this groundbreaking technology continues to evolve and shape the world around us.

The origins of cryptocurrency

Cryptocurrency, a type of digital or virtual currency that uses cryptography to secure transactions and control the creation of new units, has taken the world by storm in recent years. However, the idea of a decentralized digital currency has been around for decades. In this section, we will explore the origins of cryptocurrency, from its earliest precursors to the development of Bitcoin, the world's first and most well-known cryptocurrency.

Precursors to Cryptocurrency

The concept of digital cash, or an electronic version of physical currency that could be used for online transactions, dates back to the early days of the internet. In the 1980s and 1990s, several attempts were made to create digital currencies, but these early efforts faced a number of technical and legal challenges.

One of the earliest digital currencies was E-gold, which was founded in 1996 and allowed users to hold gold-backed digital currencies. Another early example was Liberty Reserve, which launched in 2006 and allowed users to buy and sell digital currencies that were backed by real-world assets such as gold and silver.

These early attempts at digital currency were largely centralized, meaning that they were controlled by a single entity or organization. This made them vulnerable to hacking and fraud, and they were often shut down by governments or law enforcement agencies.

The Birth of Bitcoin

The idea of a decentralized digital currency, one that could operate without a central authority or controlling entity, can be traced back to a paper published in 2008 by an unknown individual or group using the pseudonym "Satoshi Nakamoto". The paper, titled "Bitcoin: A Peer-to-Peer Electronic Cash System", outlined the technical details of a new digital currency called Bitcoin.

Bitcoin was designed to operate on a decentralized network, with transactions recorded on a public ledger called the blockchain. This allowed for a high degree of transparency and security, as every transaction was verified by multiple participants on the network.

One of the key innovations of Bitcoin was the use of cryptographic techniques to secure transactions and control the creation of new units. Unlike traditional currencies, which are issued and controlled by central banks, Bitcoin was designed to be self-regulating and decentralized.

Bitcoin also introduced the concept of mining, in which participants on the network compete to solve complex mathematical problems in order to validate transactions and earn new units of the currency. This process helps to keep the network secure and ensures that new units are created at a predictable rate.

The Rise of Cryptocurrency

Bitcoin was launched in 2009, and over the next few years, a number of other cryptocurrencies emerged. These new currencies were often based on the same principles as Bitcoin, but with different features and use cases.

One of the most well-known of these early cryptocurrencies was Litecoin, which was launched in 2011 and aimed to be a faster and more efficient alternative to Bitcoin. Other early cryptocurrencies included Namecoin, which was designed as a decentralized domain name system, and Ripple, which was aimed at providing a more efficient and cost-effective way to make cross-border payments.

Today, there are thousands of different cryptocurrencies in circulation, with a combined market capitalization of over $2 trillion as of early 2022. While Bitcoin remains the most well-known and widely used cryptocurrency, there are many other projects that are pushing the boundaries of what is possible with this technology.

Conclusion

The origins of cryptocurrency can be traced back to the early days of the internet, when pioneers were experimenting with ways to create digital currencies. However, it was not until the launch of Bitcoin in 2009 that the idea of a decentralized digital currency really took off.

Since then, cryptocurrency has become a global phenomenon, with millions of people using digital currencies to make transactions, invest, and participate in online communities. While the industry still faces a number of challenges and uncertainties, it has the potential to revolutionize the way we think about money and finance.

As cryptocurrency continues to evolve and gain mainstream acceptance, it is important for individuals and institutions alike to stay informed and up-to-date on developments in the industry. This includes understanding the underlying technology behind cryptocurrency, as well as the legal and regulatory landscape.

Overall, the story of cryptocurrency is a testament to the power of innovation and human creativity. By challenging traditional notions of money and finance, the cryptocurrency industry has opened up new possibilities for economic empowerment and financial inclusion. Whether or not cryptocurrency will eventually replace traditional forms of currency remains to be seen, but one thing is certain: the impact of cryptocurrency on our world is only just beginning.

The emergence of Bitcoin

The emergence of Bitcoin marked a significant turning point in the history of digital currencies. Bitcoin was the first decentralized digital currency, meaning it operates without a central authority, such as a government or bank. Instead, it relies on a peer-to-peer network of users to validate transactions and maintain the integrity of the currency.

In this section, we will explore the emergence of Bitcoin and how it has transformed the world of finance and technology.

The Early Days of Bitcoin

The story of Bitcoin begins in 2008, when a person or group of people under the pseudonym "Satoshi Nakamoto" released a white paper outlining the concept of a decentralized digital currency. The white paper, titled "Bitcoin: A Peer-to-Peer Electronic Cash System," described a system in which transactions would be verified by network nodes through cryptography and recorded on a public ledger known as the blockchain.

The first version of the Bitcoin software was released in January 2009, and the first Bitcoin transaction occurred between Satoshi Nakamoto and a programmer named Hal Finney. In the early days, Bitcoin was primarily used by a small community of enthusiasts, who were drawn to the idea of a currency that operated independently of governments and banks.

Bitcoin's Rise to Prominence

Over time, Bitcoin gained wider recognition and acceptance. By 2011, it had attracted the attention of mainstream media, and more merchants began accepting Bitcoin as a form of payment. In 2013, the price of a single Bitcoin surpassed $1,000 for the first time, sparking a surge of interest and investment.

The growth of Bitcoin was driven in part by its unique properties. Unlike traditional currencies, which are subject to inflation and devaluation through government policies, Bitcoin has a fixed supply cap of 21 million coins. This means that as demand for Bitcoin increases, its value is likely to rise, making it an attractive investment opportunity for many people.

In addition, Bitcoin offers a high level of privacy and security. Transactions are recorded on the blockchain, which is a decentralized, public ledger that is virtually impossible to alter or hack. This makes it an attractive option for individuals and businesses seeking to protect their financial transactions from prying eyes.

Challenges and Controversies

Despite its many benefits, Bitcoin has also faced its share of challenges and controversies. Some of the main issues include:

Volatility: Bitcoin's value is highly volatile, with prices often fluctuating wildly in short periods of time. This makes it a risky investment option for some people.

Security: While Bitcoin transactions are generally considered secure, there have been instances of theft and hacking that have raised concerns about the currency's overall security.

Regulatory challenges: As a decentralized currency, Bitcoin operates outside of the traditional regulatory framework, which has led to uncertainty and challenges in terms of taxation, money laundering, and other legal issues.

Energy consumption: Bitcoin mining, the process by which new coins are created, requires a significant amount of computational power and energy. This has raised concerns about the environmental impact of Bitcoin and other cryptocurrencies.

Conclusion

The emergence of Bitcoin has had a profound impact on the world of finance and technology. It has opened up new opportunities for investment, commerce, and innovation, while also presenting significant challenges and uncertainties. As the cryptocurrency industry continues to evolve, it will be important to monitor developments and assess the potential risks and benefits of these emerging technologies.

The benefits and drawbacks of cryptocurrency

Cryptocurrency has become a popular topic of discussion in recent years, with its proponents touting its many benefits while its critics remain skeptical. In this section, we will explore the advantages and disadvantages of cryptocurrency, and examine the different perspectives on this emerging technology.

Benefits of cryptocurrency

Decentralization and security

One of the key benefits of cryptocurrency is its decentralized nature, meaning that it operates without the need for a central authority or intermediary. This allows for greater security, as the transactions are verified and recorded on a distributed ledger called the blockchain, which is maintained by a network of nodes rather than a single entity. This makes it difficult for hackers to manipulate or corrupt the data, as the blockchain is designed to be tamper-proof.

Accessibility

Another advantage of cryptocurrency is its accessibility. Unlike traditional banking systems, which can be complicated and exclusionary, anyone with an internet connection can access and use cryptocurrency. This makes it particularly useful for people who live in areas with limited access to banking services, or who are unable to open bank accounts due to issues such as immigration status.

Speed and efficiency

Cryptocurrency transactions are also much faster and more efficient than traditional financial transactions. This is because they do not require intermediaries such as banks or other financial institutions, which can slow down the process and increase costs. Instead, cryptocurrency transactions are conducted peer-to-peer, with the funds transferred directly between users.

Transparency

Cryptocurrency is also transparent, as all transactions are recorded on the blockchain and can be viewed by anyone with an internet connection. This makes it easier to track and verify transactions, and reduces the risk of fraud and corruption.

Potential for growth

Finally, cryptocurrency has significant potential for growth, as it is still a relatively new and rapidly evolving technology. Many experts predict that the cryptocurrency market will continue to expand in the coming years, potentially offering new opportunities for investment and innovation.

Drawbacks of cryptocurrency

Volatility

One of the biggest drawbacks of cryptocurrency is its volatility. Cryptocurrencies such as Bitcoin and Ethereum are notorious for their price fluctuations, which can be dramatic and unpredictable. This makes them a risky investment, and many people are wary of putting their money into a currency that can lose value so quickly.

Lack of regulation

Another major issue facing the cryptocurrency industry is the lack of regulation. Because it operates outside of traditional banking systems, cryptocurrency is largely unregulated, which has led to concerns about money laundering, tax evasion, and other illegal activities. Governments around the world are grappling with how to regulate the cryptocurrency industry, and there is ongoing debate about whether and how to do so.

Security concerns

While the blockchain is designed to be secure, there have been several high-profile hacks and security breaches in the cryptocurrency industry in recent years. These incidents have raised concerns about the vulnerability of the technology, and have led some people to question its long-term viability.

Limited acceptance

Although cryptocurrency is becoming more widely accepted, it is still not as widely used as traditional currencies. This means that there are limited opportunities for people to spend or exchange their cryptocurrency, which can make it less attractive as a form of payment.

Complexity

Finally, cryptocurrency can be complicated and difficult to understand for people who are not familiar with the technology. The terminology and concepts can be confusing, and many people are put off by the learning curve required to use cryptocurrency effectively.

Conclusion

In conclusion, cryptocurrency has both benefits and drawbacks, and its future is still uncertain. While it offers the potential for greater security, accessibility, and efficiency, it also comes with significant risks and challenges. As the technology continues to evolve and mature, it will be important for governments, businesses, and individuals to carefully consider the opportunities and risks associated with cryptocurrency,

The future of cryptocurrency

The emergence of cryptocurrency has led to significant changes in the financial landscape, with new opportunities and challenges for investors, businesses, and governments. While the industry is still relatively new, there are many predictions and projections about where it may be headed in the future. This section will examine some of the potential developments and trends in the cryptocurrency space.

Advancements in Technology

One of the most important factors in the future of cryptocurrency is likely to be advancements in technology. The underlying blockchain technology that powers cryptocurrencies is still relatively new, and there are ongoing efforts to improve and enhance it. Some of the potential areas of development include:

Scalability: One of the biggest challenges facing blockchain technology is its limited scalability. Currently, many blockchains can only process a small number of transactions per second, which makes them unsuitable for large-scale applications. However, there are ongoing efforts to improve scalability through techniques such as sharding and off-chain transactions.

Interoperability: Another challenge for the cryptocurrency industry is interoperability, or the ability of different blockchains to communicate and work together. Currently, there are many different blockchains with their own unique protocols, which can make it difficult for them to interoperate. However, there are ongoing efforts to develop standards and protocols that will allow different blockchains to communicate and share data.

Privacy: While cryptocurrencies offer a high degree of anonymity, they are not completely private. Transactions on the blockchain are visible to anyone with access to the network, which can create privacy concerns for users. There are ongoing efforts to develop new privacy-enhancing technologies, such as zero-knowledge proofs and ring signatures, that can help address these concerns.

Regulatory Developments

Another important factor in the future of cryptocurrency is likely to be regulatory developments. As the industry continues to grow and mature, governments around the world are grappling with how to regulate it. Some of the potential regulatory developments include:

Increased Oversight: Governments may seek to increase their oversight of the cryptocurrency industry to prevent illegal activities such as money laundering and terrorist financing. This could involve more stringent KYC (know-your-customer) and AML (anti-money-laundering) regulations.

Taxation: As the use of cryptocurrencies becomes more widespread, governments may seek to tax transactions involving digital currencies. This could involve the introduction of new tax laws and regulations specifically targeted at cryptocurrencies.

Legal Recognition: Currently, many governments do not legally recognize cryptocurrencies, which can create legal and regulatory uncertainty for users and businesses. In the future, governments may seek to provide legal recognition to cryptocurrencies and establish clear legal frameworks for their use.

The Role of Central Banks

Another important factor in the future of cryptocurrency is likely to be the role of central banks. Currently, most central banks are skeptical of cryptocurrencies and view them as a potential threat to financial stability. However, there are ongoing efforts to explore the potential benefits of central bank digital currencies (CBDCs), which could offer many of the benefits of cryptocurrencies while also providing the stability and security of traditional currencies. Some potential benefits of CBDCs include:

Increased Efficiency: CBDCs could potentially offer faster and more efficient payment systems, reducing the need for intermediaries such as banks and payment processors.

Improved Financial Inclusion: CBDCs could potentially help address issues of financial exclusion, as they could be made available to anyone with a mobile phone, regardless of their access to traditional banking services.

Greater Monetary Policy Control: CBDCs could potentially allow central banks to have greater control over monetary policy, as they would have direct control over the money supply.

However, there are also potential drawbacks to the introduction of CBDCs. For example, they could potentially lead to increased surveillance of financial transactions and undermine the anonymity and privacy that many people value in cryptocurrencies.

Environmental Concerns

Another major issue facing the future of cryptocurrency is the environmental impact of mining and transactions. The process of mining cryptocurrencies like Bitcoin requires vast amounts of computing power, which in turn consumes large amounts of electricity. As the price of cryptocurrencies has soared, so too has the energy consumption associated with their mining and transactions.

This energy consumption has significant environmental implications, particularly as much of the electricity used to power mining operations comes from non-renewable sources like coal and natural gas. In addition, the process of mining cryptocurrencies generates a significant amount of electronic waste, as obsolete mining equipment is discarded and replaced.

In response to these concerns, some cryptocurrency projects are exploring more energy-efficient and environmentally-friendly alternatives. For example, the cryptocurrency Chia is designed to be mined using hard drive space rather than computing power, which is significantly less energy-intensive. Other projects are exploring the use of renewable energy sources to power mining operations.

Regulatory Challenges

As cryptocurrencies continue to grow in popularity and influence, they are also attracting increased attention from governments and regulatory bodies around the world. While some countries have embraced cryptocurrencies and are working to create regulatory frameworks that support their use, others are more skeptical and have sought to restrict or ban them outright.

The lack of a clear regulatory framework for cryptocurrencies creates a number of challenges and uncertainties for businesses and consumers alike. For example, it can be difficult for cryptocurrency exchanges and other service providers to navigate a patchwork of conflicting regulations in different jurisdictions. Additionally, consumers may be hesitant to invest in or use cryptocurrencies if they are uncertain about the legal and regulatory landscape.

Looking Ahead

Despite the challenges and uncertainties facing cryptocurrency, many experts believe that it has the potential to revolutionize the way we think about money and finance. As more businesses and individuals begin to embrace cryptocurrencies, their use is likely to become more mainstream and integrated into the global financial system.

In the short term, the development of CBDCs is likely to be a major driver of change in the cryptocurrency space. As governments around the world begin to explore the introduction of digital versions of their national currencies, the competition between cryptocurrencies and CBDCs is likely to intensify. It remains to be seen which model will ultimately emerge as the dominant force in the global financial system.

Overall, the future of cryptocurrency is likely to be shaped by a wide range of factors, including technological innovation, environmental concerns, and regulatory frameworks. While there are certainly challenges and uncertainties ahead, the potential benefits of cryptocurrency are significant, and it is clear that this is a space that will continue to evolve and develop in the years to come.

CHAPTER 6: COMMERCIAL BANKS

In today's world, banks have become an integral part of our lives. We use them to deposit our paychecks, pay bills, transfer funds, and take out loans. Banks are essential for the smooth functioning of our economy, as they facilitate the circulation of money and credit. In this chapter, we will focus on commercial banks, which are the most common type of banks that individuals and businesses use for their financial transactions.

Commercial banks have a unique position in the financial system, as they are the primary source of credit in the economy. They provide loans to individuals and businesses, which help them to finance their investments and achieve their goals. Commercial banks are also responsible for safeguarding the deposits of their customers, which makes them a crucial element of the financial infrastructure.

In this chapter, we will explore the functions of commercial banks, their organizational structure, the different types of services they offer, and the regulatory framework that governs their operations. We will also discuss the role of commercial banks in promoting economic growth, as well as the risks and challenges that they face in their day-to-day operations.

To provide a comprehensive understanding of commercial banks, we will begin by defining the concept of a bank and its historical evolution. We will then delve into the functions of commercial banks, which include accepting deposits, making loans, and providing other financial services. We will discuss the organizational structure of commercial banks, including their hierarchy, branches, and departments.

Next, we will examine the different types of services that commercial banks offer. These services include deposit accounts, credit products, and payment services. We will also look at the different types of customers that commercial banks serve, such as retail customers, small and medium-sized enterprises, and large corporations.

We will then move on to the regulatory framework that governs the operations of commercial banks. We will examine the role of the central bank, which is responsible for regulating and supervising commercial banks. We will also discuss the importance of prudential regulations, which aim to maintain the stability and soundness of the banking system.

Finally, we will conclude this chapter by looking at the role of commercial banks in promoting economic growth. We will explore the link between banking and economic development, and how commercial banks can facilitate investment, innovation, and entrepreneurship. We will also examine the challenges that commercial banks face, such as competition, technological disruption, and regulatory compliance.

Overall, this chapter aims to provide a comprehensive overview of commercial banks and their role in the economy. By the end of this chapter, readers should have a clear understanding of the functions of commercial banks, their organizational structure, the services they offer, and the regulatory framework that governs their operations.

Definition of Commercial Banks

Commercial banks are financial institutions that are licensed to accept deposits from customers and make loans to individuals, businesses, and governments. They are for-profit institutions that play a crucial role in the economy by facilitating economic activity, providing credit to businesses, and creating a stable financial system.

Commercial banks are also known as retail banks because they provide services to individual customers, such as deposit accounts, personal loans, mortgages, and credit cards. They also offer a range of financial products and services, including savings accounts, checking accounts, and certificates of deposit (CDs).

Functions of Commercial Banks

Commercial banks perform several important functions that are vital to the functioning of the economy. Some of the key functions of commercial banks include:

Accepting Deposits: Commercial banks accept deposits from customers, which can be withdrawn on demand or kept for a specified period. Deposits can be in the form of savings accounts, current accounts, and fixed deposits.

Providing Loans: Commercial banks make loans to individuals, businesses, and governments. They provide a range of loan products, including personal loans, home loans, car loans, business loans, and government loans.

Issuing Credit Cards: Commercial banks issue credit cards to customers, allowing them to make purchases on credit.

Offering Investment Products: Commercial banks offer a range of investment products, including mutual funds, insurance policies, and fixed deposits.

Providing Payment Services: Commercial banks offer payment services, such as check clearing, wire transfers, and electronic fund transfers (EFTs).

Role of Commercial Banks in the Economy

Commercial banks play a critical role in the economy by providing credit to businesses and individuals, mobilizing savings, and facilitating economic activity. Some of the key roles that commercial banks play in the economy include:

Facilitating Economic Growth: Commercial banks provide credit to businesses, which helps them to grow and expand. This, in turn, leads to increased economic activity and job creation.

Mobilizing Savings: Commercial banks mobilize savings from individuals and businesses, which can then be used to make loans and investments.

Creating a Stable Financial System: Commercial banks create a stable financial system by providing liquidity to the economy, maintaining a balance between demand and supply of credit, and managing risks.

Providing Financial Services to Underserved Communities: Commercial banks also play an important role in providing financial services to underserved communities, such as low-income households and small businesses.

International Definitions

The definition of commercial banks may vary across different countries, depending on their legal and regulatory frameworks. However, some common characteristics of commercial banks across different countries include:

Accepting Deposits: Commercial banks are licensed to accept deposits from customers, which can be withdrawn on demand or kept for a specified period.

Making Loans: Commercial banks make loans to individuals, businesses, and governments, and charge interest on those loans.

Providing Payment Services: Commercial banks offer payment services, such as check clearing, wire transfers, and electronic fund transfers (EFTs).

Offering a Range of Financial Products and Services: Commercial banks offer a range of financial products and services, including savings accounts, checking accounts, credit cards, and investment products.

Conclusion

In conclusion, commercial banks are financial institutions that play a crucial role in the economy by providing credit to businesses and individuals, mobilizing savings, and facilitating economic activity. They perform several important functions, including accepting deposits, making loans, providing payment services, and offering a range of financial products and services. The definition of commercial banks may vary across different countries, but they share common characteristics such as accepting deposits, making loans, providing payment services, and offering a range of financial products and services.

Functions of Commercial Banks

Commercial banks play a vital role in the economy by performing various functions that are essential for facilitating economic growth and development.

In this section, we will explore the primary functions of commercial banks, including deposit mobilization, lending, investment, and agency services.

Deposit Mobilization

One of the primary functions of commercial banks is deposit mobilization. Banks collect funds from the public in the form of deposits, which can be either demand deposits or time deposits. Demand deposits are those deposits that can be withdrawn by the depositor on demand, while time deposits are deposits that cannot be withdrawn for a specific period of time. Banks pay interest on these deposits to attract depositors.

Lending

Lending is another important function of commercial banks. Banks lend money to individuals, businesses, and governments for various purposes such as starting a business, buying a home, or financing a project. The interest charged on loans is the primary source of income for banks.

Investment

Commercial banks also invest the funds they collect in various types of securities and assets. These investments can be short-term or long-term and are made to generate income and increase the value of the bank's assets. Banks invest in various instruments such as government securities, corporate bonds, and stocks.

Agency Services

In addition to deposit mobilization, lending, and investment, commercial banks also provide agency services to their customers. These services include collection of cheques, payment of bills, and remittance of funds. Banks also act as intermediaries in buying and selling securities and provide advisory services to customers on investment and financial planning.

Foreign Exchange Services

Another function of commercial banks is foreign exchange services. Banks facilitate foreign trade by providing services such as currency exchange, foreign currency accounts, and letters of credit. They also provide financing for international trade transactions.

Credit Creation

One of the most significant functions of commercial banks is credit creation. When banks lend money to borrowers, they create credit in the economy. Banks create credit by keeping only a fraction of the deposits they receive as reserves and lending out the rest. This process is known as fractional reserve banking and allows banks to create credit in the economy, which can stimulate economic growth.

Innovative Financial Services

Commercial banks also offer innovative financial services such as online banking, mobile banking, and electronic funds transfer. These services enable customers to access their accounts and carry out transactions from anywhere in the world. Banks also use technology to enhance their services, such as artificial intelligence and blockchain.

Conclusion

In conclusion, commercial banks are vital institutions in the financial system that perform various functions essential for economic growth and development. The primary functions of commercial banks include deposit mobilization, lending, investment, agency services, foreign exchange services, credit creation, and innovative financial services. By performing these functions, commercial banks play a crucial role in the economy by facilitating trade, commerce, and investment, and by creating credit, which stimulates economic growth.

Types of Commercial Banks

Commercial banks can be categorized into different types based on their ownership, size, and services provided. In this section, we will explore the various types of commercial banks and their characteristics.

Public Sector Banks

Public sector banks are owned and operated by the government. In many countries, including India, China, and Brazil, public sector banks are dominant players in the banking industry. These banks are typically established to promote economic development, provide financial services to underserved populations, and support government programs. They often have a social mandate to provide credit to priority sectors, such as agriculture, small and medium-sized enterprises, and low-income households. Public sector banks may also offer concessional interest rates and other benefits to their customers.

Private Sector Banks

Private sector banks are owned and operated by private individuals or companies. They are profit-oriented institutions and are typically more competitive and innovative than public sector banks. Private sector banks are often more efficient and customer-centric, as they have to compete with other banks to attract and retain customers. They may also offer a wider range of financial products and services than public sector banks. Private sector banks may have a higher minimum balance requirement and may charge higher fees than public sector banks.

Foreign Banks

Foreign banks are commercial banks that are headquartered in a foreign country but have a presence in other countries. They may operate through branches, subsidiaries, or representative offices. Foreign banks can bring in foreign capital and technology, increase competition in the domestic banking sector, and provide access to international financial markets. However, they may also pose a risk to the domestic banking sector by transferring funds abroad and engaging in risky activities. Foreign banks may also have a different business culture and may not fully understand the local market and regulatory environment.

Regional Banks

Regional banks are commercial banks that operate in a specific region or locality. They may be owned by private individuals, companies, or the government. Regional banks often focus on serving the financial needs of local communities and businesses. They may have a better understanding of the local market and may offer customized financial products and services. Regional banks may also have lower overhead costs and may charge lower fees than larger banks.

Online Banks

Online banks are commercial banks that operate primarily through the internet or other electronic channels. They may not have physical branches or

ATMs and may offer a limited range of financial products and services. Online banks can provide convenience and accessibility to customers, as they can conduct banking transactions anytime and anywhere. They may also offer higher interest rates and lower fees than traditional banks. However, online banks may pose a security risk to customers and may not be able to provide personalized customer service.

Cooperative Banks

Cooperative banks are commercial banks that are owned and operated by their customers. They are typically established to serve the financial needs of a specific group, such as farmers, artisans, or small traders. Cooperative banks operate on the principle of mutual self-help, where the customers pool their resources to provide credit and other financial services to each other. Cooperative banks may offer lower interest rates and fees than other types of banks, as they are not profit-oriented institutions. However, they may also face challenges in terms of governance, management, and risk management.

Conclusion

Commercial banks are an essential part of the financial system, providing a range of services that help facilitate economic activity. They can be categorized into different types based on their ownership, size, and services provided. Each type of commercial bank has its own characteristics, advantages, and challenges. Understanding the types of commercial banks can help individuals and businesses choose the bank that best meets their financial needs.

Products and Services offered by Commercial Banks

Commercial banks offer a wide range of financial products and services to their customers. These products and services are designed to meet the needs of different customers, including individuals, businesses, and government institutions. In this section, we will explore the different products and services offered by commercial banks, including deposit accounts, loans, credit cards, and other financial products.

Deposit Accounts

Deposit accounts are the primary products offered by commercial banks. They are used by customers to deposit their money with the bank, and the bank pays interest on the deposits. There are several types of deposit accounts offered by commercial banks, including:

Savings accounts: Savings accounts are accounts that are designed to help customers save money. These accounts usually offer a lower interest rate than other accounts, but they may have fewer fees and charges.

Checking accounts: Checking accounts are accounts that are used for everyday transactions, such as paying bills and making purchases. These accounts usually have higher fees and charges than savings accounts, but they also offer more convenience and flexibility.

Money market accounts: Money market accounts are accounts that offer a higher interest rate than savings accounts, but they usually require a higher minimum balance.

Certificates of deposit (CDs): CDs are accounts that require customers to deposit money for a fixed period of time, usually ranging from three months to five years. CDs typically offer a higher interest rate than other types of deposit accounts.

Loans

Commercial banks also offer various types of loans to their customers. Loans are a way for customers to borrow money from the bank, and they must be repaid with interest over time. Some of the most common types of loans offered by commercial banks include:

Personal loans: Personal loans are loans that are used for personal expenses, such as home improvements, vacations, and medical bills.

Business loans: Business loans are loans that are used to finance business expenses, such as purchasing equipment or expanding operations.

Mortgage loans: Mortgage loans are loans that are used to finance the purchase of a home. They are typically paid back over a period of 15 to 30 years.

Auto loans: Auto loans are loans that are used to finance the purchase of a vehicle. They are typically paid back over a period of 3 to 7 years.

Credit Cards

Credit cards are another popular product offered by commercial banks. Credit cards are a type of loan that allows customers to borrow money from the bank to make purchases. The customer must repay the loan with interest over time. Some of the benefits of using credit cards include:

Rewards programs: Many credit cards offer rewards programs that allow customers to earn points, cash back, or other rewards for making purchases.

Convenience: Credit cards are a convenient way to make purchases, especially online or while traveling.

Credit building: Using a credit card responsibly can help customers build their credit score over time.

Other Financial Products

In addition to deposit accounts, loans, and credit cards, commercial banks offer a range of other financial products and services to their customers, including:

Investment products: Many commercial banks offer investment products, such as mutual funds, stocks, and bonds.

Insurance products: Commercial banks also offer various types of insurance products, including life insurance, home insurance, and auto insurance.

Wealth management services: Some commercial banks offer wealth management services to their high-net-worth customers. These services may include investment management, financial planning, and estate planning.

Conclusion

Commercial banks offer a wide range of financial products and services to their customers. From deposit accounts and loans to credit cards and other financial products, commercial banks are an important part of the financial system. By offering these products and services, commercial banks help individuals, businesses, and government institutions manage their finances, save for the future, and access credit when needed. In this section, we will explore the different financial products and services that commercial banks offer.

Regulation of Commercial Banks

Regulation of commercial banks is essential to maintain financial stability and ensure the safety and soundness of the banking system. Governments and regulatory authorities impose rules and regulations on commercial banks to prevent risks that can cause financial crises, and to protect consumers and depositors. In this section, we will explore the regulation of commercial banks, including the history of bank regulation, the key regulatory agencies, and the types of regulations imposed on commercial banks.

History of Bank Regulation

Bank regulation has a long history, dating back to ancient times. In ancient Mesopotamia, for example, lending was governed by the Code of Hammurabi, which established interest rate caps and penalties for loan defaults. The first modern bank regulation laws were enacted in the United States in the early 19th century, in response to the failure of many state-chartered banks.

In the United States, bank regulation is primarily the responsibility of the federal government, specifically the Federal Reserve System. The Federal Reserve System was created in 1913, following a series of financial panics, to provide stability to the banking system and regulate monetary policy. Over the years, the role of the Federal Reserve has expanded to include bank supervision and regulation.

Key Regulatory Agencies

In addition to the Federal Reserve System, several other regulatory agencies oversee and regulate commercial banks in the United States. These agencies include:

Federal Deposit Insurance Corporation (FDIC): The FDIC was created in 1933 to provide deposit insurance and ensure the safety and soundness of the banking system. The FDIC insures deposits up to $250,000 per depositor per insured bank.

Office of the Comptroller of the Currency (OCC): The OCC is an independent bureau within the U.S. Department of the Treasury that charters, regulates, and supervises all national banks with assets over $10 billion and federal savings associations.

National Credit Union Administration (NCUA): The NCUA is an independent federal agency that regulates and supervises federal credit unions and insures deposits up to $250,000 per depositor per credit union.

Types of Regulations Imposed on Commercial Banks

There are various types of regulations imposed on commercial banks, including:

Capital Requirements: Capital requirements are regulations that require banks to maintain a minimum level of capital to support their operations and absorb potential losses. Capital is the amount of money that banks have invested in their operations and can use to absorb losses. Capital requirements ensure that banks have enough financial resources to withstand losses and remain solvent.

Liquidity Requirements: Liquidity requirements are regulations that require banks to maintain a certain level of liquid assets, such as cash and government securities, to meet their short-term obligations. These requirements ensure that banks can meet their obligations to depositors and creditors, even in times of financial stress.

Reserve Requirements: Reserve requirements are regulations that require banks to hold a certain percentage of their deposits in reserve accounts at the Federal Reserve. These reserves serve as a buffer against unexpected withdrawals and provide a source of liquidity for the banking system.

Consumer Protection: Consumer protection regulations aim to ensure that consumers are treated fairly and protected from abusive or deceptive practices. These regulations include requirements for disclosure of terms and fees, limits on interest rates, and protection against discrimination.

Anti-Money Laundering (AML) Regulations: AML regulations are designed to prevent banks from being used to facilitate criminal activities such as money laundering and terrorist financing. These regulations require banks to establish and maintain effective AML programs, which include procedures for identifying and reporting suspicious activity.

Bank Secrecy Act (BSA): The BSA is a federal law that requires banks to report certain transactions to the government to prevent money laundering and other financial crimes.

Stress Testing: Stress testing is a process by which banks assess the potential impact of adverse economic events on their financial health. The Federal Reserve conducts annual stress tests on large banks to ensure that they have sufficient capital to withstand a severe economic downturn. Stress testing is an important tool for regulators to monitor the stability of the financial system and prevent another financial crisis like the one in 2008.

Consumer Protection Laws: Commercial banks are also subject to a variety of consumer protection laws designed to ensure that customers are treated fairly and protected from predatory practices. The Consumer Financial Protection Bureau (CFPB) is a federal agency responsible for enforcing many of these laws, including the Truth in Lending Act, the Fair Credit Reporting Act, and the Fair Debt Collection Practices Act. These laws require banks to disclose certain information to customers, provide access to credit reports, and prohibit certain unfair or deceptive practices.

Capital Requirements: Banks are required to hold a certain amount of capital as a buffer against potential losses. This capital requirement is set by regulators and is designed to ensure that banks have sufficient resources to withstand losses and continue operating even during periods of financial stress. The capital requirements vary depending on the size and risk profile of the bank, with larger and more complex banks generally subject to higher requirements.

Resolution Planning: The Dodd-Frank Wall Street Reform and Consumer Protection Act of 2010 requires banks to develop resolution plans, or "living wills," that outline how the bank would be resolved in the event of a failure. These plans are designed to ensure that the failure of a large bank does not cause widespread disruption to the financial system. The Federal Reserve and the FDIC review these plans annually and can require banks to make changes if they are deemed inadequate.

Conclusion: Commercial banks play a critical role in the economy by providing financial services to individuals, businesses, and government institutions. However, because of their importance and the potential risks they pose to the financial system, commercial banks are subject to extensive regulation by federal and state agencies. These regulations are designed to ensure that banks operate in a safe and sound manner, protect consumers from abusive practices, and maintain the stability of the financial system.

CHAPTER 7: CREDIT UNIONS

Credit unions are financial cooperatives that are owned and controlled by their members. These institutions offer a range of financial products and services, including loans, savings accounts, and checking accounts. Credit unions operate under the principle of "people helping people," and their primary objective is to provide affordable financial services to their members.

Credit unions have a long history, dating back to the mid-19th century when the first cooperative credit society was established in Germany. Today, credit unions are found in many countries around the world and are an important part of the financial system. In this chapter, we will explore the history, structure, and functions of credit unions, as well as the benefits and drawbacks of membership.

History of Credit Unions

The origins of credit unions can be traced back to the mid-19th century in Germany. In 1849, Franz Hermann Schulze-Delitzsch founded the first cooperative credit society in Germany, which aimed to provide affordable credit to small business owners and artisans. This model was later adopted in other countries, including France and Italy.

The credit union movement in the United States began in the early 20th century. In 1909, the St. Mary's Bank Credit Union was established in Manchester, New Hampshire, becoming the first credit union in the United States. Credit unions quickly gained popularity among workers, especially those who were not able to access traditional banking services. By 1920, there were over 1,000 credit unions in the United States, serving over 100,000 members.

Structure and Functions of Credit Unions

Credit unions are non-profit financial cooperatives that are owned and controlled by their members. Members typically share a common bond, such as working for the same employer or living in the same community. Credit unions are governed by a board of directors, which is elected by the members.

Credit unions offer a range of financial products and services, including loans, savings accounts, and checking accounts. These institutions operate under the principle of "people helping people," and their primary objective is to provide affordable financial services to their members. Credit unions are generally able to offer lower interest rates on loans and higher interest rates on savings accounts than traditional banks, as they operate on a not-for-profit basis and do not have to generate profits for shareholders.

Benefits of Credit Union Membership

Credit unions offer a number of benefits to their members, including:

Lower Fees: Credit unions typically charge lower fees than traditional banks, as they operate on a not-for-profit basis and do not have to generate profits for shareholders.

Lower Interest Rates: Credit unions are able to offer lower interest rates on loans and credit cards than traditional banks, as they operate on a not-for-profit basis and do not have to generate profits for shareholders.

Personalized Service: Credit unions are typically smaller than traditional banks, which allows them to offer more personalized service to their members. Members are often able to speak directly with a loan officer or other financial professional to discuss their financial needs.

Community Focus: Credit unions are often deeply rooted in their local communities and are committed to serving the needs of their members.

Drawbacks of Credit Union Membership

Despite the benefits of credit union membership, there are also some potential drawbacks, including:

Limited Access: Credit unions typically have a smaller network of branches and ATMs than traditional banks, which can make it more difficult for members to access their accounts when traveling or living in a different area.

Limited Services: Credit unions may not offer the same range of financial products and services as traditional banks, which can limit members' options when it comes to managing their finances.

Membership Requirements: Credit unions typically require members to meet certain eligibility requirements, such as living in a particular geographic area or working for a specific employer or industry. This can limit the pool of potential members and make it difficult for some individuals to join.

Lower Technology Investment: Due to their smaller size and limited resources, credit unions may not have the same level of technology investment as larger banks. This can result in a less user-friendly online banking experience and slower adoption of new financial technologies.

Limited Accessibility to Loans: Credit unions may have stricter lending requirements compared to traditional banks, which can make it more difficult for some members to access loans or credit products. Additionally, credit unions may have limited lending capacity due to their smaller size and resources.

Lower Interest Rates: While credit unions typically offer lower fees and interest rates compared to traditional banks, this can also be a disadvantage for savers who are looking for higher returns on their deposits.

Limited Branch Access: Credit unions may not have as many branches or ATMs as traditional banks, which can make it difficult for members to access their accounts when they need to make deposits, withdrawals or other transactions.

Difficulty Scaling: Due to their cooperative structure, credit unions may face difficulty in scaling up their operations and expanding their reach beyond their local communities. This can limit their ability to compete with larger banks and financial institutions.

Conclusion:

Overall, credit unions offer a unique alternative to traditional banks, with lower fees and interest rates, personalized customer service, and a focus on community involvement. However, they also have limitations in terms of accessibility, technology investment, and lending capacity, which can make it difficult for some individuals to access their services. As with any financial decision, it is important to carefully consider your options and choose the institution that best fits your individual needs and goals.

Definition of Credit Unions

Credit unions are financial institutions that are member-owned and democratically controlled. They provide a range of financial services to their members, including savings accounts, loans, and other financial products. Credit unions are typically formed by people who share a common bond, such as living in the same community, working for the same employer, or belonging to the same organization. In this section, we will explore the definition of credit unions, their history, and the key characteristics that set them apart from traditional banks.

What is a Credit Union?
A credit union is a not-for-profit financial institution that is owned and operated by its members. Members of credit unions pool their resources together to create a financial cooperative that provides a range of financial services to its members. Unlike traditional banks, which are owned by shareholders and focus on generating profits, credit unions are owned by their members and focus on meeting their financial needs.

Credit unions offer a range of financial products and services, including savings accounts, checking accounts, loans, mortgages, and credit cards. They also offer financial education and other services to help members manage their finances and improve their financial literacy.

History of Credit Unions
Credit unions have a long history that dates back to the 19th century. The first credit union was founded in Germany in 1852 by Friedrich Wilhelm Raiffeisen. Raiffeisen's goal was to create a cooperative financial institution that would provide affordable credit to farmers who were struggling to obtain loans from traditional banks.

The credit union movement quickly spread throughout Europe and eventually made its way to the United States. The first credit union in the United States was founded in 1908 in Manchester, New Hampshire. Since then, credit unions have grown in popularity and are now found in countries all over the world.

Key Characteristics of Credit Unions

Credit unions have several key characteristics that set them apart from traditional banks:

Member-Owned: Credit unions are owned and operated by their members. Each member has a say in how the credit union is run and can vote on important decisions, such as electing the board of directors.

Not-For-Profit: Credit unions are not-for-profit institutions, which means that they do not aim to generate profits for shareholders. Instead, they focus on meeting the financial needs of their members.

Community-Focused: Credit unions are often focused on serving a specific community, such as people who live in a particular area or work for a particular employer.

Membership Requirements: Credit unions typically have membership requirements, such as living in a particular geographic area, belonging to a particular organization, or working for a particular employer.

Limited Access: Credit unions typically have a smaller network of branches and ATMs than traditional banks, which can make it more difficult for members to access their accounts when traveling or living in a different area.

Limited Services: Credit unions may not offer the same range of financial products and services as traditional banks, which can limit members' options when it comes to managing their finances.

Conclusion
Credit unions are member-owned financial institutions that provide a range of financial products and services to their members. They are not-for-profit institutions that focus on meeting the financial needs of their members, rather than generating profits for shareholders. Credit unions have a long history that dates back to the 19th century and are now found in countries all over the world. They have several key characteristics that set them apart from traditional banks, including their community focus, membership requirements, and limited access and services.

Differences between Credit Unions and Commercial Banks

While both credit unions and commercial banks offer financial products and services, there are significant differences between the two. Credit unions are not-for-profit organizations that are owned by their members and are designed to provide financial services to a specific group of people. Commercial banks, on the other hand, are for-profit institutions that offer financial services to the general public.

Ownership and Governance:

One of the most significant differences between credit unions and commercial banks is ownership and governance. Credit unions are owned by their members, who also elect the board of directors that manages the institution. In contrast, commercial banks are typically owned by shareholders who elect a board of directors that governs the institution.

Profit Motive:

Another significant difference between credit unions and commercial banks is the profit motive. Credit unions are not-for-profit organizations that are designed to provide financial services to their members at a lower cost than traditional banks. In contrast, commercial banks are for-profit institutions that are driven by the need to generate profits for their shareholders.

Interest Rates and Fees:

Credit unions are known for offering lower interest rates on loans and higher interest rates on deposits than commercial banks. This is because credit unions are owned by their members and are not driven by the profit motive. In addition, credit unions often charge lower fees for their products and services than commercial banks.

Services and Products:

While credit unions and commercial banks both offer financial products and services, there are some differences in the types of products and services that they offer. Credit unions may offer fewer products and services than commercial banks, but they often offer more personalized service to their members. Some of the products and services that credit unions may offer include:

Savings and checking accounts
Loans, including personal loans, auto loans, and home equity loans
Credit cards
Certificates of deposit (CDs)

Financial counseling and education

Commercial banks typically offer a wider range of financial products and services than credit unions, including:

Savings and checking accounts
Loans, including personal loans, auto loans, and mortgages
Credit cards
Certificates of deposit (CDs)
Investment services, including brokerage and financial planning
Business banking services
Membership:

Credit unions are typically organized around a specific group of people, such as employees of a particular company or residents of a specific geographic area. In order to become a member of a credit union, an individual must meet certain eligibility requirements. Commercial banks, on the other hand, are open to the general public, and anyone can open an account at a commercial bank.

Regulation:

Both credit unions and commercial banks are regulated by federal and state agencies to ensure that they are operating in a safe and sound manner. Credit unions are regulated by the National Credit Union Administration (NCUA), while commercial banks are regulated by the Federal Deposit Insurance Corporation (FDIC) and the Office of the Comptroller of the Currency (OCC).

Conclusion:

Credit unions and commercial banks both play important roles in the financial services industry. While there are some differences between the two, both institutions offer valuable products and services to their customers. Ultimately, the choice between a credit union and a commercial bank will depend on an individual's specific financial needs and preferences.

Functions of Credit Unions

Credit unions are financial institutions that offer a range of financial products and services to their members, who are typically individuals with a common bond such as living in the same geographic area or working for the same employer. Credit unions are unique in that they are not-for-profit organizations, which means that they are owned by their members and operate solely for their benefit. In this section, we will explore the various functions of credit unions, including their role in providing financial services to underserved communities, promoting financial literacy, and fostering member participation.

Providing Financial Services to Underserved Communities

One of the primary functions of credit unions is to provide financial services to underserved communities, such as low-income neighborhoods, rural areas, and communities of color. These communities are often overlooked by traditional banks, which may view them as less profitable and therefore less deserving of financial services. Credit unions, on the other hand, are often established specifically to serve these communities, and they may offer a range of services that are tailored to their unique needs. For example, credit unions may offer low-cost loans, savings accounts, and financial counseling services to help members build credit and achieve their financial goals.

Promoting Financial Literacy

Another important function of credit unions is to promote financial literacy among their members and the wider community. Many credit unions offer financial education programs and resources, such as workshops, seminars, and online courses, to help members better understand personal finance topics such as budgeting, saving, investing, and debt management. By promoting financial literacy, credit unions can help members make informed financial decisions and avoid common pitfalls that can lead to financial hardship.

Fostering Member Participation

Credit unions are unique in that they are owned by their members, who have a say in how the organization is run and who are eligible to vote in board elections. This structure fosters member participation and engagement, which can help ensure that credit unions remain responsive to the needs of their members. Credit unions may also offer opportunities for members to volunteer and participate in community outreach programs, which can help build a sense of camaraderie and connection among members.

Other Functions of Credit Unions

In addition to the functions described above, credit unions may provide a range of other financial products and services, such as:

Checking and savings accounts: Credit unions may offer checking and savings accounts with competitive interest rates and low fees.

Loans: Credit unions may offer a range of loans, including personal loans, auto loans, and home loans, with favorable terms and interest rates.

Credit cards: Credit unions may offer credit cards with low interest rates and rewards programs.

Insurance: Credit unions may offer various insurance products, such as auto insurance, homeowner's insurance, and life insurance, to help members protect their assets and financial wellbeing.

Retirement planning: Credit unions may offer retirement planning services, such as individual retirement accounts (IRAs) and 401(k) plans, to help members save for retirement.

Differences Between Credit Unions and Commercial Banks

While credit unions and commercial banks offer many of the same financial products and services, there are some key differences between these types of institutions. Some of the main differences include:

Ownership: Credit unions are owned by their members, while commercial banks are owned by shareholders who expect to receive a return on their investment.

Profit status: Credit unions are not-for-profit organizations, which means that any profits are reinvested in the organization or returned to members in the form of dividends or lower fees. Commercial banks, on the other hand, are for-profit organizations that are focused on generating profits for their shareholders.

Eligibility requirements: Credit unions typically require members to meet certain eligibility requirements, such as living in a particular geographic area or working for a particular employer. Commercial banks do not typically have such requirements

Products and Services offered by Credit Unions

redit unions are financial institutions that are owned by their members and operate on a not-for-profit basis. They offer a range of products and services designed to meet the financial needs of their members, including savings accounts, loans, credit cards, and insurance. In this article, we will explore in detail the different products and services offered by credit unions.

Savings Accounts

One of the primary services offered by credit unions is savings accounts. Credit unions offer a variety of savings accounts, including share accounts, money market accounts, and certificates of deposit (CDs). Share accounts are similar to savings accounts offered by banks and typically offer competitive interest rates. Money market accounts typically offer higher interest rates than regular savings accounts and require higher minimum balances. CDs are certificates that offer higher interest rates than regular savings accounts in exchange for a commitment to keep the funds deposited for a set period of time.

Loans

Credit unions also offer a range of loans, including personal loans, auto loans, home equity loans, and mortgages. Credit union loans typically offer lower interest rates than loans offered by traditional banks. This is because credit unions are not-for-profit institutions and are able to pass on their earnings to their members in the form of lower interest rates.

Credit Cards

Credit unions also offer credit cards, which typically come with lower interest rates and fees than credit cards offered by traditional banks. Credit unions also offer rewards programs that allow members to earn points or cash back for purchases made using their credit cards.

Insurance

Credit unions also offer a range of insurance products, including auto insurance, home insurance, and life insurance. Credit unions typically offer lower insurance rates than traditional insurance companies, as they are able to negotiate better rates for their members.

Online and Mobile Banking

Credit unions also offer online and mobile banking services, allowing members to access their accounts and perform transactions from anywhere with an internet connection. Online and mobile banking services typically include features such as mobile check deposit, bill pay, and account transfers.

Financial Planning and Investment Services

Credit unions also offer financial planning and investment services, including retirement planning, investment management, and wealth management. These services are typically provided by licensed professionals who can help members develop a financial plan and invest their funds in a way that aligns with their financial goals and risk tolerance.

Community Development

Credit unions are also committed to community development, and often offer programs and services that support the communities they serve. This may include financial education programs, small business loans, and support for local charities and non-profits.

Conclusion

Credit unions offer a wide range of products and services designed to meet the financial needs of their members. From savings accounts to loans, credit cards to insurance, and online and mobile banking to financial planning and investment services, credit unions offer a variety of options to help their members achieve their financial goals. Additionally, credit unions are committed to community development and often offer programs and services that support the communities they serve.

Regulation of Credit Unions

Credit unions are financial institutions that offer a range of products and services to their members, including savings accounts, checking accounts, loans, and credit cards. Unlike traditional banks, credit unions are not-for-profit organizations owned and operated by their members, and their primary goal is to provide affordable financial services to their members. While credit unions operate independently of the federal government, they are subject to a range of regulations aimed at ensuring their safety and soundness, as well as protecting their members' interests.

In this section, we will explore the regulatory environment in which credit unions operate, including the key laws and regulations that govern credit union operations, the role of regulatory agencies, and the challenges that credit unions face in complying with these regulations.

The Laws and Regulations Governing Credit Unions

Credit unions are subject to a number of federal and state laws and regulations that are designed to ensure their safety and soundness, as well as protect the interests of their members. These laws and regulations include:

The Federal Credit Union Act: This is the primary law governing credit unions in the United States. Enacted in 1934, the Act established the National Credit Union Administration (NCUA) as the federal agency responsible for chartering, supervising, and insuring federal credit unions. The Act also sets out the basic requirements for credit union membership, governance, and operations.

NCUA Rules and Regulations: The NCUA has issued a series of rules and regulations that govern various aspects of credit union operations, including capital requirements, lending limits, and financial reporting. These regulations are designed to ensure that credit unions operate in a safe and sound manner, and that they are able to meet the needs of their members.

State Laws: In addition to federal laws and regulations, credit unions are also subject to state laws that govern their operations. These laws may vary from state to state, but they typically address issues such as credit union charters, governance, and member rights.

Role of Regulatory Agencies

Several federal and state agencies are responsible for regulating credit unions and ensuring that they operate in a safe and sound manner. These agencies include:

The National Credit Union Administration (NCUA): This is the primary federal agency responsible for regulating credit unions. The NCUA charters federal credit unions, supervises their operations, and insures their deposits up to $250,000 per account.

State Regulatory Agencies: State regulatory agencies are responsible for regulating state-chartered credit unions. These agencies may have different requirements than the NCUA, but they still play an important role in ensuring the safety and soundness of credit unions operating within their jurisdiction.

The Consumer Financial Protection Bureau (CFPB): The CFPB is responsible for enforcing federal consumer protection laws, including those that apply to credit unions. The CFPB works to protect consumers from unfair, deceptive, or abusive practices in the financial industry.

The Challenges of Compliance

Complying with federal and state laws and regulations can be a significant challenge for credit unions. Some of the key challenges include:

Regulatory Burden: Credit unions must comply with a wide range of laws and regulations, which can be complex and time-consuming. This regulatory burden can make it difficult for credit unions to focus on serving their members and meeting their needs.

Costs: Compliance with regulations can be expensive, particularly for smaller credit unions that may not have the resources to devote to compliance efforts. The costs of compliance can include hiring additional staff, investing in new technology, and conducting regular audits and reviews.

Competitive Disadvantage: Some credit unions argue that the regulatory burden they face puts them at a competitive disadvantage compared to traditional banks. Because credit unions are subject to more stringent regulations, they may be less able to offer certain products and services or to compete on price.

Conclusion

In conclusion, regulation plays a crucial role in ensuring the safety and soundness of credit unions, as well as protecting the interests of their members. The regulatory framework for credit unions is designed to promote their financial stability, limit risk-taking, and ensure that they operate in a safe and sound manner.

While credit unions may face a regulatory burden that puts them at a competitive disadvantage compared to traditional banks, it is important to note that they also enjoy certain advantages. For example, credit unions are typically more focused on serving their members and communities, and they often offer more personalized service and lower fees than traditional banks.

In recent years, there have been calls for regulatory reform that would ease some of the burden on credit unions. Some credit unions have argued that certain regulations, such as the member business lending cap, limit their ability to serve their members and compete with traditional banks. However, any regulatory reform must be carefully considered to ensure that it does not undermine the safety and soundness of credit unions or their ability to serve their members.

Overall, the regulatory environment for credit unions is complex and constantly evolving. Credit unions must stay up-to-date with changes in regulations and adapt their operations accordingly to remain compliant and competitive. Despite the challenges, credit unions remain an important and valuable part of the financial landscape, providing vital services and support to millions of Americans.

CHAPTER 8: INVESTMENT BANKS

Investment banks play a vital role in the global financial system, serving as intermediaries between investors and issuers of securities. They facilitate the buying and selling of securities, provide financial advisory services, and underwrite new securities offerings. Investment banks are distinct from traditional commercial banks in that they do not take deposits or make loans to consumers. Instead, they provide a range of specialized financial services to corporations, governments, and wealthy individuals.

Investment banking has a long and fascinating history, dating back to the Italian city-states of the Renaissance period. However, the modern investment banking industry as we know it today began to take shape in the 19th century in the United States and Europe. Over the years, investment banks have played an important role in shaping the global economy, from the financing of major infrastructure projects to the creation of innovative financial products.

This chapter will provide a comprehensive overview of investment banks, covering their history, business model, key services, regulatory framework, and challenges facing the industry today.

History of Investment Banking

The origins of investment banking can be traced back to medieval Europe, where merchant bankers would provide loans to finance trade expeditions. In the 14th and 15th centuries, Italian merchant bankers began to specialize in the underwriting of government debt, laying the foundation for the modern investment banking industry.

In the United States, investment banking emerged in the late 19th century as the country underwent a rapid period of industrialization and expansion. J.P. Morgan, the son of a prominent banker, was one of the most influential figures in the early investment banking industry, helping to finance major projects such as the construction of the first transcontinental railroad.

During the 20th century, investment banks played an important role in the growth of the U.S. economy, financing major infrastructure projects and facilitating the growth of emerging industries such as technology and healthcare.

Business Model of Investment Banks

The business model of investment banks is complex and multifaceted, reflecting the range of services they offer and the diversity of clients they serve. In general, investment banks can be divided into three main categories: advisory, sales and trading, and underwriting.

Advisory Services: Investment banks provide a range of financial advisory services to clients, including mergers and acquisitions (M&A) advisory, restructuring and recapitalization, and strategic planning. Advisory services typically involve a deep understanding of a client's business and industry, as well as strong analytical skills and strategic insight.

Sales and Trading: Investment banks facilitate the buying and selling of securities on behalf of clients, providing access to capital markets and helping clients to manage their investment portfolios. Sales and trading activities can include equities, fixed income, foreign exchange, and commodities.

Underwriting: Investment banks underwrite new securities offerings, helping to bring new companies to market and providing capital to established companies seeking to raise additional funds. Underwriting can involve a range of securities, including stocks, bonds, and derivatives.

Regulatory Framework for Investment Banks

The regulatory framework for investment banks is complex and multi-layered, reflecting the global nature of the industry and the range of financial services provided. In the United States, the primary regulatory agencies overseeing investment banks are the Securities and Exchange Commission (SEC) and the Financial Industry Regulatory Authority (FINRA).

In addition, investment banks are subject to a range of international regulatory frameworks, including the Basel Accords, which set international standards for banking supervision and risk management. Investment banks are also subject to a range of national and international laws governing financial markets and securities offerings.

Challenges Facing Investment Banks Today

The investment banking industry faces a range of challenges in the current business environment, including increased regulatory scrutiny, changing market conditions, and evolving technology.

Increased Regulatory Scrutiny: In the wake of the 2008 financial crisis, regulators have implemented a range of new rules and regulations aimed at increasing transparency, reducing risk, and preventing another crisis. Investment banks have been particularly impacted by these changes, as they are subject to stricter capital requirements and greater regulatory oversight than many other types of financial institutions. In addition, investment banks are required to adhere to a complex web of international regulations, which can be difficult to navigate and may vary significantly from country to country.

Changing Market Conditions: Investment banks operate in a highly volatile and unpredictable market environment, which can be affected by a wide range of economic, political, and social factors. Changes in interest rates, inflation, and currency exchange rates can have a significant impact on the profitability of investment banks, as can shifts in consumer and investor sentiment. In addition, investment banks must contend with increased competition from other financial institutions, such as commercial banks, asset managers, and fintech startups.

Evolving Technology: The rise of new technologies, such as blockchain, artificial intelligence, and machine learning, has the potential to fundamentally transform the investment banking industry. While these technologies offer the potential for increased efficiency, improved risk management, and new revenue streams, they also pose significant challenges for investment banks. For example, investment banks must invest heavily in new technology infrastructure and hire skilled professionals with the necessary expertise to develop and implement these technologies.

Despite these challenges, investment banks continue to play a critical role in the global financial system, providing a range of services that are essential to the functioning of the economy. In the following sections, we will explore the history of investment banks, the various services they offer, and the key players in the industry. We will also examine some of the ethical and legal issues that have arisen in the investment banking industry, as well as the future of the industry in an increasingly globalized and technologically advanced world.

Definition of Investment Banks

Investment banks are financial institutions that provide a range of services to clients, including underwriting and selling securities, advising on mergers and acquisitions, and managing assets. These services are designed to help companies and governments raise capital, manage risk, and achieve their strategic goals. Investment banks play a critical role in the global financial system, and their activities have a significant impact on the economy.

In this section, we will define investment banks, describe their primary functions, and explore the various types of investment banks that exist. We will also discuss the history of investment banking, the regulatory framework that governs their activities, and the challenges and opportunities that they face in today's business environment.

Definition of Investment Banks

An investment bank is a financial institution that specializes in providing a range of services to clients, including underwriting and selling securities, advising on mergers and acquisitions, and managing assets. Investment banks are distinct from commercial banks in that they do not accept deposits from the public or make loans. Instead, they provide fee-based services that are designed to help clients raise capital, manage risk, and achieve their strategic goals.

The primary functions of investment banks include:

Underwriting and Selling Securities: Investment banks act as intermediaries between issuers of securities and investors. They help companies and governments raise capital by underwriting new securities offerings, such as stocks and bonds, and selling these securities to investors.

Mergers and Acquisitions (M&A) Advisory: Investment banks provide advice to clients on mergers, acquisitions, and other strategic transactions. They assist clients with identifying potential acquisition targets, conducting due diligence, negotiating terms, and arranging financing.

Asset Management: Investment banks manage assets on behalf of clients, including pension funds, endowments, and high-net-worth individuals. They provide a range of investment products and services, including mutual funds, hedge funds, and private equity.

Types of Investment Banks

There are several different types of investment banks, including:

Bulge Bracket Banks: These are the largest and most well-known investment banks, such as Goldman Sachs, JPMorgan Chase, and Morgan Stanley. They have a global presence and provide a wide range of services to clients.

Middle Market Banks: These are smaller investment banks that focus on mid-sized companies. They provide a range of services, including underwriting, M&A advisory, and asset management.

Boutique Banks: These are small investment banks that specialize in specific industries or types of transactions. For example, a boutique bank may specialize in healthcare M&A or renewable energy project finance.

History of Investment Banking

The history of investment banking can be traced back to the 19th century, when financial institutions began to specialize in providing services to clients in the railroad and industrial sectors. These institutions helped finance the expansion of these industries by underwriting securities offerings and providing advice on M&A transactions.

In the early 20th century, investment banking became more closely associated with the stock market. Investment banks played a key role in the creation of the modern IPO market, helping companies raise capital by underwriting new stock offerings.

During the 1980s and 1990s, investment banking underwent a period of rapid expansion and consolidation. Many of the largest investment banks merged with commercial banks or insurance companies, leading to the creation of financial conglomerates that offered a wide range of services.

Regulation of Investment Banking

Investment banks are subject to a complex regulatory framework that is designed to protect investors and maintain the stability of the financial system. The primary regulatory bodies that oversee investment banking activities include:

Securities and Exchange Commission (SEC): The SEC is responsible for enforcing federal securities laws and regulating securities markets in the United States.

Financial Industry Regulatory Authority (FINRA): FINRA is a self-regulatory organization (SRO) that oversees investment banks and other securities firms. It was created in 2007 through the consolidation of the National Association of Securities Dealers (NASD) and the regulatory arm of the New York Stock Exchange (NYSE).

Federal Reserve System: The Federal Reserve System, often referred to simply as "the Fed," is the central banking system of the United States. It is responsible for regulating the nation's monetary policy and supervising banks and other financial institutions.

Office of the Comptroller of the Currency (OCC): The OCC is an independent bureau within the US Department of the Treasury that regulates and supervises all national banks and federal savings associations.

In addition to these regulatory bodies, investment banks are also subject to a range of international regulations and standards, including the Basel Accords, which establish minimum capital requirements for financial institutions, and the Financial Action Task Force (FATF), which sets international standards for combating money laundering and terrorist financing.

Investment banks also operate under a set of ethical and professional standards set by industry associations such as the Securities Industry and Financial Markets Association (SIFMA) and the International Capital Market Association (ICMA). These standards cover a range of topics, including conflicts of interest, insider trading, and the handling of confidential information.

Overall, the regulatory framework governing investment banks is complex and constantly evolving in response to changes in the financial markets and the broader economy. Investment banks must stay up-to-date with these regulations and comply with them in order to maintain their licenses and reputation in the industry.

Types of Investment Banks

There are several different types of investment banks that operate in the financial industry. These include:

Full-Service Investment Banks: Full-service investment banks provide a wide range of financial services to clients, including underwriting new securities offerings, providing advice on mergers and acquisitions, and managing investment portfolios.

Boutique Investment Banks: Boutique investment banks are smaller firms that specialize in a particular sector or service, such as technology or mergers and acquisitions. They typically offer more personalized service and may be more flexible in their fee structure than larger investment banks.

Investment Banking Divisions of Commercial Banks: Many commercial banks have investment banking divisions that offer similar services to full-service investment banks. However, these divisions may be subject to different regulatory requirements than standalone investment banks.

Regional Investment Banks: Regional investment banks operate in a specific geographic area, such as a single state or region of the country. They typically focus on providing services to mid-sized companies and may have a more limited range of services than larger investment banks.

Roles and Functions of Investment Banks

Investment banks play several important roles in the financial industry. Some of the key functions of investment banks include:

Underwriting Securities Offerings: Investment banks help companies raise capital by underwriting new securities offerings, such as initial public offerings (IPOs) and bond issuances. In this role, investment banks help companies price their securities and market them to potential investors.

Mergers and Acquisitions (M&A): Investment banks provide advice and assistance to companies involved in mergers and acquisitions. This can include conducting due diligence on potential acquisition targets, valuing companies, and negotiating deals.

Sales and Trading: Investment banks facilitate the trading of securities between buyers and sellers, both through traditional exchanges and through over-the-counter (OTC) markets. They may also engage in proprietary trading, buying and selling securities for their own account in order to generate profits.

Asset Management: Investment banks manage investment portfolios for clients, such as pension funds and other institutional investors. They may also offer wealth management services to high-net-worth individuals.

Research: Investment banks conduct research on companies and industries in order to provide investment recommendations to their clients. This research can include financial analysis, industry trends, and market outlooks.

Overall, investment banks play a critical role in the global financial system by providing a range of services to businesses, governments, and individuals. They serve as intermediaries between investors and companies seeking financing, as well as providing advisory and transaction services. Investment banks play a vital role in facilitating economic growth and development by providing capital to fund new ventures, expanding existing businesses, and creating jobs.

However, the role of investment banks has been the subject of intense scrutiny and debate, particularly in the aftermath of the 2008 financial crisis. Critics argue that investment banks prioritize profits over social responsibility, engaging in unethical practices such as insider trading and market manipulation. Additionally, investment banks have been accused of contributing to systemic risk by engaging in speculative investments and complex financial instruments.

Despite these criticisms, investment banks continue to play a crucial role in the global economy, providing essential services to clients and facilitating financial transactions. As the business environment continues to evolve, investment banks will need to adapt to new challenges and opportunities, such as the increasing use of technology and changing regulatory frameworks. By doing so, investment banks can continue to contribute to economic growth and development while upholding the highest standards of ethical and professional conduct.

Functions of Investment Banks

Investment banks play a vital role in the financial markets. They perform a range of functions, from underwriting securities to advising clients on mergers and acquisitions. This section will provide an in-depth analysis of the various functions performed by investment banks.

Underwriting

One of the primary functions of investment banks is underwriting securities. This involves purchasing securities from issuers and selling them to the public. Investment banks typically work with companies to determine the type and amount of securities to issue, and then purchase the securities from the issuer at a discounted price. The investment bank then sells the securities to the public at a higher price, earning a profit on the spread between the purchase price and the selling price.

Underwriting is typically used for initial public offerings (IPOs), where a company offers its shares to the public for the first time. Investment banks may also underwrite debt securities, such as bonds, which are issued by companies to raise capital.

Mergers and Acquisitions (M&A)
Investment banks also provide advisory services to clients on mergers and acquisitions (M&A). This involves assisting clients in identifying potential targets for acquisition or merger, performing due diligence, and negotiating the terms of the transaction.

Investment banks also provide financial advice on other corporate finance matters, such as capital raising, debt financing, and restructuring.

Trading and Market Making
Investment banks are also involved in trading and market making. They buy and sell securities in large quantities, both for their own account and on behalf of clients. Investment banks may also act as market makers, providing liquidity to the market by buying and selling securities at quoted prices.

Asset Management
Investment banks manage investment portfolios for clients, such as pension funds and other institutional investors. They may also offer wealth management services to high-net-worth individuals. Asset management services may include portfolio management, financial planning, and estate planning.

Research
Investment banks conduct research on companies and industries in order to provide investment recommendations to their clients. This research can include financial analysis, industry trends, and market outlooks. The research may be used to support underwriting activities, as well as to provide advice to clients on investments.

Risk Management

Investment banks are also involved in risk management. They use sophisticated models to measure and manage risk, such as credit risk, market risk, and operational risk. Investment banks may also provide risk management services to clients, such as hedging strategies to manage their exposure to market risks.

Capital Markets

Investment banks are involved in the capital markets, which include equity markets, debt markets, and derivatives markets. Investment banks may provide a range of services related to capital markets, including underwriting securities, trading securities, providing market analysis, and advising clients on capital raising activities.

Financial Advisory

Investment banks also provide financial advisory services to clients, including corporate finance advice, financial restructuring, and strategic planning. Financial advisory services may include mergers and acquisitions, divestitures, and other corporate finance transactions.

Challenges Facing Investment Banks

The investment banking industry faces a range of challenges in the current business environment, including increased regulatory scrutiny, changing market conditions, and evolving technology.

Increased Regulatory Scrutiny

In the wake of the 2008 financial crisis, the regulatory environment for investment banks has become much more stringent. Investment banks are subject to a complex regulatory framework designed to protect investors and maintain the stability of the financial system.

The primary regulatory bodies that oversee investment banking activities include the Securities and Exchange Commission (SEC) and the Financial Industry Regulatory Authority (FINRA) in the United States. Investment banks must comply with a range of regulations related to disclosure, capital requirements, and risk management.

Changing Market Conditions

Investment banks must also navigate changing market conditions that can impact their business operations and financial performance. Some of the key market trends and challenges facing investment banks include:

Volatility: The financial markets are inherently volatile, with prices of securities fluctuating rapidly in response to changes in market conditions, economic indicators, and geopolitical events. Investment banks must be able to adapt to these changes and manage the risks associated with market volatility in order to protect their clients and their own financial interests.

Low Interest Rates: The prolonged period of low interest rates in many countries has had a significant impact on the profitability of investment banks, particularly those that rely heavily on traditional banking activities such as lending and borrowing. Low interest rates can reduce the margins that investment banks can earn on their loans and investments, which can make it more difficult to generate profits.

Competition: Investment banking is a highly competitive industry, with many firms vying for the same clients and business opportunities. This competition can drive down fees and commissions, which can make it more challenging for investment banks to achieve their financial targets and remain profitable.

Evolving Technology
Technology is rapidly transforming the financial services industry, and investment banking is no exception. Investment banks are investing heavily in technology to improve their operational efficiency, reduce costs, and enhance the customer experience. Some of the key areas where technology is having an impact on investment banking include:

Trading: Advances in technology have revolutionized the way that securities are traded, with electronic trading platforms now accounting for a significant portion of trading activity. Investment banks are investing in high-speed trading systems and algorithms that can quickly execute trades and respond to market changes in real time.

Data Analytics: Investment banks are using sophisticated data analytics tools to gain insights into market trends, customer behavior, and other key factors that can impact their business operations. These insights can help investment banks make more informed investment decisions, improve risk management practices, and better understand customer needs and preferences.

Blockchain: Blockchain technology has the potential to transform the way that financial transactions are conducted, with the potential to streamline processes, reduce costs, and enhance security. Investment banks are exploring the use of blockchain technology for a range of applications, from settlement and clearance to cross-border payments and trade finance.

Conclusion

Investment banks play a critical role in the global financial system, providing a range of services that help companies and investors achieve their financial goals. While investment banks face a range of challenges and regulatory requirements, they are also well positioned to take advantage of the opportunities presented by evolving market conditions and technology trends. By staying ahead of these trends and adapting their business models and operations accordingly, investment banks can continue to serve their clients effectively and drive long-term value for their shareholders.

Types of Investment Banks

Investment banks come in different shapes and sizes, and they offer various services to clients. In this section, we will discuss the different types of investment banks and the services they provide.

Bulge Bracket Investment Banks

The bulge bracket investment banks are the largest and most prestigious investment banks in the world. These banks are known for their global presence, extensive product offerings, and large deal sizes. Some examples of bulge bracket investment banks include JPMorgan Chase, Goldman Sachs, and Morgan Stanley.

Bulge bracket investment banks typically offer a full range of investment banking services, including underwriting, M&A advisory, sales and trading, research, and asset management. These banks have a broad client base, which includes large corporations, governments, and institutional investors.

Middle Market Investment Banks

Middle market investment banks are smaller than bulge bracket investment banks and focus on mid-sized companies. These banks typically offer a more personalized and specialized approach to investment banking services. Examples of middle market investment banks include William Blair, Jefferies, and Piper Sandler.

Middle market investment banks typically offer services such as M&A advisory, private placements, and debt and equity financing. These banks work with smaller clients and often specialize in certain industries or sectors.

Boutique Investment Banks

Boutique investment banks are even smaller than middle market investment banks and offer highly specialized services. These banks often focus on a particular sector or niche market, such as technology or healthcare. Examples of boutique investment banks include Qatalyst Partners, Moelis & Company, and Centerview Partners.

Boutique investment banks typically offer services such as M&A advisory, capital raising, and strategic consulting. These banks have a highly specialized knowledge base and offer a tailored approach to investment banking services.

Investment Banking Divisions of Commercial Banks

Many commercial banks have investment banking divisions that offer investment banking services alongside their traditional banking services. These divisions may be less specialized than standalone investment banks but still offer a range of services to clients. Examples of commercial banks with investment banking divisions include Bank of America Merrill Lynch, Citigroup, and Wells Fargo.

Investment banking divisions of commercial banks typically offer services such as underwriting, M&A advisory, and sales and trading. These banks have a broad client base, which includes corporations, governments, and institutional investors.

Regional Investment Banks

Regional investment banks are smaller than bulge bracket investment banks and focus on a particular region or market. These banks typically have a strong knowledge base of the local market and offer a personalized approach to investment banking services. Examples of regional investment banks include Raymond James, Stifel Financial, and KeyBanc Capital Markets.

Regional investment banks typically offer services such as M&A advisory, debt and equity financing, and sales and trading. These banks work with clients in a particular region or market and often specialize in certain industries or sectors.

Services Offered by Investment Banks

Investment banks offer a range of services to clients, including underwriting, M&A advisory, sales and trading, research, and asset management. In this section, we will discuss these services in more detail.

Underwriting

Underwriting is the process of guaranteeing a certain amount of money will be raised through the issuance of securities, such as stocks or bonds. Investment banks act as underwriters by purchasing securities from the issuer and then selling them to the public or institutional investors.

There are two types of underwriting: firm commitment underwriting and best efforts underwriting. In firm commitment underwriting, the investment bank agrees to purchase all the securities being offered by the issuer and then resell them to investors. In best efforts underwriting, the investment bank agrees to make its best effort to sell the securities but does not guarantee the sale.

M&A Advisory

M&A advisory involves providing advice and assistance to companies seeking to merge with or acquire other companies. This type of investment banking service is typically provided by larger, full-service investment banks. M&A advisory services can include:

Target Identification: Investment banks help companies identify potential merger or acquisition targets by conducting industry research and analyzing financial data. They may also assist with initial outreach to potential targets.

Valuation: Once potential targets have been identified, investment banks can help their clients determine the value of the target company by analyzing its financial statements and market data.

Due Diligence: Investment banks perform a detailed analysis of the target company's financial statements, legal and regulatory compliance, customer contracts, and other relevant information to identify potential risks and opportunities.

Negotiation: Investment banks can help their clients negotiate the terms of the merger or acquisition, including the purchase price, payment terms, and any contingencies or warranties.

Financing: Investment banks can help their clients secure financing for the merger or acquisition, which may include arranging debt financing or underwriting the sale of new equity.

Post-Merger Integration: Investment banks may also provide support to their clients after the merger or acquisition is completed, helping to integrate the two companies' operations and systems.

M&A advisory is a complex and specialized field that requires a deep understanding of financial markets, legal and regulatory requirements, and industry dynamics. Investment banks that provide M&A advisory services must have a team of experienced professionals with expertise in areas such as valuation, due diligence, and negotiation.

Asset Management

Investment banks may also provide asset management services to clients, which can include managing investment portfolios for institutional investors such as pension funds, endowments, and sovereign wealth funds. Asset management services can also be offered to high-net-worth individuals.

Asset management services typically involve:

Portfolio Construction: Investment banks work with their clients to design and implement investment portfolios that meet their specific needs and objectives.

Investment Selection: Investment banks research and analyze potential investments to identify those that are most likely to generate returns for their clients.

Risk Management: Investment banks monitor the performance of investment portfolios and make adjustments as needed to manage risk and ensure that clients' objectives are being met.

Reporting: Investment banks provide regular reports to their clients on the performance of their investment portfolios and any changes that have been made.

Asset management services can be a significant source of revenue for investment banks, particularly for those that specialize in managing large institutional investment portfolios.

Wealth Management

In addition to asset management services, investment banks may also offer wealth management services to high-net-worth individuals. Wealth management services typically include:

Financial Planning: Investment banks work with their clients to develop a comprehensive financial plan that takes into account their goals, risk tolerance, and investment preferences.

Investment Management: Investment banks manage their clients' investment portfolios, selecting investments that are consistent with their clients' financial goals and risk tolerance.

Estate Planning: Investment banks provide guidance on estate planning, including the creation of wills and trusts.

Tax Planning: Investment banks work with their clients to develop tax-efficient investment strategies and to minimize their tax liabilities.

Wealth management services can be a lucrative business for investment banks, as high-net-worth individuals often have significant assets to manage and may require a range of specialized services.

Conclusion

Investment banks play a critical role in financial markets, providing a range of services that help companies raise capital, manage risk, and grow their businesses. Investment banks can be divided into several different categories based on their primary business activities, including securities underwriting, trading and sales, M&A advisory, asset management, and wealth management. While investment banking can be a complex and challenging field, it can also be highly rewarding for those who are able to navigate the intricacies of financial markets and provide value to their clients.

It is important to note that investment banks have faced significant regulatory scrutiny in the wake of the global financial crisis of 2008.

Regulations have been put in place to ensure that investment banks operate in a safe and sound manner, and that they do not engage in risky activities that could pose a threat to the financial system. In addition, there has been increased public scrutiny of the compensation practices of investment banks, which many people believe contributed to the financial crisis.

Despite these challenges, investment banks continue to play a vital role in the global economy. They provide a wide range of services that are essential to the functioning of financial markets, and they help companies raise the capital they need to grow and expand their businesses. As such, investment banking is likely to remain an important and dynamic field in the years to come.

Products and Services offered by Investment Banks

Investment banks offer a range of products and services to clients, including corporations, governments, and high-net-worth individuals. These services help clients raise capital, manage risk, and grow their businesses. In this section, we will explore the various products and services offered by investment banks, including securities underwriting, trading and sales, mergers and acquisitions (M&A) advisory, asset management, and wealth management.

Securities Underwriting

One of the primary services offered by investment banks is securities underwriting. Underwriting involves the purchase and resale of securities issued by companies or governments. The investment bank agrees to purchase a certain number of securities at a set price and then resells them to investors. This process helps companies raise capital and enables investors to invest in a diverse range of securities. There are two types of underwriting: firm commitment underwriting and best efforts underwriting.

Firm Commitment Underwriting

In firm commitment underwriting, the investment bank agrees to purchase all the securities being offered by the issuer and then resell them to investors. This type of underwriting provides a guarantee to the issuer that all the securities will be sold, regardless of market conditions. However, the investment bank assumes the risk of being unable to resell the securities at a profit.

Best Efforts Underwriting

In best efforts underwriting, the investment bank agrees to make its best effort to sell the securities but does not guarantee the sale. This type of underwriting is less risky for the investment bank, as it does not assume the risk of being unable to sell all the securities. However, the issuer assumes the risk of the securities not being sold.

Trading and Sales

Another key service offered by investment banks is trading and sales. Investment banks employ traders who buy and sell securities on behalf of the bank and its clients. The bank also offers sales services to its clients, providing them with access to its trading desk and market analysis.

The trading and sales division of an investment bank can be divided into several different areas, including equities, fixed income, currencies, and commodities. The equities desk focuses on buying and selling stocks, while the fixed income desk deals with bonds and other debt securities. The currencies desk trades foreign currencies, and the commodities desk deals with physical commodities such as oil and gold.

Mergers and Acquisitions (M&A) Advisory

M&A advisory involves providing advice and assistance to companies looking to merge with or acquire other companies. Investment banks help companies evaluate potential targets, negotiate deals, and structure transactions. M&A advisory can be highly lucrative for investment banks, as they typically charge fees based on the size of the transaction.

Asset Management

Investment banks also offer asset management services to clients. This involves managing investment portfolios on behalf of clients, such as pension funds and other institutional investors. Asset management services can include portfolio construction, risk management, and investment research.

Wealth Management

In addition to asset management, investment banks may also offer wealth management services to high-net-worth individuals. Wealth management services typically include investment management, financial planning, and estate planning.

Conclusion

Investment banks offer a range of products and services designed to help clients raise capital, manage risk, and grow their businesses. These services include securities underwriting, trading and sales, M&A advisory, asset management, and wealth management. Each of these services requires specialized knowledge and expertise, making investment banking a challenging but potentially lucrative career path.

Regulation of Investment Banks

Investment banks play a crucial role in the financial markets by providing a range of services that help companies raise capital, manage risk, and grow their businesses. Given their important role, it is essential that investment banks are regulated effectively to ensure they operate in a safe and sound manner and to protect investors and the wider economy from potential risks. In this section, we will discuss the regulation of investment banks, including the regulatory bodies responsible for overseeing their activities, the key regulations they must comply with, and the challenges associated with regulating these complex institutions.

Regulatory Bodies

In the United States, investment banks are regulated by a number of different regulatory bodies, including the Securities and Exchange Commission (SEC), the Financial Industry Regulatory Authority (FINRA), and the Federal Reserve. These regulatory bodies are responsible for ensuring that investment banks comply with a range of regulations related to disclosure, capital requirements, and risk management. The SEC is responsible for regulating the securities markets and enforcing federal securities laws, while FINRA is responsible for regulating broker-dealers and ensuring compliance with FINRA rules and regulations. The Federal Reserve is responsible for supervising and regulating banks, including investment banks that are members of the Federal Reserve System.

In addition to these regulatory bodies, investment banks may also be subject to regulation by other government agencies, such as the Commodity Futures Trading Commission (CFTC) or the Office of the Comptroller of the

Currency (OCC), depending on the types of activities they engage in and the products they offer.

Key Regulations

There are a number of key regulations that investment banks must comply with, including:

Disclosure Regulations: Investment banks are required to disclose information about their operations, financial condition, and risk management practices to investors and regulatory bodies. These disclosures are intended to provide transparency and promote informed decision-making by investors and other stakeholders.

Capital Requirements: Investment banks are required to maintain minimum levels of capital to ensure that they have sufficient financial resources to withstand unexpected losses or market disruptions. The specific capital requirements vary depending on the type and size of the investment bank.

Risk Management: Investment banks are required to have robust risk management practices in place to identify, measure, and manage the risks associated with their activities. This includes establishing internal controls, conducting stress tests, and monitoring risk exposure on an ongoing basis.

Anti-Money Laundering (AML) Regulations: Investment banks are required to have effective AML programs in place to detect and prevent money laundering and terrorist financing activities. This includes implementing policies and procedures for customer due diligence, transaction monitoring, and suspicious activity reporting.

Challenges in Regulating Investment Banks

Regulating investment banks presents a number of challenges, given the complex and constantly evolving nature of their activities. Some of the key challenges include:

Complexity: Investment banks engage in a wide range of complex activities, including securities underwriting, trading and sales, M&A advisory, asset management, and wealth management. Regulators must have a deep understanding of these activities in order to effectively regulate them.

Global Nature: Investment banks operate in a global market, with operations in multiple jurisdictions. This makes it difficult for regulators to ensure consistent regulation across all markets and to coordinate their efforts with regulators in other countries.

Innovation: Investment banks are constantly innovating and developing new products and services, which can create regulatory challenges. Regulators must be able to keep pace with these developments and adapt their regulatory frameworks as necessary.

Enforcement: Enforcement of regulations can be challenging, particularly in cases where investment banks engage in illegal or unethical activities. Regulators must have strong enforcement mechanisms in place to deter bad behavior and hold individuals and institutions accountable for their actions.

Conclusion

Effective regulation is essential for ensuring that investment banks operate in a safe and sound manner and to protect investors and the wider economy . While the 2008 financial crisis exposed weaknesses in the regulatory framework for investment banks, steps have since been taken to address these shortcomings and enhance oversight of the industry. Regulators have implemented a range of reforms, including increasing capital requirements, improving risk management practices, and enhancing transparency and disclosure requirements.

Despite these efforts, investment banking remains a complex and evolving industry that poses significant challenges for regulators. As new products and services emerge, regulators must be vigilant in monitoring and assessing potential risks and taking appropriate action to mitigate them.

Moreover, the regulatory landscape for investment banks varies widely across different countries and jurisdictions. While some countries have implemented stringent regulations and oversight measures, others have been criticized for their lax regulatory frameworks, which may create opportunities for misconduct and increase the risk of financial instability.

In conclusion, investment banks play a critical role in financial markets, providing a range of services that help companies raise capital, manage risk, and grow their businesses. However, the industry also poses significant risks, both to investors and to the wider economy. Effective regulation is essential for ensuring that investment banks operate in a safe and sound manner, and that investors and the wider public are protected from the potential negative consequences of their actions. As such, regulators must continue to work collaboratively with industry participants to identify potential risks and take appropriate measures to mitigate them.

CHAPTER 9: BROKERAGE FIRMS AND FINANCIAL PLANNERS

Investing can be a complex and challenging process, requiring knowledge of financial markets and various investment products. To navigate these waters successfully, many individuals turn to professionals for help. Two types of financial professionals commonly used by individuals are brokerage firms and financial planners.

Brokerage firms, also known as stockbrokers, are financial intermediaries that buy and sell securities on behalf of their clients. They provide investors with access to a wide range of financial products, including stocks, bonds, mutual funds, and exchange-traded funds (ETFs). Financial planners, on the other hand, offer more comprehensive financial planning services, including investment management, retirement planning, tax planning, and estate planning.

While brokerage firms and financial planners both offer valuable services to investors, there are important differences between them that investors should be aware of. In this chapter, we will examine these differences in detail, including the types of services offered, the regulatory environment, and the costs associated with each.

Brokerage Firms

Brokerage firms have been an important part of the financial services industry for over a century. They provide investors with access to financial markets and a wide range of investment products. In this section, we will explore the history of brokerage firms and their role in the financial services industry today.

History of Brokerage Firms

Brokerage firms have been around since the late 19th century, when the New York Stock Exchange (NYSE) was founded. The first brokerage firms were small partnerships that helped investors buy and sell stocks. As the stock market grew and became more complex, the role of brokerage firms expanded.

Today, brokerage firms are large corporations that provide investors with access to a wide range of financial products and services.

Role of Brokerage Firms Today

Brokerage firms play an important role in financial markets today. They provide investors with access to a wide range of financial products, including stocks, bonds, mutual funds, and ETFs. They also offer a range of services, including investment research, trading platforms, and investment advice.

One of the main advantages of using a brokerage firm is the convenience they offer. Investors can easily buy and sell securities online or through a broker. Brokerage firms also provide investors with access to investment research, which can help them make more informed investment decisions.

However, there are also some disadvantages to using a brokerage firm. One of the main disadvantages is the cost. Brokerage firms typically charge investors a commission or a fee for each transaction. These fees can add up quickly, particularly for investors who trade frequently.

Financial Planners

Financial planners provide more comprehensive financial planning services than brokerage firms. In addition to offering access to investment products, they provide investors with advice on retirement planning, tax planning, and estate planning. In this section, we will explore the role of financial planners in more detail.

Role of Financial Planners

Financial planners provide a range of services to investors, including investment management, retirement planning, tax planning, and estate planning. They work with clients to develop a comprehensive financial plan that takes into account their individual needs and goals.

One of the main advantages of using a financial planner is the personalized advice they offer. Financial planners work closely with clients to understand their individual needs and goals, and develop a customized investment plan that meets those needs.

Another advantage of using a financial planner is their expertise in financial planning. Financial planners are trained to help clients navigate complex financial situations, such as retirement planning and estate planning. They can provide valuable advice on tax planning, investment management, and other financial topics.

However, there are also some disadvantages to using a financial planner. One of the main disadvantages is the cost. Financial planners typically charge clients a fee based on a percentage of the assets they manage, which can be expensive for some individuals. In addition, some financial planners may have conflicts of interest, such as receiving commissions or incentives for recommending certain financial products or services.

Another potential disadvantage is the lack of transparency in the financial planning industry. While financial planners are required to disclose any potential conflicts of interest, they may not always do so, making it difficult for clients to fully understand the advice they are receiving.

Despite these disadvantages, many individuals still choose to use financial planners to help them achieve their financial goals. In the following sections, we will take a closer look at brokerage firms and financial planners, including their services, fees, and potential benefits and drawbacks.

Brokerage Firms

A brokerage firm is a financial institution that facilitates the buying and selling of financial securities, such as stocks, bonds, and mutual funds, on behalf of its clients. Brokerage firms can offer a range of investment services, including financial planning, retirement planning, and wealth management.

Services Offered by Brokerage Firms

Brokerage firms offer a wide range of services to their clients, including:

Investment Advice: Brokerage firms provide investment advice to their clients, helping them to choose investments that are appropriate for their financial goals and risk tolerance. This advice may be provided through the firm's financial advisors, or through online investment tools and resources.

Trading Services: Brokerage firms facilitate the buying and selling of financial securities on behalf of their clients. Clients can place trades through the firm's website, mobile app, or by calling a financial advisor.

Retirement Planning: Many brokerage firms offer retirement planning services, helping clients to save for retirement and create a retirement income plan. This may include assistance with setting up a 401(k) or IRA, as well as advice on how to allocate investments to maximize retirement income.

Wealth Management: Brokerage firms may offer wealth management services to high-net-worth individuals, providing customized investment solutions and financial planning advice.

Fees and Charges

Brokerage firms typically charge fees and commissions for their services. These fees can vary depending on the services provided and the amount of assets under management. Common fees charged by brokerage firms include:

Commissions: Brokerage firms may charge commissions on trades made on behalf of their clients. These commissions can vary depending on the type of security being traded and the size of the trade.

Management Fees: Brokerage firms may charge management fees for managing client assets. These fees are typically charged as a percentage of assets under management, and can range from 0.25% to 2% or more.

Transaction Fees: Brokerage firms may charge transaction fees for certain types of trades or transactions, such as mutual fund purchases or account transfers.

Benefits and Drawbacks of Using a Brokerage Firm

There are several potential benefits and drawbacks to using a brokerage firm for your investment needs.

Benefits:

Access to Professional Advice: Brokerage firms employ financial advisors who can provide professional advice on investment strategies and financial planning.

Diversification: Brokerage firms offer access to a wide range of investment products, allowing clients to diversify their portfolios and minimize risk.

Convenience: Brokerage firms offer online investment tools and resources, making it easy for clients to manage their investments from anywhere.

Drawbacks:

Fees: Brokerage firms can be expensive, particularly for clients with smaller investment portfolios.

Conflicts of Interest: Some brokerage firms may have conflicts of interest, such as receiving commissions or incentives for recommending certain investments.

Lack of Control: When working with a brokerage firm, clients may have less control over their investments than they would if managing their own portfolio.

Financial Planners

Financial planners are professionals who specialize in providing financial planning advice and services to individuals and families. Unlike brokerage firms, financial planners typically do not engage in buying and selling securities on behalf of their clients. Instead, they focus on helping clients achieve their financial goals through comprehensive financial planning, which may include:

Retirement Planning: Financial planners can help clients create a retirement savings plan, estimate retirement expenses, and determine the best retirement income strategy.

Investment Management: Financial planners can help clients develop an investment strategy that aligns with their financial goals and risk tolerance. They can also assist with investment selection and ongoing portfolio management.

Tax Planning: Financial planners can provide advice on tax-efficient investment strategies and help clients optimize their tax situation.

Estate Planning: Financial planners can help clients create an estate plan that addresses issues such as asset distribution, minimizing estate taxes, and ensuring that beneficiaries are taken care of.

Advantages:

Expertise: Financial planners are trained and experienced in financial planning, which means they can provide valuable advice and guidance on a wide range of financial topics.

Holistic Approach: Financial planners take a holistic approach to financial planning, which means they consider all aspects of a client's financial situation, including their goals, risk tolerance, and tax situation.

Objective Advice: Unlike brokerage firms, financial planners typically do not receive commissions or incentives for recommending certain investments. This means that their advice is more likely to be objective and in the best interests of their clients.

Disadvantages:

Fees: One of the main disadvantages of using a financial planner is the cost. Financial planners typically charge clients a fee for their services, which can be a percentage of assets under management or a flat fee. This can be expensive, particularly for clients with smaller investment portfolios.

Limited Investment Options: Financial planners do not typically engage in buying and selling securities on behalf of their clients, which means clients may have limited investment options. They may also have less control over their investments than if they managed their own portfolio.

Conclusion:

Both brokerage firms and financial planners offer valuable services to investors, but they have different approaches and advantages and disadvantages. Brokerage firms are primarily focused on buying and selling securities on behalf of their clients, while financial planners take a more comprehensive approach to financial planning. Clients should carefully consider their financial goals, investment objectives, and risk tolerance before choosing a brokerage firm or financial planner. They should also consider the cost of each option and any potential conflicts of interest. Ultimately, the choice between a brokerage firm and a financial planner will depend on each individual's unique financial situation and goals.

Definition of Brokerage Firms and Financial Planners

In the world of finance, there are many professionals who offer services to help individuals manage their money. Two common types of professionals are brokerage firms and financial planners. While both may offer similar services, they differ in their approach and expertise. In this section, we will define what brokerage firms and financial planners are and explore their differences and similarities.

Definition of Brokerage Firms:

A brokerage firm is a company that facilitates buying and selling of financial securities on behalf of clients. Brokerage firms act as intermediaries between buyers and sellers, executing trades on behalf of their clients. They may offer a range of investment products, such as stocks, bonds, mutual funds, exchange-traded funds (ETFs), and options.

Definition of Financial Planners:

A financial planner is a professional who helps individuals and families manage their finances. Financial planners help clients develop and implement financial plans to achieve their goals, such as saving for retirement or funding their children's education. They offer a range of services, including retirement planning, investment advice, tax planning, and estate planning.

Differences between Brokerage Firms and Financial Planners:

While both brokerage firms and financial planners may offer investment advice and services, there are some key differences between the two:

Services offered: Brokerage firms typically offer services related to buying and selling securities, such as executing trades and providing investment recommendations. Financial planners, on the other hand, may offer a broader range of services, including retirement planning, tax planning, and estate planning.

Compensation: Brokerage firms may charge commissions or transaction fees for executing trades on behalf of clients. Financial planners may charge a flat fee, hourly rate, or a percentage of the assets under management.

Expertise: Brokerage firms may employ financial advisors who have expertise in investment products and securities. Financial planners, on the other hand, typically have a broader range of expertise in financial planning topics, such as retirement planning and tax planning.

Similarities between Brokerage Firms and Financial Planners:

Despite their differences, brokerage firms and financial planners also have some similarities:

Client-centered approach: Both brokerage firms and financial planners aim to serve their clients' financial needs and goals.

Licensed professionals: Brokerage firms and financial planners must be licensed to provide investment advice and services.

Access to investment products: Both brokerage firms and financial planners offer clients access to a range of investment products and securities.

Advantages of Brokerage Firms:

Access to Investment Products: Brokerage firms offer clients access to a range of investment products, including stocks, bonds, mutual funds, and ETFs.

Investment Recommendations: Brokerage firms may provide investment recommendations to clients based on their financial goals and risk tolerance.

Flexibility: Clients can execute trades at their convenience through brokerage firms' online platforms or with the help of a financial advisor.

Drawbacks of Brokerage Firms:

Fees: Brokerage firms can be expensive, particularly for clients with smaller investment portfolios.

Conflicts of Interest: Some brokerage firms may have conflicts of interest, such as receiving commissions or incentives for recommending certain investments.

Lack of Control: When working with a brokerage firm, clients may have less control over their investments than they would if managing their own portfolio.

Advantages of Financial Planners:

Expertise: Financial planners are trained to help clients navigate complex financial situations, such as retirement planning and estate planning. They can provide valuable advice on tax planning, investment management, and other financial topics.

Holistic Approach: Financial planners take a holistic approach to financial planning, considering all aspects of their clients' financial situation and goals.

Fiduciary Duty: Many financial planners are held to a fiduciary standard, which means they are required to act in their clients' best interests.

Drawbacks of Financial Planners:

Cost: One of the main drawbacks of financial planners is the cost. Financial planners typically charge clients a fee based on a percentage of their assets under management or a flat fee for their services. The fees charged by financial planners can vary widely, depending on factors such as the level of expertise of the planner, the complexity of the client's financial situation, and the geographic location of the client.

For clients with smaller investment portfolios, the cost of working with a financial planner may be prohibitive. In addition, some financial planners may require clients to commit to a minimum investment or a minimum period of time to work with them, which can further increase the cost.

Conflicts of Interest:

Another potential drawback of working with a financial planner is the possibility of conflicts of interest. Financial planners may receive commissions or incentives for recommending certain investment products or services, which may not be in the best interest of their clients.

To mitigate these conflicts of interest, many financial planners are held to a fiduciary standard, which requires them to act in their clients' best interests. However, not all financial planners are held to this standard, and it can be difficult for clients to determine whether their planner is acting in their best interest.

Lack of Control:

When working with a financial planner, clients may have less control over their investments than they would if managing their own portfolio. Financial planners may make investment decisions on behalf of their clients, which can lead to a lack of control and transparency in the investment process.

However, some financial planners may allow clients to have more input in the investment process, such as by providing them with a range of investment options and allowing them to make the final decision.

Conclusion:

In summary, brokerage firms and financial planners offer different advantages and drawbacks for investors. Brokerage firms are a good option for investors who want to manage their own investments and have control over their portfolio. Financial planners, on the other hand, are a good option for investors who need guidance and expertise in navigating complex financial situations.

When choosing between a brokerage firm and a financial planner, it is important for investors to consider their own financial goals and needs, as well as the costs and potential conflicts of interest associated with each option. Ultimately, the right choice will depend on the individual investor's preferences and priorities.

Functions of Brokerage Firms and Financial Planners

Brokerage firms provide a variety of services to clients, including:

Investment advice: Brokerage firms offer investment advice to clients on a range of investment products such as stocks, bonds, mutual funds, and exchange-traded funds (ETFs). They can provide insights into market trends, investment opportunities, and potential risks.

Trading services: Brokerage firms act as intermediaries between buyers and sellers in financial markets. They provide trading services, allowing clients to buy and sell securities such as stocks and bonds. This includes executing trades on behalf of clients, providing market analysis, and facilitating transactions.

Portfolio management: Some brokerage firms offer portfolio management services to clients. This involves managing a client's investment portfolio, selecting investments based on the client's goals and risk tolerance, and monitoring the portfolio over time.

Research: Brokerage firms conduct research on financial markets and investment products. They provide clients with market insights and analysis to help inform investment decisions.

Retirement planning: Brokerage firms may also offer retirement planning services to clients. This can include advice on saving for retirement, selecting retirement accounts such as individual retirement accounts (IRAs) or 401(k)s, and managing retirement assets.

Functions of Financial Planners:

Financial planners provide a range of services to clients, including:

Financial planning: Financial planners offer comprehensive financial planning services to clients, taking into account their current financial situation, goals, and risk tolerance. This can include retirement planning, estate planning, tax planning, and investment management.

Investment advice: Financial planners provide investment advice to clients, offering insights into market trends, investment opportunities, and potential risks. They can help clients select investment products that align with their goals and risk tolerance.

Risk management: Financial planners can help clients manage risks associated with their financial situation. This may include insurance planning, such as selecting life insurance, disability insurance, or long-term care insurance.

Tax planning: Financial planners can help clients minimize their tax liabilities by offering advice on tax planning strategies. This may include strategies such as tax-loss harvesting, retirement account contributions, and charitable giving.

Estate planning: Financial planners can assist clients in creating and executing an estate plan. This may involve creating wills, trusts, and other legal documents to ensure that clients' assets are distributed according to their wishes after their death.

Comparison of Functions:

While there is some overlap in the functions provided by brokerage firms and financial planners, there are also some key differences. Brokerage firms tend to focus on investment-related services, while financial planners offer a more comprehensive approach to financial planning. Some key differences between the two include:

Investment advice: While both brokerage firms and financial planners offer investment advice, financial planners tend to take a more holistic approach to investment management. They consider a client's entire financial situation and goals when selecting investment products, rather than just focusing on maximizing returns.

Retirement planning: Brokerage firms may offer retirement planning services, but financial planners typically offer a more comprehensive approach. They may help clients create a retirement savings plan, select retirement accounts, and manage retirement assets.

Tax planning: While brokerage firms may offer tax planning advice, financial planners tend to have a deeper understanding of tax laws and regulations. They can offer advice on complex tax planning strategies that may help clients minimize their tax liabilities.

Estate planning: Financial planners are often more involved in estate planning than brokerage firms. They can help clients create legal documents such as wills and trusts, and provide advice on how to minimize estate taxes.

Overall, while both brokerage firms and financial planners provide valuable services to clients, the choice between the two will depend on a client's individual financial situation and goals.

Potential Conflicts of Interest:

One potential issue to consider when working with a brokerage firm or financial planner is the potential for conflicts of interest. These conflicts can arise when the interests of the advisor do not align with the interests of the client, potentially leading to biased advice or recommendations.

Conflicts of interest can arise in a number of ways:

Commission-Based Compensation: Some brokerage firms may receive commissions or other incentives for recommending certain investments, which could create a conflict of interest if the recommended investments are not the best fit for the client's needs.

In-House Products: Brokerage firms may have their own proprietary products or investment vehicles that they may recommend over other options, potentially leading to a conflict of interest if the in-house products are not the best fit for the client's needs.

Limited Product Offerings: Some brokerage firms may only offer a limited selection of investment products, potentially leading to a conflict of interest if the recommended investments are not the best fit for the client's needs but are the best fit for the firm's offerings.

Sales Quotas: Some financial advisors may be incentivized to meet sales quotas or targets, potentially leading to a conflict of interest if the advisor is recommending investments solely to meet these targets rather than with the client's best interests in mind.

To mitigate the potential for conflicts of interest, clients should ask their advisor about their compensation structure, the types of products and investments they offer, and any potential incentives or quotas they may have. It is also important for clients to educate themselves about investments and to do their own research before making any investment decisions.

Investment Management:

One of the primary functions of both brokerage firms and financial planners is investment management. Investment management involves selecting and managing investments on behalf of clients to help them achieve their financial goals.

Brokerage firms typically offer a range of investment products, including stocks, bonds, mutual funds, and exchange-traded funds (ETFs). Clients can work with a broker to select the investments that best fit their needs and goals.

Financial planners may also offer investment management services, but typically take a more holistic approach to financial planning. They will consider a client's overall financial situation and goals before making investment recommendations. Financial planners may also offer more specialized investment strategies, such as socially responsible investing or impact investing.

Retirement Planning:

Another important function of brokerage firms and financial planners is retirement planning. Retirement planning involves developing a plan to help clients achieve their financial goals during retirement.

Brokerage firms may offer retirement accounts, such as individual retirement accounts (IRAs) or 401(k) plans. Clients can work with a broker to select the investments that best fit their retirement goals.

Financial planners may also offer retirement planning services, but typically take a more comprehensive approach to retirement planning. They will consider a client's overall financial situation, including sources of retirement income, expenses, and potential tax implications. Financial planners may also help clients develop a retirement income plan to ensure they have enough income to last throughout their retirement.

Estate Planning:

Estate planning is another important function of brokerage firms and financial planners. Estate planning involves developing a plan for how a client's assets will be managed and distributed after their death.

Brokerage firms may offer services such as trust accounts, which can help clients manage their assets and ensure they are distributed according to their wishes.

Financial planners may also offer estate planning services, including the development of a will, trusts, and other estate planning documents. They can also work with clients to develop a plan to minimize estate taxes and ensure their assets are distributed according to their wishes.

Insurance Planning:

Insurance planning is another area where brokerage firms and financial planners can provide valuable advice and services. Insurance planning involves developing a plan to manage risk and protect against potential financial losses.

Brokerage firms may offer insurance products, such as life insurance or long-term care insurance. Clients can work with a broker to select the insurance products that best meet their needs and budget. Brokerage firms may also offer investment products that have insurance components, such as variable annuities.

On the other hand, financial planners can also provide guidance on insurance planning. They can analyze a client's current insurance coverage and recommend changes or additional coverage as needed. Financial planners may also provide advice on insurance products that are not typically offered by brokerage firms, such as disability insurance or umbrella liability insurance.

Retirement Planning:

Retirement planning is another area where both brokerage firms and financial planners can offer valuable services. Retirement planning involves developing a plan to accumulate and manage assets in order to achieve a desired standard of living in retirement.

Brokerage firms can help clients with retirement planning by offering investment products that are specifically designed for retirement accounts, such as Individual Retirement Accounts (IRAs) or 401(k)s. Brokerage firms can also offer retirement planning tools and resources to help clients plan and manage their retirement savings.

Financial planners can also provide guidance on retirement planning. They can help clients determine how much they need to save in order to achieve their retirement goals and recommend investment strategies to help them get there. Financial planners can also help clients with other aspects of retirement planning, such as determining when to claim Social Security benefits or developing a retirement income plan.

Estate Planning:

Estate planning is another area where both brokerage firms and financial planners can offer valuable services. Estate planning involves developing a plan to manage and transfer assets in the event of a client's death or incapacity.

Brokerage firms can help clients with estate planning by offering investment products that are specifically designed to transfer wealth to heirs, such as trusts or investment accounts with beneficiary designations. Brokerage firms can also offer tools and resources to help clients plan and manage their estates.

Financial planners can also provide guidance on estate planning. They can help clients develop an estate plan that addresses their goals and concerns, such as minimizing estate taxes or ensuring that assets are distributed according to their wishes. Financial planners can also work with clients' attorneys and other professionals to implement an estate plan.

Risk Management:

Risk management is another area where both brokerage firms and financial planners can provide valuable services. Risk management involves developing a plan to identify and manage potential risks that could negatively impact a client's financial situation.

Brokerage firms can help clients with risk management by offering investment products that are designed to manage risk, such as diversification or hedging strategies. Brokerage firms can also offer tools and resources to help clients assess and manage their risk exposure.

Financial planners can also provide guidance on risk management. They can help clients identify potential risks and develop a plan to manage them, such as purchasing insurance or diversifying their investment portfolio. Financial planners can also work with clients' other professional advisors, such as attorneys or insurance agents, to develop a comprehensive risk management plan.

Conclusion:

Overall, both brokerage firms and financial planners can provide valuable advice and services to clients in a variety of areas, including investment management, financial planning, insurance planning, retirement planning, estate planning, and risk management. While there are some differences between the two, the choice between a brokerage firm and a financial planner will depend on a client's individual financial situation and goals. Clients should carefully consider their options and work with a professional who can help them achieve their financial objectives.

Types of Brokerage Firms and Financial Planners

Full-Service Brokerage Firms:
Full-service brokerage firms provide a range of services to clients, including investment advice, research, and trading services. They often have large research departments staffed with analysts who provide research reports and investment recommendations to clients. They may also offer financial planning services, including retirement planning, estate planning, and tax

planning. Full-service brokerage firms typically charge higher fees than discount or online brokerage firms due to the level of service provided.

Examples of Full-Service Brokerage Firms: Merrill Lynch, Morgan Stanley, and Wells Fargo Advisors.

Discount Brokerage Firms:
Discount brokerage firms provide basic trading services to clients at a lower cost than full-service brokerage firms. They may offer online trading platforms and research tools to help clients make investment decisions. However, they generally do not offer investment advice or financial planning services. Discount brokerage firms typically charge lower fees than full-service brokerage firms.

Examples of Discount Brokerage Firms: Charles Schwab, TD Ameritrade, and E-Trade.

Online Brokerage Firms:
Online brokerage firms are similar to discount brokerage firms but operate entirely online. They typically offer lower fees than both full-service and discount brokerage firms. However, they may not offer the same level of research or trading tools as discount brokerage firms.

Examples of Online Brokerage Firms: Robinhood, Webull, and Ally Invest.

Types of Financial Planners:

Fee-Only Financial Planners:
Fee-only financial planners are compensated solely through fees paid by clients for their services. They do not receive commissions or other compensation for recommending specific investments. This helps to eliminate potential conflicts of interest and ensures that the planner is acting in the best interests of the client. Fee-only financial planners may offer a range of services, including investment management, financial planning, and tax planning.

Examples of Fee-Only Financial Planning Firms: XY Planning Network, Garret Planning Network, and NAPFA.

Commission-Based Financial Planners:
Commission-based financial planners receive commissions or other compensation for recommending specific investments or financial products. This can create potential conflicts of interest, as the planner may be

incentivized to recommend investments that may not be in the best interests of the client. Commission-based financial planners may offer a range of services, including investment management, financial planning, and insurance planning.

Examples of Commission-Based Financial Planning Firms: Edward Jones, Ameriprise Financial, and Northwestern Mutual.

Fee-Based Financial Planners:
Fee-based financial planners receive both fees paid by clients for their services and commissions or other compensation for recommending specific investments or financial products. This can create potential conflicts of interest, as the planner may be incentivized to recommend investments that may not be in the best interests of the client. Fee-based financial planners may offer a range of services, including investment management, financial planning, and insurance planning.

Examples of Fee-Based Financial Planning Firms: Merrill Lynch, Morgan Stanley, and Wells Fargo Advisors.

Conclusion:

The choice between different types of brokerage firms and financial planners ultimately depends on a client's individual financial situation and goals. Full-service brokerage firms may be a good choice for clients who require a high level of investment advice and financial planning services. Discount or online brokerage firms may be more suitable for clients who prefer to manage their own investments and require basic trading services. Similarly, fee-only financial planners may be a good choice for clients who want to ensure that their planner is acting in their best interests, while commission-based or fee-based financial planners may be more suitable for clients who require a range of financial services.

Products and Services offered by Brokerage Firms and Financial Planners

Brokerage firms and financial planners offer a range of products and services to their clients to help them manage their finances and achieve their financial goals. These products and services can vary widely, depending on the firm or planner and the needs of the client. In this section, we will discuss some of the common products and services offered by brokerage firms and financial planners.

Investment Products:

Investment products are the most common products offered by brokerage firms and financial planners. These products can range from stocks, bonds, and mutual funds to alternative investments such as real estate, private equity, and hedge funds. Brokerage firms often have access to a wide range of investment products, which they can offer to clients based on their investment goals and risk tolerance.

Financial planners may also recommend investment products, but their approach is typically more holistic, taking into account the client's overall financial situation and goals. They may recommend a diversified portfolio of investments based on the client's risk tolerance and investment goals, and may use strategies such as dollar-cost averaging or rebalancing to help the client achieve their goals.

Retirement Planning Services:

Many brokerage firms and financial planners offer retirement planning services to help clients prepare for retirement. These services can include:

Retirement income planning: Helping clients develop a plan to generate income during retirement, taking into account factors such as Social Security benefits, pensions, and investment income.
Retirement savings planning: Helping clients determine how much they need to save for retirement and develop a plan to achieve their savings goals.
Tax planning: Helping clients minimize taxes during retirement, such as by taking advantage of tax-advantaged retirement accounts.
Estate Planning Services:

Estate planning is another area where brokerage firms and financial planners can provide valuable advice and services. Estate planning involves developing a plan to manage a client's assets in the event of their death or incapacity. These services can include:

Developing a will: Helping clients create a legal document that outlines their wishes for the distribution of their assets after their death.
Trusts: Helping clients create trusts to manage their assets during their lifetime and after their death.
Tax planning: Helping clients minimize estate taxes and other taxes related to the transfer of assets.

Insurance Products:

Insurance planning is another area where brokerage firms and financial planners can provide valuable advice and services. Insurance planning involves developing a plan to manage risk and protect against potential financial losses. Insurance products that may be recommended by brokerage firms and financial planners include:

Life insurance: Providing financial protection for the client's family in the event of their death.

Health insurance: Providing coverage for medical expenses.

Disability insurance: Providing income replacement if the client becomes disabled and is unable to work.

Long-term care insurance: Providing coverage for the cost of long-term care in the event of a chronic illness or disability.

Education Planning:

Many brokerage firms and financial planners also offer education planning services to help clients save for their children's education. These services can include:

529 college savings plans: Helping clients set up tax-advantaged savings plans to fund their children's education.

Coverdell Education Savings Accounts: Helping clients set up tax-advantaged accounts to save for elementary, secondary, or college education expenses.

Tax Planning Services:

Tax planning is an important part of overall financial planning, and brokerage firms and financial planners may offer tax planning services to help clients minimize their tax liability. These services can include:

Tax-efficient investment strategies: Helping clients structure their investments to minimize taxes.

Retirement account contributions: Advising clients on the tax benefits of contributing to retirement accounts such as IRAs and 401(k)s.

Tax-loss harvesting: Helping clients offset capital gains with capital losses to reduce their tax liability.

Other Services:

In addition to the services listed above, brokerage firms and financial planners may also offer other products and services to their clients, such as:

Education Planning: Brokerage firms and financial planners can help clients develop a plan for saving for their children's education. This may include advising on tax-advantaged savings accounts, such as 529 plans, and helping clients understand the financial aid process.

Estate Planning: Estate planning involves developing a plan for the distribution of one's assets after death. Brokerage firms and financial planners can provide guidance on estate planning strategies, including trusts and other estate planning tools.

Charitable Giving: Many clients are interested in charitable giving, and brokerage firms and financial planners can help clients develop a plan for giving to charity that maximizes tax benefits and aligns with their values.

Risk Management: Risk management involves identifying and managing potential risks to one's financial security. Brokerage firms and financial planners may offer risk management services, such as insurance planning and liability management.

Business Planning: For clients who own a business or are self-employed, brokerage firms and financial planners can provide advice on business planning and financial management.

Debt Management: Many clients struggle with managing debt, and brokerage firms and financial planners can provide guidance on debt management strategies, such as debt consolidation and debt repayment plans.

Behavioral Finance: Behavioral finance is an emerging field that examines how emotions and biases influence financial decision-making. Brokerage firms and financial planners may incorporate behavioral finance insights into their advice to help clients make better financial decisions.

Conclusion:

In conclusion, brokerage firms and financial planners offer a wide range of products and services to their clients to help them achieve their financial goals. Whether a client chooses to work with a brokerage firm or a financial planner will depend on their individual financial situation and goals. While brokerage firms may be more focused on transactional services, financial planners may provide a more comprehensive approach to financial planning, including retirement planning, tax planning, and estate planning. Ultimately, it is important for clients to carefully evaluate their options and choose a provider that aligns with their needs and goals.

Regulation of Brokerage Firms and Financial Planners

Brokerage firms and financial planners play a crucial role in managing individuals' and businesses' financial portfolios. To ensure the fair and ethical practices of the financial industry, regulatory bodies exist to oversee and monitor the activities of brokerage firms and financial planners. These regulatory bodies establish rules and regulations that govern the conduct of financial advisors and firms, and failure to comply with these regulations can result in disciplinary actions, fines, and even criminal charges. In this section, we will discuss the various regulatory bodies that oversee brokerage firms and financial planners, the regulations they impose, and the consequences of non-compliance.

Regulatory Bodies

There are several regulatory bodies in the United States that oversee the activities of brokerage firms and financial planners, including:

Securities and Exchange Commission (SEC): The SEC is the primary federal regulatory body responsible for overseeing the securities industry, including brokerage firms and financial planners.

Financial Industry Regulatory Authority (FINRA): FINRA is a self-regulatory organization that oversees brokerage firms and their registered representatives. FINRA establishes rules and regulations that govern the conduct of firms and their representatives.

State Securities Regulators: State securities regulators oversee the securities industry at the state level. They are responsible for licensing and regulating brokerage firms and financial planners that operate within their state.

Department of Labor (DOL): The DOL oversees the Employee Retirement Income Security Act (ERISA), which governs the conduct of financial advisors who provide advice to retirement plan participants.

Regulations

Regulatory bodies impose various regulations on brokerage firms and financial planners to ensure the fair and ethical practices of the financial industry. Some of the key regulations include:

Registration Requirements: Brokerage firms and financial planners must register with regulatory bodies to operate legally. The registration process includes background checks, fingerprinting, and completion of various exams to demonstrate competence in the financial industry.

Disclosure Requirements: Brokerage firms and financial planners must disclose certain information to clients, including fees, conflicts of interest, and disciplinary history.

Suitability Requirements: Financial advisors must ensure that any investment recommendations they make are suitable for their clients' financial situation, investment objectives, and risk tolerance.

Fiduciary Duty: Financial advisors who operate as fiduciaries must act in their clients' best interests and avoid conflicts of interest.

Consequences of Non-Compliance

Failure to comply with regulatory requirements can result in disciplinary actions, fines, and even criminal charges. The consequences of non-compliance can be severe and can include:

Revocation of Registration: Regulatory bodies can revoke the registration of brokerage firms and financial planners that fail to comply with regulatory requirements.

Fines: Regulatory bodies can impose fines on brokerage firms and financial planners that violate regulatory requirements.

Suspension: Regulatory bodies can suspend the registration of brokerage firms and financial planners for a certain period if they violate regulatory requirements.

Criminal Charges: In severe cases, regulatory bodies can refer cases to law enforcement agencies for criminal charges.

Conclusion

Regulatory bodies play a crucial role in overseeing the activities of brokerage firms and financial planners and ensuring the fair and ethical practices of the financial industry. The regulations imposed by these bodies are designed to protect consumers and ensure that financial advisors act in their clients' best interests. Compliance with these regulations is essential for the reputation and success of brokerage firms and financial planners, and failure to comply can result in severe consequences. Therefore, it is important for brokerage firms and financial planners to be aware of the regulations that govern their activities and ensure that they comply with them.

CHAPTER 10: INSURANCE COMPANIES

Insurance is a form of risk management that involves the transfer of risk from one party to another in exchange for a premium. Insurance companies play a critical role in this process by providing a mechanism for individuals and businesses to protect themselves from financial losses that may result from unforeseen events such as accidents, illnesses, or natural disasters.

In this chapter, we will explore the world of insurance companies, their role in the economy, and how they operate. We will examine the different types of insurance policies that are available, including life insurance, health insurance, auto insurance, and property and casualty insurance. We will also look at the underwriting process and how insurance companies assess risk when determining premiums.

Finally, we will examine the regulatory environment that governs insurance companies and how they are held accountable for their practices. The insurance industry is heavily regulated, and insurance companies must comply with a range of federal and state laws and regulations to ensure that they operate in a fair and ethical manner.

Overview of Insurance Companies

Insurance companies are businesses that specialize in the business of risk management. They provide insurance policies to individuals and businesses in exchange for a premium. Insurance companies are regulated by state and federal laws, and they must comply with strict regulations to ensure that they operate in a fair and ethical manner.

Insurance companies collect premiums from their policyholders, which they use to pay claims when policyholders experience losses. Insurance companies use actuarial science to calculate premiums and determine the likelihood of a particular event occurring.

Types of Insurance Policies

There are many different types of insurance policies that are available to individuals and businesses. Some of the most common types of insurance policies include:

Life Insurance: Life insurance policies provide financial protection for the policyholder's beneficiaries in the event of the policyholder's death. There are two main types of life insurance policies: term life insurance and whole life insurance.

Health Insurance: Health insurance policies provide financial protection for medical expenses incurred by the policyholder. Health insurance policies can be purchased individually or through an employer.

Auto Insurance: Auto insurance policies provide financial protection in the event of an accident or theft involving the policyholder's vehicle.

Property and Casualty Insurance: Property and casualty insurance policies provide financial protection for damage to property and liability for injuries caused by the policyholder.

Underwriting Process

The underwriting process is the process by which insurance companies assess risk and determine premiums. The underwriting process involves collecting information about the policyholder, including age, health status, driving history, and other factors that may impact the likelihood of a loss occurring.

Insurance companies use actuarial science to calculate premiums based on the likelihood of a loss occurring. Premiums are generally higher for policies that involve higher levels of risk.

Regulation of Insurance Companies

The insurance industry is heavily regulated, both at the state and federal level. Insurance companies must comply with a range of laws and regulations to ensure that they operate in a fair and ethical manner. Some of the key regulations that govern the insurance industry include:

State Insurance Regulations: Each state has its own insurance regulations that insurance companies must comply with.

Federal Insurance Regulations: The federal government also regulates the insurance industry through agencies such as the National Association of Insurance Commissioners (NAIC) and the Federal Insurance Office.

Consumer Protection Laws: Consumer protection laws, such as the Fair Credit Reporting Act and the Health Insurance Portability and Accountability Act (HIPAA), govern how insurance companies collect and use customer information.

Financial Regulations: Insurance companies are subject to financial regulations, such as the Dodd-Frank Wall Street Reform and Consumer Protection Act, which requires insurance companies to maintain minimum levels of capital.

Conclusion

Insurance companies play a critical role in our economy by providing individuals and businesses with a mechanism to manage risk. As discussed in this chapter, insurance companies offer a wide range of products and services, including life insurance, health insurance, property and casualty insurance, and annuities. These products help individuals and businesses protect against financial losses due to unexpected events.

Insurance companies use actuarial science and risk management techniques to determine the premiums they charge for their products. Actuaries analyze data on mortality, morbidity, and other risk factors to calculate the likelihood of an event occurring and the potential cost of that event. This information is used to set premiums that are sufficient to cover the cost of claims while also generating a profit for the insurer.

Insurance companies are subject to a wide range of regulations at both the state and federal levels. These regulations are designed to protect consumers and ensure the financial stability of the insurance industry. State insurance departments oversee the licensing of insurance companies and agents, the solvency of insurers, and the rates they charge for their products. The National Association of Insurance Commissioners (NAIC) provides a framework for state insurance regulation and also works to coordinate regulation among states.

In recent years, insurance companies have faced a number of challenges, including low interest rates, increased competition, and changing customer expectations. To remain competitive, insurers have had to innovate and adapt their products and services to meet changing consumer needs. This has led to the development of new products such as cyber insurance and usage-based auto insurance, as well as the use of technology to streamline underwriting and claims processing.

Overall, insurance companies provide a vital service to individuals and businesses by helping them manage risk and protect against financial losses. As our economy continues to evolve and new risks emerge, insurance companies will need to continue to innovate and adapt to remain relevant and meet the changing needs of their customers.

Definition of Insurance Companies

An insurance company is a type of financial institution that provides financial protection or coverage to individuals and businesses against the risk of uncertain future events, such as accidents, illnesses, natural disasters, and death, in exchange for a fee, known as a premium. Insurance companies offer a range of insurance products, including life insurance, health insurance, property and casualty insurance, and other specialized insurance products.

In this section, we will explore the concept of insurance and insurance companies in more detail, including the various types of insurance products offered by insurance companies, how insurance companies operate, and how they are regulated.

What is Insurance?

Insurance is a financial tool that allows individuals and businesses to transfer the risk of loss from uncertain future events to a third party, the insurance company. In exchange for a premium, the insurance company agrees to compensate the insured in the event of a loss covered by the insurance policy.

The concept of insurance is based on the law of large numbers, which states that the larger the number of similar exposure units, the more accurately the probability of loss can be predicted. In other words, insurance companies use statistical models to predict the likelihood of loss based on the number of policyholders and historical data on the frequency and severity of similar events.

Types of Insurance Products

Insurance companies offer a variety of insurance products to meet the needs of individuals and businesses. Some of the most common types of insurance products include:

Life Insurance: Life insurance provides financial protection to beneficiaries in the event of the insured's death. There are two main types of life insurance: term life insurance and permanent life insurance.

Health Insurance: Health insurance covers the cost of medical expenses incurred by the insured, including hospitalization, surgery, and prescription drugs.

Property and Casualty Insurance: Property and casualty insurance provides coverage for property damage and liability claims, such as those arising from automobile accidents, natural disasters, and other types of losses.

Other Specialized Insurance Products: Insurance companies also offer a range of specialized insurance products, such as disability insurance, long-term care insurance, and travel insurance.

How Insurance Companies Operate

Insurance companies operate by collecting premiums from policyholders and investing those premiums in a range of financial instruments, such as stocks, bonds, and real estate. The investment income generated by insurance companies helps to offset the cost of claims paid to policyholders.

Insurance companies also use actuarial science to price insurance policies based on the likelihood of loss and the expected cost of claims. Actuarial science is the discipline of using mathematics, statistics, and financial theory to assess the risk of uncertain future events and to quantify the financial impact of those events.

Insurance companies also employ underwriters, who are responsible for evaluating insurance applications and determining the appropriate premium to charge based on the level of risk posed by the applicant. Underwriters use a range of factors to assess risk, including the applicant's age, health status, occupation, and past claims history.

Regulation of Insurance Companies

Insurance companies are regulated by state and federal government agencies to ensure that they are financially sound and able to meet their obligations to policyholders. State insurance departments are responsible for regulating insurance companies at the state level, while federal agencies such as the National Association of Insurance Commissioners (NAIC) and the Federal Insurance Office (FIO) provide oversight at the national level.

State insurance departments are responsible for reviewing insurance company financial statements and monitoring their solvency. They also oversee the licensing of insurance agents and brokers, investigate consumer complaints, and enforce state insurance laws and regulations.

The NAIC is a national organization of state insurance regulators that develops model laws and regulations for insurance companies and provides a forum for state regulators to share information and coordinate their efforts. The FIO is a federal agency that monitors the insurance industry and provides advice to federal policymakers on insurance issues.

Conclusion

Insurance companies are a vital component of the global financial industry, providing individuals and businesses with a means to manage risk and protect their assets. As a highly regulated industry, insurance companies are subject to numerous laws and regulations designed to ensure the stability and fairness of the marketplace. The regulatory framework includes state and federal oversight, with the NAIC and FIO playing key roles in developing and enforcing regulations.

Despite the challenges facing the insurance industry, including rising costs and evolving consumer demands, insurance companies remain an essential part of modern society. The ability to manage risk and protect against unforeseen events is critical for individuals and businesses alike, and insurance companies provide a valuable service in fulfilling this need. As the industry continues to evolve, regulatory oversight will be essential in maintaining a stable and fair marketplace for all stakeholders.

Overall, the insurance industry is a complex and multifaceted sector that plays a critical role in the global economy. From life insurance and health insurance to property and casualty insurance, insurance companies offer a wide range of products and services designed to protect individuals and businesses from a variety of risks. By understanding the key players and regulations that govern the industry, individuals can make informed decisions about their insurance needs and ensure that they are adequately protected in the event of unforeseen events.

Functions of Insurance Companies

Insurance companies play a crucial role in modern society by providing individuals and businesses with protection against the financial consequences of unforeseen events. However, their functions go beyond simply paying claims. In this section, we will explore the various functions of insurance companies, including risk assessment and management, underwriting, claims handling, and investment management.

Risk Assessment and Management

One of the primary functions of insurance companies is to assess and manage risk. This involves evaluating the likelihood of a particular event occurring and the potential financial consequences if it does. Insurance companies use a variety of techniques to assess risk, including statistical analysis, actuarial modeling, and risk profiling.

Statistical Analysis

Insurance companies rely heavily on statistical analysis to evaluate risk. By analyzing historical data and trends, insurance companies can identify patterns and assess the likelihood of certain events occurring. For example, an insurance company may analyze the frequency and severity of car accidents in a particular region to determine the risk of insuring drivers in that area.

Actuarial Modeling

Actuarial modeling is a more sophisticated approach to risk assessment. It involves using complex mathematical models to predict the likelihood of specific events occurring and the associated financial consequences. Actuaries are trained professionals who use these models to help insurance companies develop pricing models and risk management strategies.

Risk Profiling

Risk profiling is a process of identifying the specific risks that an individual or business faces. Insurance companies use risk profiling to develop customized insurance products that provide coverage for specific risks. For example, a business that operates in a high-risk industry may require specialized insurance coverage to protect against specific risks associated with that industry.

Underwriting

Once an insurance company has assessed the risks associated with a particular policy, it must decide whether to accept or reject the application for coverage. This process is known as underwriting. Underwriters are responsible for evaluating the risks associated with each policy and determining the appropriate premium to charge based on those risks.

Underwriters use a variety of factors to evaluate risk, including age, health, occupation, driving record, and credit history. They also consider the type of policy being requested and the potential financial consequences of a claim. Once the underwriter has evaluated all of these factors, they will determine whether to accept or reject the application for coverage.

Claims Handling

If an insured event occurs, the policyholder will file a claim with the insurance company. Claims handlers are responsible for evaluating the claim, determining whether it is covered by the policy, and processing the payment if it is covered. Claims handlers also work to prevent fraudulent claims and ensure that the payment is made in a timely manner.

Claims handlers must have a thorough understanding of the insurance policy, including the coverage limits, exclusions, and deductibles. They must also be skilled in negotiation and communication to ensure that the claim is resolved quickly and fairly.

Investment Management

Insurance companies generate revenue by collecting premiums from policyholders and investing those funds to earn a return. Investment managers are responsible for managing these funds and ensuring that they are invested in a way that maximizes returns while minimizing risk.

Insurance companies typically invest in a mix of fixed-income securities, such as bonds, and equities, such as stocks. They also invest in alternative assets, such as real estate, private equity, and hedge funds. Investment managers must balance the need for income generation with the need to maintain adequate reserves to pay claims.

Conclusion

Insurance companies play a critical role in modern society by providing individuals and businesses with protection against financial losses due to unforeseen events. They perform a variety of functions, including risk assessment and management, underwriting, claims handling, and investment management. By understanding these functions, individuals and businesses can make informed decisions about their insurance needs and choose the right insurance products to meet those needs.

Types of Insurance Companies

Insurance companies come in various shapes and sizes, offering different types of coverage to meet the diverse needs of consumers and businesses. In this section, we will explore the different types of insurance companies, their characteristics, and the types of insurance policies they offer.

Life Insurance Companies

Life insurance companies specialize in offering coverage that pays out a sum of money to beneficiaries upon the death of the insured person. These policies provide financial protection for families and loved ones who depend on the insured person's income.

Life insurance policies come in two main types: term life insurance and whole life insurance. Term life insurance provides coverage for a specific period, typically 10, 20, or 30 years, while whole life insurance provides coverage for the entire life of the insured person.

Health Insurance Companies

Health insurance companies provide coverage for medical expenses, including doctor visits, hospital stays, and prescription drugs. These policies help to protect individuals and families from the high costs of healthcare.

Health insurance policies come in different types, including:

Health Maintenance Organizations (HMOs): HMOs provide coverage through a network of healthcare providers and require policyholders to choose a primary care physician.

Preferred Provider Organizations (PPOs): PPOs offer more flexibility in choosing healthcare providers but usually charge higher premiums and out-of-pocket expenses.

Point-of-Service (POS) plans: POS plans are a combination of HMOs and PPOs, allowing policyholders to choose between in-network or out-of-network providers.

Property and Casualty Insurance Companies

Property and casualty insurance companies provide coverage for damage to property and liability for injury or damage caused by the insured person. These policies protect individuals and businesses from financial losses due to unexpected events, such as natural disasters, accidents, or lawsuits.

Property and casualty insurance policies come in different types, including:

Homeowners insurance: Homeowners insurance provides coverage for damage to a person's home and belongings due to natural disasters, theft, or vandalism.

Automobile insurance: Automobile insurance provides coverage for damage to a person's vehicle, as well as liability for injuries or damage caused to other people or property in an accident.

Commercial insurance: Commercial insurance provides coverage for businesses and organizations, including liability, property damage, and worker's compensation.

Reinsurance Companies

Reinsurance companies provide insurance to other insurance companies. These companies help to spread the risk of large losses by providing backup coverage to insurance companies when they face significant claims.

Reinsurance policies come in different types, including:

Catastrophe reinsurance: Catastrophe reinsurance provides coverage for losses due to natural disasters, such as hurricanes, earthquakes, or floods.

Excess of loss reinsurance: Excess of loss reinsurance provides coverage for claims that exceed a predetermined limit set by the primary insurance company.

Proportional reinsurance: Proportional reinsurance shares the risk and premiums between the primary insurance company and the reinsurer.

Conclusion

Insurance companies provide critical services that protect individuals and businesses from financial risks. Different types of insurance companies offer a variety of policies to meet the diverse needs of their clients, from life insurance to property and casualty insurance. Understanding the different types of insurance companies and the policies they offer is essential for consumers and businesses to make informed decisions about their insurance needs.

Products and Services offered by Insurance Companies

Insurance companies offer a wide range of products and services to meet the needs of individuals, businesses, and other organizations. These products and services can vary depending on the type of insurance company, the market segment it serves, and the regulatory environment in which it operates. In this section, we will discuss some of the common products and services offered by insurance companies.

Life Insurance

Life insurance is a type of insurance that provides a death benefit to the beneficiaries of the policyholder upon their death. The purpose of life insurance is to provide financial protection to the policyholder's loved ones in the event of their death. Life insurance policies can be term life insurance or permanent life insurance. Term life insurance policies provide coverage for a specific period, such as 10 or 20 years, while permanent life insurance policies provide coverage for the policyholder's entire life.

Health Insurance

Health insurance is a type of insurance that provides coverage for medical expenses incurred by the policyholder. Health insurance policies can cover a wide range of medical expenses, including doctor visits, hospital stays, prescription drugs, and more. Health insurance policies can be purchased by individuals or provided by employers as part of an employee benefits package. Health insurance policies can be fee-for-service, where the policyholder pays for services as they are received, or they can be a managed care plan, where the policyholder pays a fixed amount each month and receives care from a network of providers.

Disability Insurance

Disability insurance is a type of insurance that provides income replacement in the event that the policyholder becomes disabled and is unable to work. Disability insurance policies can be short-term or long-term, and they can be purchased by individuals or provided by employers as part of an employee benefits package.

Auto Insurance

Auto insurance is a type of insurance that provides coverage for damage or injury caused by the policyholder's vehicle. Auto insurance policies can cover a wide range of incidents, including accidents, theft, and vandalism. Auto insurance policies are required by law in most states.

Homeowners Insurance

Homeowners insurance is a type of insurance that provides coverage for damage or loss of the policyholder's home and personal property. Homeowners insurance policies can cover a wide range of incidents, including fire, theft, and natural disasters. Homeowners insurance policies are often required by mortgage lenders.

Commercial Insurance

Commercial insurance is a type of insurance that provides coverage for businesses and other organizations. Commercial insurance policies can cover a wide range of incidents, including property damage, liability, and business interruption. Commercial insurance policies can be tailored to meet the specific needs of the business or organization.

Other Products and Services

In addition to the products and services mentioned above, insurance companies offer a wide range of other products and services, including:

Annuities: Annuities are a type of financial product that provide a guaranteed income stream to the policyholder for a set period of time or for the rest of their life.

Long-term care insurance: Long-term care insurance provides coverage for the cost of long-term care services, such as nursing home care, for individuals who are unable to care for themselves.

Travel insurance: Travel insurance provides coverage for medical expenses, trip cancellation, and other incidents that may occur while traveling.

Pet insurance: Pet insurance provides coverage for veterinary expenses and other costs associated with pet ownership.

Conclusion

Insurance companies offer a wide range of products and services to meet the needs of individuals, businesses, and other organizations. These products and services can vary depending on the type of insurance company, the market segment it serves, and the regulatory environment in which it operates. Understanding the products and services offered by insurance companies can help individuals and businesses make informed decisions about their insurance needs.

Regulation of Insurance Companies

The insurance industry plays a crucial role in modern economies by providing protection against various risks that individuals and businesses face. Insurance companies are subject to various regulations to ensure that they are financially stable and able to fulfill their obligations to policyholders. In this section, we will examine the regulation of insurance companies, including the laws and policies that govern their operations and the entities responsible for enforcing them.

Overview of Insurance Regulation

Insurance regulation is the process of overseeing the insurance industry to ensure that it operates in a fair, transparent, and financially stable manner. The primary objective of insurance regulation is to protect policyholders from insolvency and other risks that may arise from the failure of an insurance company. In the United States, insurance regulation is primarily the responsibility of state governments, although there are also federal laws and regulations that apply to certain aspects of insurance.

State Insurance Departments

Each state has a department of insurance that is responsible for regulating insurance companies operating within its borders. The state insurance department is responsible for enforcing insurance laws and regulations, licensing insurance companies and agents, approving insurance policies, and overseeing insurance company financial stability. The state insurance department also conducts examinations of insurance companies to ensure that they are complying with state laws and regulations.

National Association of Insurance Commissioners (NAIC)

The National Association of Insurance Commissioners (NAIC) is a national organization of state insurance regulators that develops model laws and regulations for insurance companies and provides a forum for state regulators to share information and coordinate their efforts. The NAIC also provides a central repository for insurance company financial information, which is used by state regulators to monitor the financial health of insurance companies.

Federal Insurance Office (FIO)

The Federal Insurance Office (FIO) is a federal agency that monitors the insurance industry and provides advice to federal policymakers on insurance issues. The FIO is part of the U.S. Department of the Treasury and was created by the Dodd-Frank Wall Street Reform and Consumer Protection Act of 2010. The FIO's responsibilities include identifying issues and gaps in the regulation of insurance companies, monitoring the insurance industry's systemic risk, and representing the United States in international insurance matters.

Types of Insurance Regulation

Insurance regulation can be divided into several categories, including solvency regulation, market conduct regulation, and consumer protection regulation.

Solvency Regulation

Solvency regulation is the process of ensuring that insurance companies have sufficient financial resources to meet their obligations to policyholders. Solvency regulation typically involves the following:

Minimum capital and surplus requirements: Insurance companies must maintain a certain amount of capital and surplus to ensure that they can meet their financial obligations to policyholders.

Risk-based capital requirements: Insurance companies must hold additional capital if they assume more risk.

Statutory accounting rules: Insurance companies must follow specific accounting rules that differ from Generally Accepted Accounting Principles (GAAP) to ensure that their financial statements accurately reflect their financial condition.

Market Conduct Regulation

Market conduct regulation is the process of ensuring that insurance companies operate in a fair and transparent manner. Market conduct regulation typically involves the following:

Advertising and marketing practices: Insurance companies must not engage in false, misleading, or deceptive advertising and marketing practices.

Underwriting practices: Insurance companies must not engage in discriminatory underwriting practices that unfairly affect certain groups of people.

Claims handling practices: Insurance companies must handle claims in a fair and timely manner and must not engage in bad faith practices that unfairly deny claims.

Consumer Protection Regulation

Consumer protection regulation is the process of protecting insurance consumers from unfair or abusive practices. Consumer protection regulation typically involves the following:

Disclosure requirements: Insurance companies must provide consumers with clear and accurate information about their policies, including the coverage provided, the premiums, and any limitations or exclusions.

Complaint handling: Insurance companies must have procedures in place for handling consumer complaints and must respond to complaints in a timely and effective manner.

Prohibition of unfair practices: Insurance companies are prohibited from engaging in unfair or deceptive practices, such as misrepresenting policy benefits or denying valid claims.

Non-discrimination: Insurance companies are prohibited from discriminating against individuals based on factors such as race, gender, age, or pre-existing medical conditions.

Financial solvency regulation: Insurance companies are required to maintain sufficient financial reserves to ensure they can meet their obligations to policyholders.

The regulation of insurance companies is primarily the responsibility of state governments. Each state has its own insurance department or commission that is responsible for regulating insurance companies operating within its borders. These state regulators are responsible for enforcing state laws and regulations, investigating complaints against insurance companies, and ensuring that insurance companies operating in their state are financially sound and able to meet their obligations to policyholders.

In addition to state regulation, the federal government also plays a role in regulating the insurance industry. The Federal Insurance Office (FIO) was established under the Dodd-Frank Wall Street Reform and Consumer Protection Act to monitor the insurance industry and provide advice to federal policymakers on insurance issues. The FIO is responsible for coordinating federal efforts on insurance matters and promoting uniformity in insurance regulation across the states.

International regulatory bodies, such as the International Association of Insurance Supervisors (IAIS), also play a role in regulating the insurance industry. The IAIS is a global standard-setting organization that promotes international cooperation among insurance supervisors and develops principles, standards, and guidance for the regulation and supervision of the insurance industry.

Overall, the regulation of insurance companies is crucial for protecting consumers and ensuring the stability of the insurance industry. Without adequate regulation, insurance companies may engage in unfair or abusive practices, and policyholders may be left without the protection they need. State and federal regulators, as well as international organizations, play important roles in overseeing the insurance industry and promoting a stable and fair marketplace for consumers.

CHAPTER 11: ALTERNATIVE INVESTMENT FUNDS

Alternative investment funds (AIFs) are investment vehicles that are not publicly traded and are used by high net worth individuals, institutional investors, and other sophisticated investors to access a wide range of investment strategies and asset classes that are not available through traditional investments such as stocks, bonds, and mutual funds. AIFs include hedge funds, private equity funds, real estate funds, and other types of investment vehicles.

In recent years, alternative investment funds have become increasingly popular among investors seeking higher returns and diversification in their portfolios. This section will provide an overview of alternative investment funds, their importance in the financial industry, and the various types of AIFs.

Explanation of Alternative Investment Funds

Alternative investment funds are investment vehicles that are not registered with the Securities and Exchange Commission (SEC) and are not publicly traded on a stock exchange. These funds are typically managed by experienced investment professionals and are only available to accredited investors, who are defined as individuals with a net worth of at least $1 million or annual income of at least $200,000 for the past two years.

AIFs are designed to provide investors with access to a wide range of investment strategies and asset classes that are not available through traditional investments such as stocks, bonds, and mutual funds. For example, hedge funds are known for their ability to generate high returns through sophisticated investment strategies such as short selling, leverage, and derivatives trading. Private equity funds, on the other hand, invest in private companies that are not publicly traded and are often involved in the management of those companies.

Importance of Alternative Investment Funds in the Financial Industry

Alternative investment funds play an important role in the financial industry by providing investors with access to a wide range of investment opportunities that are not available through traditional investments. They also offer the potential for higher returns and diversification in a portfolio, which is important for managing risk.

AIFs also benefit the economy by providing capital to businesses and entrepreneurs who might not have access to traditional sources of funding. For example, private equity funds can provide financing to small and medium-sized businesses that are looking to expand their operations or develop new products.

Types of Alternative Investment Funds

There are several types of alternative investment funds, each with their own unique investment strategies and asset classes.

Hedge Funds

Hedge funds are perhaps the most well-known type of alternative investment fund. They are typically structured as limited partnerships and are managed by investment professionals who use a variety of strategies to generate returns. These strategies can include long and short positions, derivatives trading, and leverage. Hedge funds are known for their ability to generate high returns, but they are also associated with higher risk due to their use of complex investment strategies.

Private Equity Funds

Private equity funds invest in private companies that are not publicly traded. These funds can provide financing to businesses that are looking to expand their operations or develop new products. Private equity funds can also take an active role in the management of these companies and work to improve their operations and profitability.

Real Estate Funds

Real estate funds invest in real estate assets such as commercial properties, residential properties, and mortgages. These funds can provide investors with exposure to real estate markets that are not available through traditional investments. Real estate funds can also provide regular income in the form of rent and other sources of revenue.

Venture Capital Funds

Venture capital funds invest in early-stage companies that are often in the technology or biotech sectors. These funds can provide financing to companies that are developing new technologies or products. Venture capital funds can also take an active role in the management of these companies and work to improve their operations and profitability.

Conclusion

Alternative investment funds are an important part of the financial industry, providing investors with access to a wide range of investment opportunities and offering the potential for higher returns and diversification in their portfolios. However, it is important to understand that these funds can also come with greater risks and potential drawbacks compared to traditional investment options.

Despite the challenges and criticisms facing alternative investment funds, they are likely to continue to play a significant role in the financial industry. As investors seek to diversify their portfolios and look for new opportunities for growth, alternative investment funds offer a range of options to meet these needs.

As the financial industry continues to evolve and adapt to changing economic and regulatory conditions, it is likely that alternative investment funds will also continue to evolve and develop in response to these changes. By staying informed and educated about these investment options, investors can make informed decisions and maximize their chances for success in the financial markets.

I. Hedge Funds

Hedge funds are alternative investment funds that have become increasingly popular over the past few decades. They are known for their unique investment strategies and ability to generate high returns for investors. However, hedge funds are also associated with high risk and have been subject to controversy and criticism. In this section, we will provide an in-depth look at hedge funds, including their history, structure, investment strategies, and impact on the financial industry.

History of Hedge Funds

Hedge funds have a long history that dates back to the 1940s. The first hedge fund was started by Alfred Winslow Jones in 1949. Jones was a journalist and economist who decided to start his own investment fund using a unique investment strategy that involved buying stocks he believed would increase in value and selling short stocks he believed would decrease in value. This strategy was designed to hedge against market risk, which is where the term "hedge fund" comes from.

In the decades that followed, hedge funds became increasingly popular among wealthy investors, and the industry grew rapidly. Today, hedge funds manage trillions of dollars in assets and are considered an important part of the financial industry.

Structure of Hedge Funds

Hedge funds are private investment funds that are typically only available to accredited investors, such as high net worth individuals, pension funds, and endowments. They are not open to the general public and are not required to register with the Securities and Exchange Commission (SEC).

Hedge funds are typically structured as limited partnerships, with the fund manager serving as the general partner and the investors serving as limited partners. The fund manager is responsible for making investment decisions and managing the fund, while the limited partners provide the capital.

Investment Strategies of Hedge Funds

Hedge funds are known for their unique investment strategies, which can be complex and often involve a high degree of risk. Some of the most common hedge fund investment strategies include:

Long/Short Equity: This strategy involves buying stocks the hedge fund manager believes will increase in value (going long) and selling short stocks the manager believes will decrease in value. This strategy is designed to hedge against market risk and can generate high returns if the manager makes the right investment decisions.

Global Macro: This strategy involves investing in a wide range of assets, including stocks, bonds, commodities, and currencies, based on the manager's macroeconomic outlook. This strategy is designed to take advantage of global economic trends and can be highly profitable if the manager's predictions are accurate.

Event-Driven: This strategy involves investing in companies that are going through a significant event, such as a merger, acquisition, or bankruptcy.

This strategy is designed to take advantage of the market inefficiencies that can occur during these events and can generate high returns if the manager makes the right investment decisions.

Arbitrage: This strategy involves taking advantage of price discrepancies between different markets or securities. For example, the hedge fund may buy a security in one market where it is undervalued and sell it in another market where it is overvalued. This strategy is designed to generate profits from market inefficiencies and can be highly profitable if the manager makes the right investment decisions.

Impact of Hedge Funds on the Financial Industry

Hedge funds have had a significant impact on the financial industry, both positive and negative. Some of the ways hedge funds have impacted the industry include:

Increased competition: Hedge funds have increased competition in the financial industry, particularly in the areas of asset management and investment banking. This has led to lower fees and better investment opportunities for investors.

Increased risk: Hedge funds are known for their high-risk investment strategies, which can lead to significant losses for investors. In addition, some hedge funds have been involved in controversial activities, such as insider trading and market manipulation.

Increased market efficiency: Hedge funds have been credited with increasing market efficiency by identifying and exploiting pricing inefficiencies. This can help to prevent market bubbles and reduce volatility in the financial markets.

Innovations in investment strategies: Hedge funds are known for their innovative investment strategies, which have led to the development of new financial products and investment vehicles. For example, many hedge funds have been involved in the development of structured products, such as collateralized debt obligations (CDOs), which played a significant role in the 2008 financial crisis.

Employment opportunities: The growth of the hedge fund industry has created employment opportunities in a variety of fields, including finance, law, and technology. Many hedge funds are headquartered in major financial centers such as New York and London, which has led to the development of a significant industry ecosystem in these cities.

Despite these positive impacts, hedge funds have also been associated with negative consequences, including:

Systemic risk: The high leverage and interconnectedness of many hedge funds can create systemic risk in the financial system. If a large hedge fund were to fail, it could have significant ripple effects throughout the financial industry.

Lack of transparency: Hedge funds are often not subject to the same regulatory requirements as other financial institutions, which can lead to a lack of transparency in their operations. This lack of transparency can make it difficult for investors to assess the risks and potential rewards of investing in a hedge fund.

Inequality: Hedge funds are often only available to high-net-worth individuals and institutional investors, which can exacerbate wealth inequality by providing exclusive investment opportunities to a select few.

Regulatory challenges: Regulating hedge funds can be difficult due to their complexity and the wide range of investment strategies they employ. As a result, regulators may struggle to keep pace with the rapid evolution of the industry and ensure that investors are adequately protected.

Overall, hedge funds have had a significant impact on the financial industry, both positive and negative. While they offer the potential for high returns and innovative investment strategies, they also pose risks to investors and the broader financial system. As a result, the regulation of hedge funds remains a contentious issue, with policymakers and industry participants weighing the costs and benefits of increased oversight.

Definition and explanation of hedge funds

Hedge funds are alternative investment vehicles that use a range of strategies to generate high returns for their investors. They are typically available only to high net worth individuals and institutional investors, and are not subject to the same regulatory requirements as mutual funds and other traditional investment vehicles. This section will provide a comprehensive definition and explanation of hedge funds, including their history, characteristics, and investment strategies.

Definition of Hedge Funds

A hedge fund is a private investment vehicle that is typically structured as a limited partnership or limited liability company. It is managed by an investment advisor or team of advisors, who make investment decisions on behalf of the fund's investors. Hedge funds are designed to be flexible investment vehicles, with the ability to invest in a wide range of assets, including stocks, bonds, commodities, currencies, and derivatives.

Characteristics of Hedge Funds

Hedge funds have several distinctive characteristics that set them apart from other types of investment vehicles:

Limited access: Hedge funds are generally only available to accredited investors, which include high net worth individuals, institutional investors, and other entities that meet certain financial criteria. This limited access helps to create a sense of exclusivity among investors, and can also help to attract large amounts of capital.

High fees: Hedge funds typically charge higher fees than other investment vehicles, including management fees and performance fees. These fees can range from 1% to 2% of assets under management for management fees, and 20% of profits for performance fees. These fees are justified by the expectation of high returns and the complexity of the investment strategies employed by hedge funds.

Flexibility: Hedge funds are designed to be flexible investment vehicles, with the ability to invest in a wide range of assets and use a variety of investment strategies. This flexibility allows hedge funds to adapt to changing market conditions and take advantage of new investment opportunities.

Transparency: Hedge funds are not subject to the same regulatory requirements as mutual funds and other traditional investment vehicles, and are not required to disclose their holdings or investment strategies to the public. This lack of transparency can make it difficult for investors to evaluate the risks and potential returns of hedge funds.

Investment Strategies of Hedge Funds

Hedge funds use a variety of investment strategies to generate returns for their investors. Some of the most common investment strategies used by hedge funds include:

Long/short equity: This strategy involves buying stocks that the fund manager believes will increase in value, while simultaneously selling short stocks that are expected to decrease in value. This strategy allows hedge funds to generate returns even in a declining market.

Global macro: This strategy involves making investments based on macroeconomic trends and events, such as changes in interest rates or currency values. This strategy allows hedge funds to take advantage of global market trends and generate returns across a wide range of assets.

Distressed debt: This strategy involves investing in companies or securities that are in financial distress or are expected to be in financial distress. This strategy allows hedge funds to generate high returns by buying assets at a discount and then selling them at a profit once the company or security has recovered.

Event-driven: This strategy involves investing in companies that are expected to undergo a significant event, such as a merger or acquisition, a spin-off, or a bankruptcy. This strategy allows hedge funds to generate returns by anticipating and capitalizing on market reactions to these events.

Impact of Hedge Funds on the Financial Industry

Hedge funds have had a significant impact on the financial industry, both positive and negative. Some of the ways hedge funds have impacted the industry include:

Increased competition: Hedge funds have increased competition in the financial industry, particularly in the areas of asset management and investment banking. This has led to lower fees and better investment opportunities for investors.

Increased risk: Hedge funds are known for their high-risk investment strategies, which can lead to significant losses for investors.

Increased regulation: In response to some of the negative impacts of hedge funds, there has been an increase in regulation of the industry. This includes requirements for hedge funds to register with regulatory bodies, such as the Securities and Exchange Commission (SEC) in the United States, and increased reporting requirements. While this has increased transparency and oversight, it has also led to increased costs for hedge funds and made it more difficult for smaller funds to enter the market.

Innovations in investing: Hedge funds have also been responsible for many innovations in the investing world, such as the development of quantitative strategies and the use of derivatives. These innovations have contributed to the growth of the financial industry and have led to new investment opportunities for investors.

Impact on the economy: The impact of hedge funds on the wider economy is a subject of debate. Some argue that hedge funds can contribute to economic growth by providing funding to new businesses and industries. Others argue that the high-risk investment strategies of hedge funds can contribute to financial instability and market volatility.

Overall, while hedge funds have had a significant impact on the financial industry, their role and impact on the wider economy is still the subject of debate and scrutiny.

History and development of hedge funds

Hedge funds have a relatively short history compared to other types of investment funds, but they have quickly become an important part of the financial industry. This section will explore the origins of hedge funds and their development over time.

Origins of Hedge Funds

The term "hedge fund" originated in the 1940s, when a group of investors used complex investment strategies to protect their portfolios against market downturns. These early hedge funds were primarily focused on managing risk rather than maximizing returns.

One of the earliest hedge funds was created in 1949 by Alfred Winslow Jones, a journalist and economist. Jones used a strategy called "long-short equity" to protect his clients' investments during market downturns. This strategy involved buying stocks that were expected to increase in value (long positions) while simultaneously selling short stocks that were expected to decrease in value. This allowed Jones to profit from both rising and falling markets.

Over time, other investment managers began using similar strategies and the hedge fund industry began to grow.

Development of Hedge Funds

The 1970s saw significant growth in the hedge fund industry, as more investors began to recognize the potential benefits of these investment vehicles. In 1970, there were only a handful of hedge funds in existence. By 1980, there were more than 200.

During the 1980s, hedge funds began to attract more institutional investors, such as pension funds and endowments. This helped to fuel further growth in the industry.

In the 1990s, hedge funds began to diversify their investment strategies beyond long-short equity. Some hedge funds began investing in commodities, while others used derivatives to hedge their portfolios against market risks. The use of leverage also became more prevalent during this time.

The early 2000s saw continued growth in the hedge fund industry, with more investors seeking exposure to alternative investments. However, the financial crisis of 2008 had a significant impact on the industry, as many hedge funds suffered significant losses. Since then, the industry has experienced both growth and contraction, with some investors expressing concern about the high fees and lack of transparency associated with many hedge funds.

Types of Hedge Funds

There are many different types of hedge funds, each with its own investment strategy and risk profile. Some of the most common types of hedge funds include:

Equity Hedge Funds: These funds primarily invest in stocks, using long-short strategies or other techniques to generate returns.

Event-Driven Hedge Funds: These funds focus on events such as mergers, acquisitions, and bankruptcies, seeking to profit from changes in the market that result from these events.

Macro Hedge Funds: These funds invest in a range of asset classes, including currencies, commodities, and bonds. They use economic and political analysis to identify trends and make investment decisions.

Relative Value Hedge Funds: These funds seek to exploit pricing inefficiencies in the market, using strategies such as pairs trading and convertible arbitrage.

Credit Hedge Funds: These funds invest in debt securities, such as bonds, and use strategies such as distressed debt investing and credit arbitrage to generate returns.

Regulation of Hedge Funds

Hedge funds are subject to less regulation than other types of investment funds, such as mutual funds. This is because they are typically only available to accredited investors, who are considered to have a higher level of financial sophistication.

However, there has been increased scrutiny of the hedge fund industry in recent years, particularly in the aftermath of the financial crisis. Some regulators have called for more oversight of hedge funds, while others argue that increased regulation could stifle innovation and limit investors' access to alternative investments.

Conclusion

Hedge funds have become an important part of the financial industry, offering investors access to a wide range of investment strategies and opportunities. Despite their relatively short history, they have grown to become a significant force in the financial markets. Their ability to generate high returns in good times, combined with their reputation for taking on significant risk, has made them attractive to wealthy individuals and institutional investors alike.

While hedge funds have been associated with controversy and criticism over the years, they have also been responsible for significant innovations in the financial industry. Some of the most influential investment strategies used by hedge funds, such as the use of derivatives and the creation of new financial products, have had a profound impact on the wider financial industry.

The future of hedge funds remains uncertain, particularly in light of the increasing regulatory scrutiny they face. However, as long as there are investors looking for high returns and the ability to diversify their portfolios, hedge funds are likely to remain an important part of the financial landscape. As the financial markets continue to evolve and new investment opportunities emerge, hedge funds will continue to adapt and innovate, seeking out new strategies and opportunities to generate returns for their investors.

In conclusion, hedge funds are a complex and multifaceted aspect of the financial industry. Their history, development, and impact have been significant, and they continue to play an important role in the financial markets. While they are not without controversy or risk, they offer investors the potential for high returns and diversification, and they will likely remain an important investment option for years to come.

Types of hedge funds

Hedge funds come in different shapes and sizes, with each fund employing a different investment strategy. Some hedge funds specialize in a specific investment sector, while others invest in a broad range of assets. Here are some of the most common types of hedge funds:

Long/Short Equity Hedge Funds
Long/Short equity hedge funds are one of the most popular types of hedge funds. These funds invest in a mix of long and short equity positions, with the goal of generating returns that are uncorrelated to the broader market. Long/Short equity hedge funds use a variety of strategies to achieve this, including fundamental analysis, quantitative analysis, and technical analysis.

Long/Short equity hedge funds aim to profit from both rising and falling stock prices. They do this by taking long positions in stocks they believe will increase in value and short positions in stocks they believe will decrease in value.

Event-Driven Hedge Funds
Event-driven hedge funds invest in companies that are going through a significant corporate event, such as a merger, acquisition, or bankruptcy. These funds aim to profit from the market inefficiencies that arise during these events. Event-driven hedge funds use a variety of strategies to generate returns, including merger arbitrage, distressed debt, and special situations.

Merger arbitrage involves investing in companies that are involved in mergers or acquisitions. The goal is to profit from the price discrepancies between the acquiring company's stock and the target company's stock.

Distressed debt involves investing in the debt of companies that are in financial distress. The goal is to profit from the price discrepancies between the face value of the debt and the market price of the debt.

Special situations involve investing in companies that are undergoing a significant change, such as a spin-off or a restructuring. The goal is to profit from the price discrepancies that arise during these events.

Global Macro Hedge Funds

Global macro hedge funds invest in a mix of assets, including currencies, commodities, and equities, with the goal of profiting from macroeconomic trends. These funds use a top-down approach to investing, analyzing global economic and political events to identify investment opportunities.

Global macro hedge funds invest based on their outlook for the global economy. For example, if the fund manager believes that the U.S. economy is going to enter a recession, they may invest in safe-haven assets, such as gold or U.S. Treasury bonds.

Relative Value Hedge Funds

Relative value hedge funds invest in assets that are mispriced relative to each other. These funds aim to profit from the price discrepancies that arise between these assets. Relative value hedge funds use a variety of strategies to identify these discrepancies, including statistical arbitrage, pairs trading, and convertible arbitrage.

Statistical arbitrage involves using statistical models to identify mispricings in assets. The goal is to profit from the price discrepancies that arise between these assets.

Pairs trading involves investing in two assets that are correlated with each other. The goal is to profit from the price discrepancies that arise between these assets.

Convertible arbitrage involves investing in convertible bonds and shorting the underlying stock. The goal is to profit from the price discrepancies that arise between the bond and the stock.

Multi-Strategy Hedge Funds

Multi-strategy hedge funds invest in a mix of assets and use a variety of strategies to generate returns. These funds may invest in equities, fixed income securities, commodities, currencies, and other assets. They may use a variety of investment strategies, including long/short equity, event-driven, global macro, and relative value.

Multi-strategy hedge funds aim to provide investors with a diversified portfolio of investment strategies. By investing in a variety of assets and strategies, multi-strategy hedge funds aim to provide investors with a way to mitigate risk and potentially generate higher returns. Some common investment strategies employed by multi-strategy hedge funds include:

Long/short equity: Long/short equity is a popular strategy employed by many hedge funds, including multi-strategy funds. This strategy involves taking long positions in stocks that are expected to appreciate in value and short positions in stocks that are expected to decline in value. By simultaneously holding both long and short positions, the fund manager can potentially profit from both upward and downward price movements in the market.

Event-driven: Event-driven strategies involve investing in companies that are undergoing significant corporate events, such as mergers and acquisitions, bankruptcies, and restructurings. The fund manager will typically take long or short positions in the target company's stock or debt, depending on their view of the outcome of the event.

Global macro: Global macro strategies involve investing in a range of asset classes, including stocks, bonds, currencies, and commodities, based on macroeconomic trends and global events. Fund managers will take long or short positions in these assets based on their analysis of the economic and political environment.

Relative value: Relative value strategies involve taking long and short positions in related assets, such as two different stocks in the same industry or two different bonds issued by the same company. The fund manager will attempt to profit from the difference in price between the two assets, which is known as the "spread."

Managed futures: Managed futures strategies involve investing in futures contracts, which are agreements to buy or sell an asset at a predetermined price at a future date. Fund managers will typically take long or short positions in futures contracts based on their analysis of the underlying asset's price movements.

Credit: Credit strategies involve investing in fixed income securities, such as corporate bonds and loans, with the goal of generating income and capital gains. Fund managers may take long or short positions in these securities based on their analysis of the creditworthiness of the issuer.

Equity market neutral: Equity market neutral strategies involve taking equal long and short positions in stocks with the aim of generating returns that are independent of the broader market. The fund manager will typically identify pairs of stocks that have a similar risk profile and take opposite positions in each stock.

Quantitative: Quantitative strategies involve using mathematical models and algorithms to identify and exploit market inefficiencies. Fund managers will typically use statistical analysis and computer programs to analyze large amounts of market data and identify patterns and trends.

While multi-strategy hedge funds invest in a variety of assets and strategies, some funds may have a greater emphasis on certain strategies depending on their investment objectives and the current market environment. For example, a fund that expects a market downturn may increase its allocation to the long/short equity and global macro strategies to profit from market declines.

It is worth noting that while multi-strategy hedge funds aim to provide investors with a diversified portfolio of investment strategies, they are not immune to market risks and losses. Investors should carefully consider the risks associated with each strategy and conduct thorough due diligence before investing in any hedge fund.

Role of hedge funds in the financial industry

Hedge funds have played a significant role in the financial industry since their inception. While they have been criticized for their high-risk investment strategies and lack of transparency, they have also provided investors with access to a wide range of investment opportunities and contributed to the growth of the financial industry as a whole. In this section, we will explore the role of hedge funds in the financial industry in more detail.

Providing Investors with Access to Alternative Investment Strategies

One of the primary roles of hedge funds in the financial industry is to provide investors with access to alternative investment strategies that may not be available through traditional investment vehicles such as mutual funds or exchange-traded funds (ETFs). Hedge funds use a wide range of investment strategies, including short-selling, leverage, and derivatives, to generate returns for investors.

These strategies can be complex and require a high level of expertise to execute effectively. As a result, hedge funds typically require investors to meet certain criteria before they are allowed to invest, such as having a minimum net worth or income. While this may limit the number of investors who can participate, it also ensures that investors have a certain level of financial sophistication and can handle the risks associated with these strategies.

Contributing to the Growth of the Financial Industry

Hedge funds have also contributed to the growth of the financial industry as a whole by providing liquidity and creating new investment opportunities. By investing in a wide range of assets and strategies, hedge funds can help to increase liquidity in the market, making it easier for investors to buy and sell securities. This can help to reduce transaction costs and improve market efficiency.

In addition, hedge funds often invest in emerging markets and other less liquid assets that may not be widely available to other investors. This can create new investment opportunities and help to diversify the portfolios of investors.

Challenging Traditional Investment Strategies

Hedge funds have also challenged traditional investment strategies by demonstrating that there are alternative ways to generate returns. While traditional investment vehicles such as mutual funds and ETFs typically focus on long-only strategies, hedge funds use a wide range of strategies to generate returns, including both long and short positions.

This has led to increased competition in the financial industry, particularly in the areas of asset management and investment banking. Hedge funds have forced traditional investment managers to become more innovative and to explore new investment strategies in order to remain competitive.

However, the increased competition has also led to concerns about the impact of hedge funds on the financial industry. Some critics argue that hedge funds contribute to market volatility and can destabilize the financial system.

Controversies Surrounding Hedge Funds

Hedge funds have been the subject of numerous controversies over the years, particularly in the wake of the 2008 financial crisis. Some of the controversies surrounding hedge funds include:

Lack of transparency: Hedge funds are often criticized for their lack of transparency, particularly with regard to their investment strategies and performance. Unlike traditional investment vehicles such as mutual funds, hedge funds are not required to disclose their holdings or performance to the public. This lack of transparency can make it difficult for investors to assess the risks associated with investing in hedge funds.

High fees: Hedge funds typically charge higher fees than traditional investment vehicles. In addition to a management fee, which is typically 2% of assets under management, hedge funds often charge a performance fee, which can be as high as 20% of profits. These fees can significantly reduce the returns that investors receive.

Risky investment strategies: Hedge funds are known for their high-risk investment strategies, which can lead to significant losses for investors. In addition, the use of leverage and derivatives can amplify these losses, increasing the risk to investors.

Market volatility: Some critics argue that hedge funds contribute to market volatility and can destabilize the financial system. Because hedge funds often use leverage and engage in short-term trading, they can exacerbate market movements, particularly during times of market stress. This can lead to a ripple effect throughout the financial system, causing market-wide instability.

However, proponents of hedge funds argue that they can actually have a stabilizing effect on the financial system. By taking contrarian positions and betting against overvalued assets, hedge funds can help correct market imbalances and prevent bubbles from forming. Additionally, hedge funds can provide liquidity to the market by taking on risky investments that other investors may be unwilling to take on.

Regulatory concerns

The hedge fund industry has long been a subject of regulatory scrutiny. In the wake of the 2008 financial crisis, policymakers and regulators around the world took a closer look at the role of hedge funds in the crisis and began implementing a variety of new regulations aimed at mitigating systemic risk.

Some of the key regulatory concerns around hedge funds include:

Systemic risk: Because of their size and interconnectedness with other financial institutions, hedge funds have the potential to create systemic risk that can destabilize the financial system as a whole. Regulators have been particularly concerned with the potential for a run on hedge funds, which could lead to widespread market disruption.

Lack of transparency: Hedge funds are notoriously secretive, and many critics argue that this lack of transparency makes it difficult for regulators and investors to fully understand the risks associated with these investments.

Investor protection: Because hedge funds are typically limited to high net worth individuals and institutional investors, regulators are concerned about the potential for retail investors to be lured into these investments without fully understanding the risks involved.

Fraud and misconduct: As with any industry, there is always the potential for fraud and misconduct in the hedge fund industry. Regulators have taken steps to increase transparency and oversight in order to mitigate this risk.

Despite these concerns, many hedge fund managers and industry advocates argue that increased regulation can have unintended consequences, such as stifling innovation and limiting investment opportunities. Some also argue that the increased scrutiny of the industry has led to a more transparent and accountable hedge fund sector.

Conclusion

Hedge funds have become an important part of the financial industry, offering investors access to a wide range of investment strategies and potentially higher returns than traditional investments. However, they also carry a significant amount of risk and are subject to regulatory scrutiny and criticism.

As with any investment, it is important for investors to carefully consider the risks and benefits of investing in hedge funds and to do their due diligence in selecting a fund that aligns with their investment goals and risk tolerance. Additionally, policymakers and regulators must continue to monitor the hedge fund industry and take steps to mitigate potential systemic risks while also fostering innovation and growth within the industry.

Risks and benefits of investing in hedge funds

Hedge funds are a popular investment vehicle for many investors, ranging from high net worth individuals to institutional investors such as pension funds and endowments. While hedge funds offer the potential for high returns, they also come with a number of risks that investors must consider. In this section, we will discuss the risks and benefits of investing in hedge funds.

Benefits of Investing in Hedge Funds

Potential for High Returns
One of the main benefits of investing in hedge funds is the potential for high returns. Hedge funds are known for their ability to generate significant returns in both bull and bear markets. This is because hedge fund managers have the flexibility to invest in a wide range of assets and use a variety of investment strategies. Some hedge funds specialize in long/short equity strategies, while others focus on fixed income, commodities, or currencies. By diversifying their investments, hedge fund managers can potentially generate higher returns than traditional asset classes such as stocks and bonds.

Access to Alternative Investments
Hedge funds offer investors access to a wide range of alternative investments that are not available through traditional investment vehicles. For example, hedge funds can invest in private equity, venture capital, real estate, and other non-traditional assets. By diversifying their portfolios with alternative investments, investors can potentially reduce their overall portfolio risk.

Active Management

Hedge funds are actively managed, which means that the fund manager makes investment decisions based on market conditions and other factors. This active management can potentially result in higher returns and better risk management compared to passive investment strategies.

Flexibility

Hedge funds offer greater flexibility compared to traditional investment vehicles. For example, hedge funds can use leverage to increase their returns, and can also use derivatives to hedge against market risk. This flexibility allows hedge fund managers to respond quickly to changing market conditions and potentially generate higher returns.

Risks of Investing in Hedge Funds

High Fees

One of the main risks of investing in hedge funds is the high fees associated with these investments. Hedge funds typically charge a management fee of 2% of assets under management, as well as a performance fee of 20% of any profits generated by the fund. These fees can significantly reduce the overall returns generated by the fund and may not be justified by the returns generated.

Lack of Transparency

Hedge funds are not required to disclose their holdings to the public, which can make it difficult for investors to evaluate the risks associated with these investments. Additionally, hedge funds are not required to disclose their investment strategies, which can make it difficult for investors to understand how the fund is investing their money.

Lack of Liquidity

Many hedge funds have restrictions on when investors can withdraw their money, which can make it difficult for investors to access their funds when they need them. Some hedge funds also have lock-up periods, which require investors to keep their money in the fund for a certain period of time.

Higher Risk

Hedge funds are known for their high-risk investment strategies, which can result in significant losses for investors. Some hedge funds use leverage to amplify their returns, which can also amplify losses in a down market. Additionally, hedge funds may use complex investment strategies that are difficult for investors to understand, which can increase the risk associated with these investments.

Lack of Regulation

Hedge funds are not subject to the same regulations as traditional investment vehicles such as mutual funds. This lack of regulation can make it difficult for investors to evaluate the risks associated with these investments and can increase the potential for fraud and other illegal activities.

Conclusion

Investing in hedge funds can offer investors the potential for high returns and access to a wide range of alternative investments. However, hedge funds also come with a number of risks, including high fees, lack of transparency, and the potential for losses.

Overall, the decision to invest in a hedge fund should be carefully considered, taking into account the investor's risk tolerance, investment goals, and overall portfolio diversification strategy. It is important to thoroughly research potential hedge fund investments and carefully evaluate the investment manager's track record, investment strategy, and risk management practices.

While hedge funds can offer diversification benefits and potentially higher returns than traditional investments, investors should also be aware of the potential risks and downsides. Ultimately, a well-diversified portfolio that includes a mix of traditional and alternative investments may be the best approach for achieving long-term investment goals.

Performance of hedge funds compared to other investments

Hedge funds are a popular investment vehicle that can offer investors access to a range of alternative investment strategies. One of the key selling points of hedge funds is the potential for high returns. However, it is important for investors to understand how hedge funds perform compared to other types of investments, such as mutual funds, exchange-traded funds (ETFs), and individual stocks and bonds.

In this section, we will explore the performance of hedge funds compared to other investments. We will examine historical data and consider the factors that can impact the performance of different types of investments. We will also discuss the limitations of performance comparisons and the importance of considering risk and other factors when evaluating investment performance.

Historical Performance of Hedge Funds

Hedge funds have a reputation for delivering strong returns. In the early days of the hedge fund industry, many funds were able to achieve returns that far exceeded those of traditional investments. However, as the industry has grown and become more competitive, it has become more difficult for hedge funds to consistently outperform other types of investments.

According to data from Hedge Fund Research, Inc. (HFR), the average annualized return for hedge funds between 1990 and 2020 was 8.25%. This compares to an annualized return of 10.62% for the S&P 500 index over the same period.

However, it is important to note that hedge fund returns can vary widely depending on the strategy employed by the fund. For example, a study by Vanguard found that between 2008 and 2018, the average annualized return for long/short equity hedge funds was 6.02%, while the average annualized return for global macro hedge funds was 2.61%.

Comparing Hedge Funds to Other Investments

When evaluating the performance of hedge funds, it is important to compare them to other types of investments. This can help investors understand how hedge funds fit into their overall investment strategy and determine whether they are an appropriate choice given their risk tolerance and investment goals.

Some of the key types of investments that investors may consider when comparing hedge funds include:

Mutual funds: Mutual funds are a type of investment vehicle that pools money from many investors to invest in a diversified portfolio of stocks, bonds, and other assets. According to data from Morningstar, the average annualized return for mutual funds between 1990 and 2020 was 9.18%, slightly higher than the average return for hedge funds over the same period.

Exchange-traded funds (ETFs): ETFs are similar to mutual funds in that they are investment vehicles that hold a diversified portfolio of assets. However, they trade on an exchange like individual stocks. According to data from Vanguard, the average annualized return for ETFs between 2003 and 2020 was 8.1%.

Individual stocks and bonds: Investors can also choose to invest directly in individual stocks and bonds. According to data from JP Morgan, the average annualized return for stocks between 1926 and 2020 was 10.2%, while the average annualized return for bonds over the same period was 5.5%.

Factors That Impact Investment Performance

There are a number of factors that can impact the performance of different types of investments, including hedge funds. Some of the key factors to consider when evaluating investment performance include:

Economic conditions: Economic conditions, such as interest rates, inflation, and GDP growth, can have a significant impact on investment performance. For example, when interest rates are low, bonds tend to perform poorly, while stocks may perform well.

Investment strategy: The investment strategy employed by a fund can have a significant impact on its performance. For example, a fund that invests primarily in high-growth technology stocks may perform well during periods of economic growth but may suffer during a recession. On the other hand, a fund that employs a more conservative, value-oriented strategy may be less affected by market fluctuations.

Market trends: Market trends can have a major impact on investment performance, particularly in the short term. For example, a sudden drop in the stock market can cause even the best-performing stocks to decline in value.

Fund manager skill: The skill of the fund manager can play a significant role in investment performance. A skilled manager with a strong track record may be able to navigate market fluctuations more effectively than a less experienced manager.

Asset allocation: The way in which a fund allocates its assets can have a significant impact on performance. A well-diversified portfolio that includes a mix of stocks, bonds, and other assets may be more resilient to market fluctuations than a portfolio that is heavily weighted towards a single asset class.

Fees and expenses: Fees and expenses can eat into investment returns, particularly for actively managed funds like hedge funds. It's important to consider the fees associated with an investment when evaluating its performance.

Overall, there are many factors that can impact the performance of hedge funds and other investments. It's important for investors to carefully evaluate these factors and to choose investments that align with their risk tolerance and investment goals.

II. Pension Funds

A pension fund is a type of investment vehicle that is designed to provide income to retirees in the form of pension payments. Pension funds are often sponsored by employers, labor unions, or government agencies, and are typically funded by contributions from both employers and employees. The money that is contributed to a pension fund is invested in a variety of assets, such as stocks, bonds, and real estate, with the goal of earning returns that will help to fund pension payments in the future.

Pension funds play a critical role in retirement planning for millions of people around the world. They offer a number of benefits, including:

Long-term investment horizon: Pension funds typically have a long-term investment horizon, which allows them to invest in assets that may be too volatile or illiquid for other types of investors. This long-term approach can help to generate higher returns over time.

Professional management: Pension funds are typically managed by professional investment managers who have the expertise and resources to identify and evaluate investment opportunities. This can help to improve the overall performance of the fund.

Diversification: Pension funds are often invested in a wide range of assets, which can help to reduce risk and volatility. This diversification can help to protect the fund against losses in any one asset class.

Tax benefits: Pension funds may offer tax benefits to both employers and employees. For example, contributions to a pension fund may be tax-deductible for employers, while employees may be able to defer taxes on their contributions until they begin receiving pension payments.

Despite these benefits, pension funds are not without their challenges and risks. In this section, we will explore some of the key factors that impact the performance of pension funds, as well as some of the potential risks and drawbacks of investing in them.

Factors That Impact Pension Fund Performance

There are a number of factors that can impact the performance of pension funds, including:

Economic conditions: Economic conditions, such as interest rates, inflation, and GDP growth, can have a significant impact on the performance of pension funds. For example, when interest rates are low, pension funds may struggle to earn sufficient returns to fund future pension payments.

Investment strategy: The investment strategy employed by a pension fund can also have a significant impact on its performance. For example, a pension fund that invests heavily in equities may experience greater volatility than one that invests primarily in fixed-income securities.

Management fees: Pension funds are typically managed by professional investment managers, who are compensated for their services through management fees. These fees can impact the overall performance of the fund, as higher fees can eat into returns over time.

Demographics: The demographic profile of a pension fund's members can also impact its performance. For example, if the fund's members are largely elderly, the fund may face greater pressure to generate returns that can support pension payments in the near term.

Potential Risks and Drawbacks of Investing in Pension Funds

While pension funds offer a number of benefits, they also come with a range of potential risks and drawbacks. Some of the key risks and drawbacks to consider when evaluating pension fund investments include:

Market risk: Pension funds are invested in a variety of assets, which can expose the fund to market risk. This risk refers to the potential for losses due to fluctuations in the value of the underlying assets.

Liquidity risk: Some of the assets in which pension funds invest may be illiquid, meaning that they cannot be easily sold or converted to cash. This can create liquidity risk, which refers to the potential for losses due to the inability to sell assets when needed.

Management risk: Pension funds are typically managed by professional investment managers, who may make investment decisions that do not align with the interests of the fund's members.

Longevity risk: Pension funds are designed to provide retirement income to their members for the duration of their lifetimes. However, as people are living longer, there is a risk that the pension fund may not be able to sustain payments for as long as necessary. This is known as longevity risk and is a significant concern for pension fund managers.

Inflation risk: Inflation risk refers to the potential for the purchasing power of the pension fund's investments to be eroded over time due to inflation. This can impact the ability of the fund to provide retirement income that keeps up with the cost of living.

Fees: Pension funds are typically subject to management fees, which can eat into returns and reduce the amount of retirement income available to members.

Regulatory risk: Pension funds are subject to a range of regulations and oversight, which can impact their investment strategies and returns. Changes in regulations or government policies can create regulatory risk, which may impact the performance of the fund.

Social risk: Pension funds can also face social risks, such as public opinion and pressure. For example, if the public becomes concerned about the environmental or social impact of a particular industry, the pension fund may face pressure to divest from that industry.

Overall, pension funds can be a valuable tool for retirement planning, but they also come with a range of risks that need to be carefully considered. Investors should weigh the potential benefits against the potential risks and ensure that they have a solid understanding of the fund's investment strategy, fees, and risk management policies before investing.

Definition and explanation of pension funds

Pension funds are investment vehicles that are specifically designed to provide retirement benefits to individuals. These funds are typically funded by contributions from employers, employees, or both, and the contributions are invested in a range of different assets, such as stocks, bonds, and real estate, with the goal of generating returns that can be used to pay out retirement benefits.

Pension funds can take different forms depending on the country and the specific regulations that govern them. Some pension funds are operated by private companies, while others are operated by the government. Additionally, some pension funds are mandatory, meaning that employers are required by law to offer them to their employees, while others are voluntary.

Types of Pension Funds

There are several different types of pension funds, each with its own unique characteristics and investment strategies. Some of the most common types of pension funds include:

Defined Benefit Plans: Defined benefit plans are pension plans that guarantee a specific level of retirement income to the plan's participants. These plans are typically funded by contributions from employers, although some plans may require employee contributions as well. The amount of retirement income that participants receive is typically based on a formula that takes into account factors such as the participant's salary and years of service.

Defined Contribution Plans: Defined contribution plans are pension plans in which participants contribute a portion of their salary to the plan, and the contributions are invested in a range of different assets. The retirement income that participants receive is based on the performance of the underlying investments, and there is no guarantee of a specific level of retirement income.

Hybrid Plans: Hybrid plans are pension plans that combine elements of defined benefit and defined contribution plans. These plans typically guarantee a minimum level of retirement income to participants, while also allowing participants to make contributions and invest in a range of different assets.

Benefits of Pension Funds

Pension funds offer a number of benefits to individuals who participate in them, including:

Tax Benefits: Contributions to pension funds are typically tax-deductible, which can reduce an individual's taxable income and lower their tax bill.

Diversification: Pension funds typically invest in a range of different assets, which can help to diversify an individual's portfolio and reduce their overall risk.

Professional Management: Pension funds are typically managed by professional investment managers who have expertise in managing large portfolios of assets.

Long-Term Focus: Pension funds have a long-term investment horizon, which allows them to take a patient approach to investing and focus on generating returns over the long-term.

Guaranteed Retirement Income: Defined benefit plans provide a guaranteed level of retirement income to participants, which can provide peace of mind and financial security in retirement.

Risks and Drawbacks of Pension Funds

While pension funds offer a number of benefits, they also come with a range of potential risks and drawbacks. Some of the key risks and drawbacks to consider when evaluating pension fund investments include:

Market Risk: Pension funds are invested in a variety of assets, which can expose the fund to market risk. This risk refers to the potential for losses due to fluctuations in the value of the underlying assets.

Liquidity Risk: Some of the assets in which pension funds invest may be illiquid, meaning that they cannot be easily sold or converted to cash. This can create liquidity risk, which refers to the potential for losses due to the inability to sell assets when needed.

Management Risk: Pension funds are typically managed by professional investment managers, who may make investment decisions that do not align with the interests of the fund's members. Additionally, poor management can lead to underperformance and lower returns.

Pension Fund Solvency Risk: Defined benefit plans are subject to pension fund solvency risk, which refers to the risk that the fund will not have sufficient assets to pay out promised benefits to plan participants. This risk can arise due to a variety of factors, including poor investment returns, changes in demographic trends, and unexpected increases in life expectancy.

To mitigate solvency risk, pension funds must carefully manage their assets and liabilities. This involves ensuring that the fund has sufficient assets to cover its long-term obligations, while also generating sufficient returns to meet those obligations over time. Pension funds typically use a range of investment strategies to achieve these goals, including diversifying their holdings across different asset classes and employing active investment management techniques.

Pension funds are also subject to regulatory requirements designed to protect plan participants and ensure the financial stability of the fund. For example, many countries require pension funds to maintain a certain level of solvency at all times, and may impose penalties or other sanctions on funds that fail to meet these requirements.

Pension Fund Management

Pension funds are typically managed by professional investment managers, who are responsible for overseeing the fund's investments and ensuring that they are aligned with the fund's objectives and risk profile. These managers may be employed directly by the fund, or may be hired by an external investment management firm.

Pension fund managers must make a range of investment decisions in order to meet the fund's objectives, including deciding how to allocate the fund's assets across different asset classes, selecting specific securities or other investments to hold within each asset class, and determining when to buy or sell these investments.

To make these decisions, pension fund managers typically rely on a range of quantitative and qualitative analysis techniques, including financial modeling, risk analysis, and market research. They also work closely with other professionals, such as actuaries and legal experts, to ensure that the fund is compliant with all relevant regulations and is being managed in the best interests of its participants.

Pension Fund Fees

Like other investment vehicles, pension funds typically charge fees for their services. These fees can vary widely depending on a number of factors, including the size of the fund, the investment strategies employed, and the level of active management involved.

Some of the most common fees associated with pension funds include:

Management fees: These fees are charged by the investment manager for managing the fund's assets. They are typically calculated as a percentage of the fund's total assets under management, and can range from a few basis points to several percentage points per year.

Performance fees: Some pension funds may also charge performance fees, which are based on the fund's investment returns over a certain period of time. These fees are typically structured as a percentage of any returns that exceed a certain benchmark, and are intended to incentivize the investment manager to generate strong returns for the fund.

Administrative fees: Pension funds may also charge administrative fees, which are intended to cover the costs of maintaining the fund's infrastructure and providing other services to participants. These fees may be charged as a flat rate, or as a percentage of assets under management.

It is important for investors to carefully consider the fees associated with a pension fund before investing, as high fees can significantly impact long-term returns.

Conclusion

Pension funds play a critical role in helping individuals save for retirement and providing financial security in old age. These funds offer a range of benefits, including access to professional investment management, diversification across a range of asset classes, and tax advantages.

However, pension funds also come with a range of risks and drawbacks, including exposure to market risk, liquidity risk, and management risk. In addition, defined benefit plans are subject to pension fund solvency risk, which can arise due to a range of factors and requires careful management by pension fund managers.

Investors considering pension fund investments should carefully evaluate the risks and benefits of these funds, and consider working with a financial advisor to develop a retirement savings strategy that meets their unique needs and goals.

Types of pension funds

There are several types of pension funds, each with its own characteristics and advantages. Some of the most common types of pension funds are:

Defined Benefit Pension Plans

Defined benefit pension plans are a type of pension plan in which the employer guarantees a certain level of retirement income to the employee. This income is based on a formula that takes into account factors such as the employee's length of service and salary history. Under a defined benefit plan, the employer is responsible for investing the contributions and managing the assets of the plan.

Defined benefit plans were once the most common type of pension plan offered by employers, but their popularity has declined in recent years due to their cost and complexity. Defined benefit plans can be expensive for employers to maintain, as they must ensure that they have sufficient funds to meet their obligations to plan participants. Additionally, the rules governing defined benefit plans can be complex, and employers must comply with a variety of regulatory requirements.

Defined Contribution Pension Plans

Defined contribution pension plans are a type of pension plan in which the employer and/or employee make contributions to the plan, which are then invested on behalf of the employee. Unlike defined benefit plans, there is no guarantee of a specific level of retirement income under a defined contribution plan. Instead, the amount of retirement income that a participant will receive is determined by the performance of the investments in the plan.

The most common type of defined contribution plan is the 401(k) plan, which is offered by many employers in the United States. Under a 401(k) plan, employees can contribute a portion of their salary to the plan on a pre-tax basis, and employers may also make contributions on behalf of their employees. The funds in the plan are typically invested in a range of mutual funds, which offer varying levels of risk and return.

One advantage of defined contribution plans is that they are typically less expensive for employers to maintain than defined benefit plans. Additionally, they offer participants more flexibility and control over their retirement savings, as they can choose how to invest their funds and when to retire.

Cash Balance Pension Plans

Cash balance pension plans are a type of defined benefit plan that combines features of defined benefit and defined contribution plans. Under a cash balance plan, the employer guarantees a specific retirement benefit to the employee, but the benefit is expressed as a hypothetical account balance rather than a traditional pension. The employer contributes to the account on behalf of the employee, and the account grows over time with interest credits.

When the employee retires, they have the option of receiving the balance in their account as a lump sum or as a stream of annuity payments. Cash balance plans have become increasingly popular in recent years, as they offer the benefits of a traditional defined benefit plan with the simplicity and portability of a defined contribution plan.

Public Pension Plans
Public pension plans are pension plans offered by government entities, such as state or local governments, to their employees. These plans are similar to defined benefit plans, but they are subject to different regulatory requirements and may be funded in different ways.

Public pension plans have come under scrutiny in recent years due to concerns about their sustainability and funding levels. Some states and municipalities have struggled to meet their obligations to pension plan participants, which has led to calls for reforms to the public pension system.

Multi-Employer Pension Plans
Multi-employer pension plans are pension plans that are sponsored by multiple employers, typically within the same industry or geographic region. These plans are designed to provide retirement benefits to employees who work for small businesses or who do not have access to a traditional pension plan.

Multi-employer pension plans are subject to a unique set of regulatory requirements, as they must ensure that contributions from multiple employers are pooled and invested appropriately. Additionally, these plans may face challenges in maintaining solvency

Importance of pension funds for retirement planning

the possibility of losses due to fluctuations in the value of the underlying assets. As a result, the value of a pension fund can rise and fall with the performance of the financial markets.

This market risk can be particularly concerning for individuals who are nearing retirement age, as they may not have enough time to recover from a market downturn before they need to start drawing on their pension funds. This risk can be mitigated through proper diversification of the pension fund's investments, but it still remains a potential concern for retirees.

Liquidity Risk

Another potential risk associated with pension funds is liquidity risk. Some of the assets in which pension funds invest may be illiquid, meaning that they cannot be easily sold or converted to cash. This can create a situation where the fund is unable to sell assets when needed, potentially leading to losses.

Liquidity risk can be particularly concerning during economic downturns, when there may be a limited market for certain assets. Additionally, if the pension fund is unable to sell illiquid assets, it may be forced to sell other assets at a loss to cover expenses, further reducing the fund's value.

Inflation Risk

Pension funds can also be subject to inflation risk, which refers to the potential for the value of the payments to be eroded over time by inflation. This risk can be particularly concerning for retirees, as they may be reliant on their pension payments to cover living expenses.

To mitigate inflation risk, some pension funds offer inflation-linked payments, which adjust the payment amount to keep pace with inflation. However, not all pension funds offer this option, and those that do may offer lower payment amounts initially.

Conclusion

Despite the potential risks and drawbacks associated with pension funds, they remain an important tool for retirement planning. By providing a steady income stream during retirement, pension funds can help individuals achieve financial security in their golden years.

However, it is important to carefully evaluate the risks and benefits of any pension fund investment, taking into account factors such as the fund's solvency, investment strategy, and flexibility. By doing so, individuals can make informed decisions that help to ensure a comfortable retirement.

Role of pension funds in the financial industry

Pension funds are a crucial component of the financial industry, playing a significant role in the management of assets and investment in the economy. Pension funds serve as long-term investors and provide a stable source of funding for businesses and infrastructure projects. In this section, we will explore the role of pension funds in the financial industry and their impact on the economy.

Investment in the Economy

Pension funds play a crucial role in the economy by investing in a wide range of assets such as stocks, bonds, and real estate. Pension funds invest in various industries, including technology, healthcare, energy, and consumer goods. By investing in various sectors of the economy, pension funds help to diversify risk and achieve long-term growth.

Pension funds invest in the economy in several ways. First, they invest directly in businesses, providing a source of long-term capital for companies to expand their operations. Second, they invest in infrastructure projects such as airports, highways, and railways, which help to build and maintain critical infrastructure and support economic growth.

Stable Source of Funding

Pension funds provide a stable source of funding for businesses and infrastructure projects. Unlike other investors, pension funds have a long-term investment horizon and can tolerate short-term market volatility. Pension funds invest in a variety of assets, including equities, bonds, and real estate, which provide a stable source of income over the long-term.

Pension funds provide a source of stable funding for businesses in several ways. First, they invest directly in businesses, providing long-term capital for companies to expand their operations. Second, they invest in the debt of companies, providing a source of long-term financing for businesses to manage their cash flow needs.

Risk Management

Pension funds play an essential role in managing risk in the financial industry. Pension funds invest in a variety of assets, which helps to diversify risk and reduce volatility. Additionally, pension funds have a long-term investment horizon, which allows them to ride out short-term market fluctuations.

Pension funds are subject to various risks, including market risk, interest rate risk, and credit risk. Market risk refers to the risk of losses due to changes in the value of the securities held by the pension fund. Interest rate risk refers to the risk of losses due to changes in interest rates, while credit risk refers to the risk of losses due to default by the issuer of the securities held by the pension fund.

However, pension funds manage these risks by investing in a diverse range of assets, including equities, bonds, and real estate. By investing in a range of assets, pension funds can reduce risk and achieve long-term growth.

Impact on Corporate Governance

Pension funds play a critical role in promoting good corporate governance. As significant shareholders of companies, pension funds have a vested interest in ensuring that companies are run efficiently and ethically.

Pension funds promote good corporate governance in several ways. First, they exercise their voting rights to support shareholder resolutions that promote ethical business practices and support long-term shareholder value. Second, they engage with company management to encourage companies to adopt sustainable business practices and reduce their environmental impact.

Influence on Financial Markets

Pension funds are significant investors in the financial markets and have a significant influence on market trends. As long-term investors, pension funds tend to hold stocks and other assets for an extended period, which helps to stabilize markets and reduce volatility.

Additionally, pension funds are a significant source of demand for stocks, bonds, and other assets, which helps to support the overall performance of the financial markets. Pension funds can also provide liquidity in times of market stress, which can help to stabilize markets during times of crisis.

Conclusion

In conclusion, pension funds play a vital role in the financial industry, providing a stable source of funding for businesses and infrastructure projects.

They also serve as an important retirement savings vehicle for individuals, offering tax advantages and the potential for higher returns than traditional savings accounts.

Pension funds are managed by highly skilled professionals who strive to balance risk and return in order to maximize the value of the fund's assets. However, as with any investment, there are risks involved, such as market volatility and interest rate changes. It is important for individuals and businesses to carefully consider their investment options and seek professional advice before making any decisions.

Overall, pension funds are an essential component of the financial industry, helping to support economic growth and provide financial security for individuals. As the global population ages and retirement becomes an increasingly important issue, pension funds are likely to become even more important in the years to come.

Risks and benefits of investing in pension funds

Pension funds are an essential component of retirement planning and investment management, as they provide a stable source of income for individuals during their retirement years. However, like any investment, there are risks and benefits associated with investing in pension funds. In this section, we will explore the risks and benefits of investing in pension funds.

Benefits of Investing in Pension Funds

Steady Income Stream
One of the primary benefits of investing in a pension fund is the steady income stream that it provides during retirement. Pension funds are designed to provide regular payments to retirees, which can help to cover living expenses and ensure a comfortable retirement.

Professional Management
Pension funds are managed by experienced investment professionals, who are responsible for making investment decisions on behalf of the fund's participants. This professional management can help to minimize investment risk and increase returns over the long-term.

Tax Advantages
Investing in a pension fund can provide tax advantages for individuals, such as tax-deferred growth and tax-deductible contributions. These tax advantages can help to maximize retirement savings and reduce tax liabilities.

Diversification
Pension funds are typically invested in a diversified portfolio of assets, such as stocks, bonds, and real estate. This diversification can help to minimize risk and ensure that the fund is well-positioned to weather changes in the market.

Employer Contributions
Many pension funds are sponsored by employers, who make contributions on behalf of their employees. This employer contribution can help to boost retirement savings and provide a valuable benefit to employees.

Risks of Investing in Pension Funds

Market Risk
Pension funds are exposed to market risk, which refers to the potential for investment losses due to fluctuations in the market. Market risk can be particularly problematic during times of economic volatility or recession, as pension funds may experience significant losses.

Inflation Risk
Inflation risk refers to the potential for the value of the pension fund to be eroded over time due to inflation. Inflation can reduce the purchasing power of retirement savings, which can be particularly problematic for retirees who rely on their pension fund as a primary source of income.

Limited Flexibility
Pension funds offer limited flexibility, as retirees are typically locked into a payment amount for life. This lack of flexibility can be problematic if a retiree's expenses change, or if they need additional funds for unexpected expenses.

Fees
Pension funds may charge fees for management and administration, which can reduce the overall return on investment. These fees can vary significantly depending on the pension fund and may be difficult for investors to fully understand.

Solvency Risk

Pension funds are subject to solvency risk, which refers to the risk that the fund will not have sufficient assets to pay out promised benefits. Defined benefit pension funds are particularly vulnerable to solvency risk, as they guarantee a specific payment amount to retirees, regardless of the performance of the fund's investments.

Conclusion

Investing in a pension fund can provide a steady source of income during retirement and offer tax advantages and professional management. However, it is important for investors to be aware of the risks associated with pension funds, such as market risk, inflation risk, limited flexibility, fees, and solvency risk. By understanding these risks and benefits, investors can make informed decisions about their retirement planning and investment strategies.

Performance of pension funds compared to other investments

Pension funds are investment vehicles designed to provide a steady stream of income during retirement. They are managed by professional fund managers who invest the funds' assets in a variety of assets, such as stocks, bonds, and real estate, with the goal of generating returns. However, the performance of pension funds can vary widely, and many investors wonder how they compare to other investment options.

This section will examine the performance of pension funds compared to other investments, including stocks, bonds, and mutual funds.

Performance of Pension Funds Compared to Stocks

Stocks are a popular investment option because they offer the potential for high returns. However, they are also associated with higher risk and volatility compared to other investments. When comparing the performance of pension funds to stocks, it is important to consider the long-term performance of both.

Research has shown that the long-term performance of pension funds is comparable to that of the stock market. According to a study by Vanguard, the average annual return for U.S. pension funds was 7.6% between 1990 and 2019, compared to 7.7% for the S&P 500 index. This indicates that pension funds have performed relatively well compared to stocks over the long term.

Performance of Pension Funds Compared to Bonds

Bonds are a type of investment that involves lending money to an organization or government in exchange for regular interest payments. Bonds are typically considered a lower-risk investment option than stocks, as they are less volatile. However, they also offer lower potential returns.

When comparing the performance of pension funds to bonds, it is important to consider the long-term performance of both. According to Vanguard, the average annual return for U.S. pension funds was 7.6% between 1990 and 2019, compared to 5.5% for long-term government bonds over the same period. This indicates that pension funds have performed better than bonds over the long term.

Performance of Pension Funds Compared to Mutual Funds

Mutual funds are investment vehicles that pool money from multiple investors to invest in a variety of assets. Mutual funds can be actively managed or passively managed, with the goal of generating returns for investors. When comparing the performance of pension funds to mutual funds, it is important to consider the differences in management style and fees.

Research has shown that the long-term performance of pension funds is generally similar to that of mutual funds. According to a study by Morningstar, the average annual return for U.S. pension funds was 7.2% between 2005 and 2019, compared to 7.4% for actively managed mutual funds and 7.5% for passively managed mutual funds. However, it is important to note that mutual funds may have higher fees compared to pension funds, which can impact overall returns.

Benefits of Investing in Pension Funds

Despite the risks associated with investing in pension funds, there are several benefits to consider:

Diversification: Pension funds invest in a variety of assets, which can help to reduce risk and increase returns over the long term.

Professional Management: Pension funds are managed by professional fund managers who have extensive knowledge and experience in the financial industry. This can help to ensure that investments are made wisely and with a long-term perspective.

Tax Benefits: Pension funds may offer tax benefits, such as tax-deferred growth and tax-free withdrawals in retirement.

Guaranteed Income: Pension funds are designed to provide a steady stream of income during retirement, which can help to ensure financial stability in later years.

Risks of Investing in Pension Funds

While there are benefits to investing in pension funds, there are also several risks to consider:

Market Risk: Pension funds are exposed to market risk, which can lead to fluctuations in returns. In times of market volatility, the value of pension fund investments can drop significantly, potentially leading to losses for investors. This risk is particularly relevant for defined contribution pension funds, where the investment risk is borne by the individual rather than the employer.

Inflation Risk: Inflation can erode the purchasing power of pension fund returns, particularly for fixed-income investments. Over time, the cost of living increases, and if the returns on pension fund investments do not keep pace with inflation, retirees may find that their retirement income does not go as far as they had anticipated.

Interest Rate Risk: Interest rates can have a significant impact on the performance of pension funds, particularly for fixed-income investments. If interest rates rise, the value of existing fixed-income investments will fall, potentially leading to losses for investors. Conversely, if interest rates fall, the value of existing fixed-income investments will rise, but the returns on new investments will be lower.

Liquidity Risk: Pension funds are typically long-term investments, and it can be challenging to access funds quickly in the event of an emergency or unexpected expense. This lack of liquidity can be a disadvantage for some investors who may need access to their funds at short notice.

Management Risk: The performance of a pension fund is dependent on the skills and expertise of the fund manager. Poor investment decisions or mismanagement can lead to losses for investors.

Counterparty Risk: Pension funds are typically invested in a variety of assets, and there is always a risk that one of the counterparties involved in these investments may default. This risk is particularly relevant for alternative investments such as hedge funds and private equity, where the counterparties are often less well-known and less transparent than those involved in more traditional investments.

Regulatory Risk: Changes to regulations can have a significant impact on the performance of pension funds. For example, changes to tax laws or accounting standards can affect the value of pension fund investments and lead to losses for investors.

Overall, it is important for investors to consider both the risks and benefits of investing in pension funds and to carefully weigh their options before making a decision. While pension funds can provide a stable source of retirement income, they are not without risks, and investors should be prepared to weather market volatility and other risks over the long term.

III. Mutual Funds

Mutual funds are a type of investment vehicle that pools money from multiple investors to purchase a diversified portfolio of securities, such as stocks, bonds, and money market instruments. They offer investors a convenient and cost-effective way to gain exposure to a wide range of assets, which may be difficult or expensive to access on their own. In this section, we will explore the basics of mutual funds, including their history, types, benefits, and drawbacks.

History of Mutual Funds

The concept of mutual funds dates back to the 18th century, when Dutch merchant Adriaan van Ketwich created a fund to invest in bonds. However, it wasn't until the 20th century that mutual funds became widely available in the United States. The first mutual fund in the US, the Massachusetts Investors Trust, was established in 1924 by a group of investors led by Edward C. Johnson II. Since then, mutual funds have grown in popularity and diversity, with thousands of funds now available to investors worldwide.

Types of Mutual Funds

Mutual funds can be classified into several categories based on their investment objectives, asset classes, and management styles. Some common types of mutual funds include:

Equity Funds: These funds invest primarily in stocks, providing investors with exposure to the potential growth of companies. Equity funds can be further classified based on the size of the companies they invest in, such as large-cap, mid-cap, and small-cap funds.

Bond Funds: These funds invest primarily in fixed-income securities, such as government and corporate bonds, providing investors with regular income and relatively stable returns.

Money Market Funds: These funds invest in short-term debt securities, such as Treasury bills and commercial paper, providing investors with a safe and liquid place to park their cash.

Index Funds: These funds seek to replicate the performance of a specific market index, such as the S&P 500 or the Nasdaq. They offer investors a low-cost way to gain exposure to a broad market.

Actively Managed Funds: These funds are managed by professional investment managers who select and trade securities based on their research and analysis of market trends and opportunities.

Benefits of Mutual Funds

Mutual funds offer several benefits to investors, including:

Diversification: By pooling money from multiple investors, mutual funds can purchase a diversified portfolio of securities, reducing the risk of individual securities.

Professional Management: Mutual funds are managed by professional investment managers who have the expertise and resources to make informed investment decisions on behalf of their investors.

Affordability: Mutual funds allow investors to access a diversified portfolio of securities at a relatively low cost, compared to purchasing individual securities.

Liquidity: Mutual funds can be bought and sold on any business day, providing investors with a high degree of liquidity and flexibility.

Drawbacks of Mutual Funds

Despite their benefits, mutual funds also have some drawbacks, including:

Fees: Mutual funds charge fees for management, administration, and other expenses, which can reduce returns over time.

Limited Control: Investors in mutual funds have limited control over the specific securities held in the portfolio, as well as the timing of buys and sells.

Taxation: Mutual funds can generate capital gains and income, which are taxable to investors.

Conclusion

In summary, mutual funds are a popular investment vehicle that offer investors a convenient and cost-effective way to gain exposure to a diversified portfolio of securities. They come in various types, including equity, bond, money market, index, and actively managed funds, each with its unique investment objective and risk profile. While mutual funds offer several benefits, including diversification, professional management, affordability, and liquidity, they also have some drawbacks, including fees, limited control, and taxation. As with any investment, it is important for investors to carefully consider their investment objectives, risk tolerance, and investment horizon before investing in mutual funds.

Definition and explanation of mutual funds

Investing in the financial markets can be a daunting task for individual investors. With numerous investment options available, ranging from stocks and bonds to commodities and currencies, investors need to have a comprehensive understanding of the markets and the ability to research and analyze individual investments. Mutual funds offer an alternative investment approach that allows investors to pool their money together and invest in a diversified portfolio of securities, managed by a professional fund manager.

A mutual fund is a type of investment vehicle that pools money from multiple investors to invest in a diversified portfolio of securities, such as stocks, bonds, and money market instruments. The fund manager then uses the pooled money to purchase a portfolio of securities, based on the fund's investment objective and strategy.

The mutual fund is owned collectively by all the investors who have purchased shares in the fund. Each investor receives a proportional share of the fund's returns, based on the number of shares they hold. Mutual funds are regulated by the Securities and Exchange Commission (SEC) and are subject to strict rules regarding transparency, disclosure, and investor protection.

Types of Mutual Funds

There are several types of mutual funds available to investors, each with its unique investment objective and risk profile. Some of the most common types of mutual funds include:

Equity Funds: These mutual funds invest primarily in stocks or equity securities. Equity funds are categorized based on the size of the companies they invest in, such as large-cap, mid-cap, or small-cap companies.

Bond Funds: These mutual funds invest primarily in bonds or debt securities. Bond funds are categorized based on the credit quality of the bonds they invest in, such as investment-grade or high-yield bonds.

Money Market Funds: These mutual funds invest in short-term, low-risk securities, such as Treasury bills and commercial paper. Money market funds are considered to be low-risk investments, with low returns.

Index Funds: These mutual funds aim to replicate the performance of a particular market index, such as the S&P 500 or the Dow Jones Industrial Average. Index funds are considered to be low-cost investments, as they require minimal management and have low fees.

Actively Managed Funds: These mutual funds are managed by a professional fund manager who actively manages the fund's portfolio in an attempt to outperform the market. Actively managed funds are considered to be higher risk than index funds, as they require more management and have higher fees.

Benefits of Mutual Funds

Mutual funds offer several benefits to investors, including:

Diversification: By pooling money together and investing in a diversified portfolio of securities, mutual funds offer investors a way to spread their risk across multiple investments.

Professional Management: Mutual funds are managed by professional fund managers who have expertise in the financial markets and can make informed investment decisions.

Affordability: Mutual funds allow investors to invest in a diversified portfolio of securities, even with a small amount of money. This makes mutual funds a cost-effective investment option for individual investors.

Liquidity: Mutual funds are traded on an exchange, making them a liquid investment option. Investors can buy and sell mutual fund shares on any business day, allowing them to access their money quickly.

Drawbacks of Mutual Funds

While mutual funds offer several benefits, they also have some drawbacks, including:

Fees: Mutual funds charge fees, such as management fees and expense ratios, which can eat into investors' returns.

Limited Control: Mutual fund investors have limited control over the fund's investment decisions, as these decisions are made by the fund manager.

Taxation: Mutual funds are subject to capital gains taxes, which can reduce investors' returns.

Conclusion

Mutual funds offer investors a convenient and cost-effective way to gain exposure to a diversified portfolio of securities, managed by professional investment managers. They are a popular investment vehicle that comes in various types, including equity, bond, money market, index, and actively managed funds, each with its unique investment objective and risk profile. While mutual funds offer several benefits, including diversification, professional management, affordability, and liquidity, they also have some drawbacks, including fees, limited control, and taxation.

In conclusion, mutual funds have become a ubiquitous investment option for both individual and institutional investors. They offer several advantages over traditional investment options, such as stocks and bonds, including diversification and professional management. However, they also have some limitations, including fees, limited control, and taxation. Investors must carefully evaluate their investment objectives, risk tolerance, and investment horizon before investing in mutual funds. Additionally, they must choose the right type of mutual fund that aligns with their investment goals and risk appetite.

Despite the drawbacks, mutual funds remain a popular and effective investment option for investors looking to grow their wealth over the long term. With the right research and investment strategy, mutual funds can be an effective way to achieve your financial goals and build a diversified investment portfolio.

Types of mutual funds

Mutual funds come in different types, each with its unique investment objective, risk profile, and investment strategy. Understanding the different types of mutual funds can help investors choose the one that best suits their investment goals and risk tolerance. In this section, we will discuss the most common types of mutual funds, including equity funds, bond funds, money market funds, index funds, and actively managed funds.

Equity funds

Equity funds, also known as stock funds, invest primarily in stocks or shares of companies. Equity funds can be further categorized into different types based on the size, sector, and geography of the companies they invest in. Some common types of equity funds include:

Large-cap funds: Large-cap funds invest in stocks of large-cap companies with a market capitalization of over $10 billion. Large-cap companies are generally considered to be more stable and less volatile than small-cap companies.

Mid-cap funds: Mid-cap funds invest in stocks of mid-cap companies with a market capitalization between $2 billion and $10 billion. Mid-cap companies are generally considered to have more growth potential than large-cap companies, but they are also riskier.

Small-cap funds: Small-cap funds invest in stocks of small-cap companies with a market capitalization of less than $2 billion. Small-cap companies are generally considered to have the most growth potential, but they are also the riskiest.

Sector funds: Sector funds invest in stocks of companies in a specific sector, such as technology, healthcare, energy, or financials. Sector funds can provide investors with exposure to a specific sector of the economy, but they are also riskier than diversified funds.

Bond funds

Bond funds, also known as fixed-income funds, invest primarily in bonds or other fixed-income securities issued by governments or corporations. Bond funds can be further categorized into different types based on the maturity, credit quality, and type of bonds they invest in. Some common types of bond funds include:

Government bond funds: Government bond funds invest primarily in bonds issued by governments, such as U.S. Treasury bonds. Government bond funds are generally considered to be less risky than corporate bond funds.

Corporate bond funds: Corporate bond funds invest primarily in bonds issued by corporations. Corporate bond funds can be further categorized into investment-grade and high-yield bond funds based on the credit quality of the bonds they invest in.

Municipal bond funds: Municipal bond funds invest primarily in bonds issued by state and local governments. Municipal bond funds can provide investors with tax-free income, but they are also subject to credit risk.

Money market funds

Money market funds invest in short-term, low-risk securities, such as Treasury bills, certificates of deposit, and commercial paper. Money market funds are generally considered to be the safest type of mutual fund, but they also offer the lowest potential returns.

Index funds

Index funds are designed to track the performance of a specific market index, such as the S&P 500 or the Dow Jones Industrial Average. Index funds are passively managed, meaning that they do not require active management by a fund manager. Instead, index funds are designed to replicate the performance of the underlying index. Index funds are generally considered to be low-cost and tax-efficient.

Actively managed funds

Actively managed funds are mutual funds that are managed by a fund manager who selects the securities to invest in based on the fund's investment objective and investment strategy. Actively managed funds can be further categorized into different types based on the investment style of the fund manager. Some common types of actively managed funds include:

Value funds: Value funds invest in stocks that are considered to be undervalued by the market. Value funds are generally considered to be less risky than growth funds, but they also offer lower potential returns.

Growth funds: Growth funds invest in stocks of companies that are expected to grow at a faster rate than the overall market. Growth funds are generally considered to be more risky than value funds, but they also offer higher potential returns.

Blend funds: Blend funds invest in a combination of both value and growth stocks. Blend funds aim to provide investors with a diversified portfolio of stocks that have both growth and value characteristics.

Sector funds: Sector funds invest in stocks of companies that belong to a specific industry or sector, such as technology, healthcare, or energy. Sector funds offer investors the opportunity to invest in a specific industry or sector that they believe will perform well in the future.

International funds: International funds invest in stocks of companies that are based outside of the investor's home country. International funds offer investors the opportunity to diversify their portfolio by investing in companies that operate in different countries and economies.

Specialty funds: Specialty funds invest in securities that are considered to be outside the mainstream, such as real estate investment trusts (REITs), commodities, or alternative investments. Specialty funds are generally considered to be more risky than other types of mutual funds, but they also offer the potential for higher returns.

Actively managed funds typically have higher expense ratios than index funds due to the higher costs associated with active management. However, some investors may be willing to pay these higher fees in exchange for the potential for higher returns that active management can offer. It is important for investors to carefully consider their investment objectives, risk tolerance, and investment horizon before investing in actively managed funds.

Benefits of investing in mutual funds

Investing in mutual funds can offer several benefits to investors. Below, we will discuss some of the main advantages of investing in mutual funds.

Diversification

Diversification is the process of spreading investments across different securities to minimize the risk of loss. Investing in a single stock or bond can be risky, as the price of the security may fluctuate greatly. In contrast, mutual funds invest in a portfolio of securities, which reduces the risk associated with investing in a single security. Mutual funds allow investors to gain exposure to a diversified portfolio of securities without the need for a large amount of capital.

Professional Management

One of the main benefits of investing in mutual funds is that they are managed by experienced and knowledgeable fund managers. Fund managers have the expertise to conduct research and analysis on different securities, identify investment opportunities, and make informed investment decisions. They also monitor the performance of the portfolio and adjust the holdings to reflect changes in the market or the investment objective of the fund.

Affordability

Mutual funds offer investors the opportunity to invest in a diversified portfolio of securities at an affordable price. Since mutual funds pool the money of multiple investors, the cost of investing is shared among all the investors in the fund. The cost of buying individual stocks or bonds can be high due to transaction fees and commissions. In contrast, mutual funds typically have lower fees and expenses, making them a cost-effective investment option.

Liquidity

Mutual funds are generally considered to be a liquid investment option, as investors can buy and sell shares in the fund on any business day. This makes it easy for investors to access their money when they need it. In contrast, some other investment options, such as real estate or private equity, may have restrictions on when investors can sell their holdings.

Flexibility

Mutual funds offer investors the flexibility to choose from a wide range of investment options, based on their investment objective and risk tolerance. There are mutual funds that invest in different types of securities, including equities, bonds, money market securities, and alternative assets. There are also mutual funds that are focused on specific sectors or regions, allowing investors to target their investments in a particular area.

Tax Efficiency

Mutual funds are generally considered to be tax-efficient investment options. Mutual funds are structured as pass-through entities, which means that any capital gains or dividends earned by the fund are passed on to the investors. This can be beneficial for investors, as they can benefit from lower tax rates on capital gains and dividends. Additionally, mutual funds may use tax-loss harvesting strategies to offset gains with losses, which can further reduce the tax liability for investors.

Transparency

Mutual funds are required by law to disclose their holdings and performance to investors. This transparency allows investors to make informed decisions about their investments and to monitor the performance of the fund. Mutual funds are also required to disclose their fees and expenses, which allows investors to evaluate the cost of investing in the fund.

Conclusion

Mutual funds offer several benefits to investors, including diversification, professional management, affordability, liquidity, flexibility, tax efficiency, and transparency. These benefits make mutual funds an attractive investment option for both novice and experienced investors. However, it is important for investors to carefully consider their investment objectives, risk tolerance, and investment horizon before investing in mutual funds. It is also important for investors to evaluate the fees and expenses associated with investing in a mutual fund, as these costs can impact the overall return on investment. Overall, mutual funds can be a valuable addition to an investor's portfolio, but investors should always conduct their due diligence before making any investment decisions.

How to invest in mutual funds

Investing in mutual funds can be a great way for individuals to diversify their portfolio and potentially earn higher returns. However, it is important to understand the process of investing in mutual funds to make informed decisions. In this section, we will discuss the steps involved in investing in mutual funds.

Determine Your Investment Goals and Risk Tolerance
Before investing in mutual funds, it is essential to determine your investment goals and risk tolerance. This will help you choose the right type of mutual fund to invest in. Ask yourself the following questions:

What is my investment objective? Am I looking for capital appreciation or regular income?
What is my investment time horizon? Do I need the money in the short term or can it be invested for the long term?
What is my risk tolerance? Am I comfortable with a high degree of risk or do I prefer low-risk investments?
Based on your answers, you can narrow down your options and choose the right mutual fund.

Choose the Right Type of Mutual Fund
As discussed earlier, mutual funds can be classified into various types based on their investment objectives, investment style, and asset class. Choose the type of mutual fund that aligns with your investment goals and risk tolerance.

Research Mutual Funds
Once you have narrowed down your options, research the mutual funds that interest you. This will help you understand the fund's investment strategy, historical performance, and fees. Consider the following factors when researching mutual funds:

Historical Performance: Look at the fund's past performance over the long term (5 to 10 years) and compare it to the benchmark index. However, past performance does not guarantee future results.

Expense Ratio: The expense ratio is the fee charged by the mutual fund company for managing the fund. Look for funds with low expense ratios, as high fees can eat into your returns over time.

Fund Manager: Research the fund manager's experience, performance track record, and investment philosophy. This can help you assess the fund manager's ability to deliver consistent returns over time.

Investment Minimums: Some mutual funds have a minimum investment amount. Make sure you can meet the minimum investment requirement before investing in the fund.

Open a Brokerage Account

To invest in mutual funds, you need to open a brokerage account with a financial institution or a brokerage firm. The brokerage firm will allow you to buy and sell mutual fund shares. Look for a brokerage firm that offers low fees and a user-friendly platform.

Place an Order

Once you have opened a brokerage account, you can place an order to buy mutual fund shares. You can place an order online, over the phone, or through a financial advisor. Make sure you have the necessary funds available in your account before placing the order.

Monitor Your Investment

After investing in mutual funds, it is essential to monitor your investment periodically. Review the fund's performance, expenses, and your investment goals to make sure your investment is on track. Rebalance your portfolio if necessary to maintain your desired asset allocation.

In conclusion, investing in mutual funds can be a great way to diversify your portfolio and potentially earn higher returns. However, it is important to understand the steps involved in investing in mutual funds to make informed decisions. Determine your investment goals and risk tolerance, choose the right type of mutual fund, research mutual funds, open a brokerage account, place an order, and monitor your investment regularly to ensure it aligns with your investment goals.

Risks and benefits of investing in mutual funds

Mutual funds are a popular investment option for individuals who want to invest in the stock market but do not have the time or expertise to manage their investments. Mutual funds offer a convenient and cost-effective way to gain exposure to a diversified portfolio of securities, managed by professional fund managers. However, like any investment, mutual funds come with their own set of risks and benefits. In this section, we will discuss the risks and benefits of investing in mutual funds.

Benefits of Investing in Mutual Funds:

Diversification: One of the main benefits of investing in mutual funds is diversification. By investing in a mutual fund, investors can gain exposure to a diversified portfolio of securities, which can help to reduce the risk of loss.

Professional Management: Mutual funds are managed by professional fund managers who have the expertise and knowledge to manage the portfolio of securities. This can help to improve the performance of the mutual fund and provide investors with better returns.

Accessibility: Mutual funds are easily accessible to investors, as they can be bought and sold through brokerage firms, financial advisors, or directly from the mutual fund company.

Flexibility: Mutual funds come in a variety of types and investment strategies, which can provide investors with flexibility in their investment choices.

Low minimum investment: Mutual funds generally have low minimum investment requirements, making them accessible to investors with limited funds.

Liquidity: Mutual funds are generally highly liquid, which means that investors can easily buy and sell their shares at any time.

Risks of Investing in Mutual Funds:

Market Risk: Like all investments in the stock market, mutual funds are subject to market risk. The value of the mutual fund can go up or down based on changes in the market.

Fees and Expenses: Mutual funds charge fees and expenses, which can reduce the overall return of the mutual fund. Investors should be aware of the fees and expenses associated with the mutual fund before investing.

Management Risk: The performance of the mutual fund is dependent on the performance of the fund manager. Poor performance by the fund manager can lead to lower returns for the investors.

Concentration Risk: Some mutual funds may invest in a particular industry or sector, which can lead to concentration risk. If the industry or sector experiences a downturn, the value of the mutual fund can decline.

Redemption Fees: Some mutual funds charge redemption fees if the investor sells their shares within a certain period of time. This can reduce the liquidity of the mutual fund and limit the investor's ability to sell their shares.

Lack of Control: Investors in mutual funds do not have direct control over the portfolio of securities. The fund manager makes all investment decisions on behalf of the investors.

Conclusion:
Investing in mutual funds can offer a variety of benefits, such as diversification, professional management, accessibility, flexibility, low minimum investment, and liquidity. However, like any investment, mutual funds come with their own set of risks, such as market risk, fees and expenses, management risk, concentration risk, redemption fees, and lack of control. Investors should carefully consider the risks and benefits of investing in mutual funds before making any investment decisions. It is recommended that investors consult with a financial advisor before investing in mutual funds.

Performance of mutual funds compared to other investments

Investors often compare the performance of mutual funds to other investment vehicles such as individual stocks, exchange-traded funds (ETFs), and index funds. In this section, we will discuss the performance of mutual funds compared to other investments.

Individual Stocks

Individual stocks are shares of ownership in a single company. They are often bought and sold on stock exchanges such as the New York Stock Exchange (NYSE) or NASDAQ. While stocks can offer potentially high returns, they can also be quite risky. The performance of individual stocks is highly dependent on the success of the underlying company, which can be influenced by a wide range of factors, including economic conditions, industry trends, and company-specific events.

Compared to individual stocks, mutual funds offer a level of diversification by holding multiple stocks within the fund. This diversification can help to reduce the risk associated with owning individual stocks. Additionally, mutual fund managers have the expertise to conduct thorough research on individual stocks and can make informed investment decisions based on that research. While individual stocks can offer higher potential returns, the risk of loss is also higher compared to mutual funds.

Exchange-Traded Funds (ETFs)

Exchange-traded funds (ETFs) are similar to mutual funds in that they hold a basket of stocks, bonds, or other securities. However, ETFs trade like individual stocks on stock exchanges, whereas mutual funds are priced and traded once per day at the end of the trading day. ETFs are often designed to track a specific index, such as the S&P 500, and aim to provide returns similar to the index they track.

ETFs can offer a level of diversification similar to mutual funds and can also be bought and sold throughout the trading day. However, ETFs can be subject to brokerage commissions and trading fees, which can reduce returns. Additionally, ETFs may be more complex than mutual funds, and investors should carefully consider the underlying holdings and investment strategy before investing.

Index Funds

Index funds are similar to ETFs in that they aim to track a specific index, such as the S&P 500. However, index funds are mutual funds, not ETFs, and are priced and traded once per day at the end of the trading day. Index funds can offer a level of diversification similar to mutual funds and can also provide exposure to a broad range of securities within a specific index.

Compared to actively managed mutual funds, index funds typically have lower fees and expenses since they are not actively managed. However, index funds are not designed to outperform the market, but rather to provide returns similar to the market they track.

Performance of Mutual Funds

The performance of mutual funds can vary widely depending on the type of fund, the investment strategy, and the market conditions. While past performance does not guarantee future results, examining historical performance can provide insights into the potential returns and risks associated with investing in mutual funds.

Historically, actively managed mutual funds have generally underperformed index funds. According to a report by S&P Dow Jones Indices, over a 10-year period ending in 2020, 85% of large-cap fund managers, 87% of mid-cap fund managers, and 92% of small-cap fund managers underperformed their respective benchmarks. This underperformance is largely attributed to the higher fees and expenses associated with actively managed funds.

In contrast, index funds have generally performed better than actively managed funds due to their lower fees and expenses. According to the same report by S&P Dow Jones Indices, over the same 10-year period ending in 2020, 87% of large-cap index funds outperformed their actively managed counterparts. Similarly, 88% of mid-cap index funds and 90% of small-cap index funds outperformed their actively managed counterparts.

However, it is important to note that past performance does not guarantee future results. While index funds have historically performed well, there is no guarantee that they will continue to do so in the future. Additionally, there may be certain market conditions or economic events that could impact the performance of index funds.

Furthermore, it is important to consider the specific investment goals and risk tolerance of each individual investor. While index funds may be a good choice for some investors, others may prefer the potential higher returns that actively managed funds may offer, despite the higher fees and expenses.

Another factor to consider when comparing mutual funds to other investments is the level of risk involved. Mutual funds, both actively managed and index, come with varying levels of risk depending on the underlying assets held in the fund. Some mutual funds may be invested in stocks, which carry a higher level of risk compared to bonds or other fixed-income securities.

When compared to other investments such as individual stocks or bonds, mutual funds offer the benefit of diversification. Diversification means spreading your investments across different assets to minimize the overall risk of your portfolio. Mutual funds offer a convenient way for investors to achieve diversification without having to purchase individual securities.

In addition, mutual funds also offer the benefit of professional management. Experienced fund managers make investment decisions on behalf of the fund's investors, based on their knowledge and expertise. This can be particularly beneficial for investors who lack the time or expertise to research individual investments on their own.

However, it is important to consider the fees and expenses associated with mutual funds, as they can significantly impact returns over time. Mutual funds typically charge an expense ratio, which covers the costs of managing the fund, as well as any other fees such as sales loads or redemption fees.

Overall, when comparing mutual funds to other investments, it is important to consider factors such as performance, risk, diversification, fees, and professional management. Each investor should carefully consider their own individual goals and risk tolerance before making any investment decisions.

IV. Sovereign Wealth Funds

Sovereign Wealth Funds (SWFs) have become increasingly significant players in the global financial market over the past few decades. SWFs are funds created by national governments and central banks to manage their wealth and diversify their investment portfolios. These funds invest in various asset classes, such as stocks, bonds, real estate, and infrastructure projects, both domestically and internationally. They have become major investors in various industries, including energy, technology, and real estate.

Despite their increasing prominence, SWFs have faced controversies and criticisms over their lack of transparency, potential for political influence, and impact on global financial stability. This essay will provide an overview of Sovereign Wealth Funds, their history, objectives, investment strategies, and controversies surrounding them.

History of Sovereign Wealth Funds

The origins of SWFs can be traced back to the 1950s and 1960s, when oil-producing countries such as Kuwait, Saudi Arabia, and Qatar established funds to manage their oil revenues. These early funds were mainly focused on investing in fixed income securities and were relatively small in size. However, their investment activities expanded over time as they began to invest in various asset classes and diversify their portfolios.

The growth of SWFs accelerated in the late 1990s and early 2000s, when several Asian countries established funds to manage their surpluses from trade and investment. These funds were initially created to stabilize their currencies, but they soon began to invest in various asset classes to generate higher returns. This trend continued in the 2000s, as several other countries established SWFs, including Russia, China, and Norway.

Objectives of Sovereign Wealth Funds

The primary objective of SWFs is to manage the excess funds generated by national governments and central banks and to diversify their investment portfolios. SWFs are typically established to achieve the following objectives:

Stabilization of national economies: SWFs are often established by countries that rely heavily on a single commodity or industry. These funds can help stabilize the national economy by investing in various industries and diversifying the sources of national revenue.

Saving for future generations: Some SWFs are established to save for future generations by investing in long-term assets such as infrastructure projects and real estate. These funds are often created by countries that have a high dependence on non-renewable resources and want to ensure that their wealth is preserved for future generations.

Support for domestic industries: Some SWFs invest in domestic industries to support their growth and development. These funds can provide capital for startups and help to finance research and development in strategic industries.

Investment Strategies of Sovereign Wealth Funds

SWFs employ various investment strategies, ranging from passive to active management, to achieve their objectives. These strategies include:

Passive management: Some SWFs follow a passive investment strategy by investing in index funds or ETFs. This strategy aims to achieve the returns of the broader market while minimizing costs and fees.

Active management: Other SWFs follow an active investment strategy by investing in individual stocks, bonds, and other assets. This strategy aims to generate higher returns by identifying undervalued assets and taking advantage of market inefficiencies.

Diversification: Most SWFs invest in a diversified portfolio of assets to reduce risk and achieve stable returns. This strategy involves investing in various asset classes, sectors, and regions to avoid concentration risk.

Controversies Surrounding Sovereign Wealth Funds

SWFs have faced controversies and criticisms since their inception, with concerns raised about their lack of transparency, potential for political influence, and impact on global financial stability. Some of the controversies surrounding SWFs include:

Lack of transparency: SWFs are often criticized for their lack of transparency in their investment activities. Some SWFs do not disclose their investment strategies or holdings, which can create uncertainty and raise suspicions about their intentions. Critics argue that without proper disclosure, it is difficult to know whether SWFs are pursuing their own interests or those of their governments.

Political influence: Another controversy surrounding SWFs is their potential for political influence. Some critics argue that SWFs could be used as tools for political purposes, such as promoting national interests or gaining influence in foreign countries. For example, if a government were to use its SWF to invest heavily in a particular country, it could potentially influence that country's policies or decision-making.

Impact on global financial stability: Some experts have raised concerns that SWFs, with their large amounts of capital, could have a destabilizing effect on global financial markets. This concern arises from the fact that SWFs are not subject to the same regulations and oversight as traditional financial institutions, which could create a risk of market distortion or manipulation. Additionally, there are concerns about the potential for SWFs to engage in predatory behavior, such as buying up strategic assets or engaging in aggressive pricing strategies.

In response to these concerns, many SWFs have taken steps to increase transparency and accountability, such as disclosing more information about their investment strategies and holdings. Some SWFs have also established codes of conduct and adopted best practices to ensure that their activities are consistent with international norms and standards.

Overall, while SWFs have faced controversies and criticisms, they have also played an important role in global finance, providing a source of capital for investment and contributing to economic growth and development. As the global economy continues to evolve, it is likely that SWFs will continue to be an important player in the financial landscape.

Definition and explanation of sovereign wealth funds

Sovereign Wealth Funds (SWFs) are investment funds established by national governments and central banks to manage their wealth and diversify their investment portfolios. These funds typically invest in various asset classes, such as stocks, bonds, real estate, and infrastructure projects, both domestically and internationally. SWFs can be classified into three main types: stabilization funds, savings funds, and development funds.

Stabilization funds are established by governments to manage windfall revenues from commodity exports, such as oil or gas. These funds are used to stabilize the country's economy and protect it from fluctuations in commodity prices. Savings funds are created to save a portion of a country's budget surplus or foreign exchange reserves for future generations. Development funds are established to support economic development initiatives and infrastructure projects.

SWFs are typically managed by professional investment managers and are subject to strict regulations and investment guidelines. These guidelines ensure that the funds are managed in a prudent and responsible manner, and that the investments are aligned with the long-term interests of the country.

SWFs have emerged as a significant force in global financial markets, with assets under management of around $8 trillion. The largest SWFs are based in countries with large reserves of natural resources, such as Norway, Saudi Arabia, and China.

Investment Strategies of Sovereign Wealth Funds

SWFs employ various investment strategies, ranging from passive to active management. Passive investment strategies involve investing in a portfolio of securities that replicate the performance of a market index, such as the S&P 500 or the FTSE 100. These funds are known as index funds or exchange-traded funds (ETFs) and are typically low-cost and highly diversified.

Active investment strategies involve actively managing a portfolio of securities with the aim of outperforming the market index. These strategies involve extensive research and analysis of the securities in the portfolio, and may include buying and selling securities based on market conditions and economic trends.

SWFs also invest in various asset classes, including stocks, bonds, real estate, and infrastructure projects. Some SWFs also invest in alternative asset classes, such as private equity and hedge funds, which can provide higher returns but also carry higher risks.

Controversies Surrounding Sovereign Wealth Funds

SWFs have faced controversies and criticisms since their inception, with concerns raised about their lack of transparency, potential for political influence, and impact on global financial stability. Some of the controversies surrounding SWFs include:

Lack of transparency: SWFs are often criticized for their lack of transparency in their investment activities. Some SWFs do not disclose their investment strategies, holdings, or returns, which makes it difficult for investors to evaluate their performance and risk profile. Lack of transparency can also fuel suspicion about the political motivations behind some investment decisions.

Potential for political influence: Some observers have raised concerns about the potential for SWFs to exert political influence through their investment decisions. Since SWFs are often established by national governments or central banks, they may be used to further political objectives, such as promoting economic development or influencing foreign policy. This can create tensions with host countries and other stakeholders, who may view the investments as a form of political influence.

Impact on global financial stability: SWFs have also been criticized for their potential impact on global financial stability. Some observers worry that the large size of some SWFs and their tendency to invest in strategic sectors, such as energy and telecommunications, could create systemic risks for the global financial system. Others argue that SWFs can be a stabilizing force in times of financial turmoil, by providing liquidity to distressed markets and investing in undervalued assets.

Conclusion

SWFs have emerged as a significant force in global financial markets, with assets under management of around $8 trillion. They are established by national governments and central banks to manage their wealth and diversify their investment portfolios. SWFs employ various investment strategies, ranging from passive to active management, and invest in various asset classes such as stocks, bonds, real estate, and infrastructure projects.

However, SWFs have faced controversies since their inception, with concerns raised about their lack of transparency, potential for political influence, and impact on global financial stability. It is important for SWFs to address these concerns and maintain transparency and accountability in their investment activities.

Overall, SWFs have played an important role in global financial markets and have contributed to the diversification of investment portfolios. As the global economic landscape continues to evolve, SWFs are likely to remain a significant player in financial markets, with their investment strategies and activities shaping the future of the global economy.

Types of sovereign wealth funds

Sovereign wealth funds (SWFs) are created to manage the national wealth of countries and central banks. These funds have a variety of investment strategies, asset classes, and governance structures. In this section, we will discuss the different types of SWFs and their characteristics.

Stabilization funds
Stabilization funds are created to stabilize the economy of a country during periods of economic volatility or in times of financial crisis. These funds receive inflows from the government's budget surplus, natural resource revenues, or foreign currency reserves. The primary objective of a stabilization fund is to cushion the impact of external shocks and prevent macroeconomic imbalances. The funds are invested in short-term and liquid instruments, such as government bonds, treasury bills, and money market funds.

Example: The Kuwait Investment Authority (KIA) is a stabilization fund established in 1953 to manage the excess oil revenues of the country.

Savings funds

Savings funds are created to save for future generations and provide a source of income when natural resources become scarce. These funds receive inflows from the government's budget surplus, natural resource revenues, or taxes. The primary objective of a savings fund is to preserve the national wealth and provide long-term benefits to the citizens. The funds are invested in a diversified portfolio of assets, such as equities, bonds, real estate, and infrastructure projects.

Example: The Government Pension Fund Global (GPFG) of Norway is a savings fund established in 1990 to manage the surplus revenues from the country's oil and gas sector.

Development funds

Development funds are created to promote economic development and diversification of a country. These funds receive inflows from the government's budget, natural resource revenues, or foreign aid. The primary objective of a development fund is to finance infrastructure projects, such as roads, ports, airports, and energy facilities, and support the growth of local industries. The funds are invested in a mix of public and private assets, such as equities, bonds, private equity, and real estate.

Example: The China Investment Corporation (CIC) is a development fund established in 2007 to diversify China's foreign exchange reserves and support the country's economic development.

Reserve investment corporations

Reserve investment corporations are created to manage the foreign exchange reserves of a country. These funds receive inflows from the government's foreign currency reserves or borrowings. The primary objective of a reserve investment corporation is to generate returns on the foreign currency reserves and mitigate currency risks. The funds are invested in a diversified portfolio of assets, such as equities, bonds, foreign exchange, and commodities.

Example: The State Administration of Foreign Exchange (SAFE) Investment Company of China is a reserve investment corporation established in 2011 to manage China's foreign exchange reserves.

Pension reserve funds

Pension reserve funds are created to provide retirement benefits to the citizens of a country. These funds receive inflows from the government's budget, social security contributions, or taxes. The primary objective of a pension reserve fund is to provide long-term financial security to the citizens and alleviate the burden of aging population on the government's finances. The funds are invested in a diversified portfolio of assets, such as equities, bonds, real estate, and infrastructure projects.

Example: The National Social Security Fund (NSSF) of China is a pension reserve fund established in 2000 to manage the social security contributions of the citizens.

Future generations funds

Future generations funds are created to save for future generations and promote sustainable development. These funds receive inflows from natural resource revenues, such as oil, gas, and minerals. The primary objective of a future generations fund is to preserve the national wealth for the benefit of future generations and support the transition to a low-carbon economy. These funds typically have long-term investment horizons and a high degree of diversification to mitigate risks and achieve stable returns. Norway's Government Pension Fund Global is an example of a future generations fund. The fund's mandate is to invest Norway's surplus revenues from its oil and gas reserves for future generations, and it has a target to achieve a real return of 4% per year.

Green funds

Green funds, also known as environmental funds, are sovereign wealth funds that focus on investing in sustainable projects and companies that have positive environmental impacts. These funds aim to address environmental challenges, such as climate change, by investing in renewable energy, green technologies, and other sustainable businesses. The primary objective of green funds is to promote sustainable development while generating financial returns. Examples of green funds include the Green Climate Fund, which was established by the United Nations Framework Convention on Climate Change to help developing countries transition to low-carbon economies, and the China Green Development Fund, which aims to invest in renewable energy and other environmentally sustainable projects in China.

Infrastructure funds

Infrastructure funds are sovereign wealth funds that invest in infrastructure projects such as roads, airports, railways, and other public infrastructure. These funds aim to provide long-term financing for critical infrastructure projects that are often too large or too risky for traditional investors. The primary objective of infrastructure funds is to generate stable, long-term returns while promoting economic development and improving the quality of life for citizens. Examples of infrastructure funds include the Abu Dhabi Investment Authority's Infrastructure Investment Fund, which invests in transportation, energy, and utilities infrastructure projects globally, and Singapore's Temasek Holdings' Infrastructure Fund, which invests in infrastructure projects in Asia and other emerging markets.

Social welfare funds

Social welfare funds, also known as social security funds, are sovereign wealth funds that aim to provide retirement and other social benefits to citizens. These funds are established to manage and invest government contributions to social welfare programs such as pension plans, healthcare, and unemployment insurance. The primary objective of social welfare funds is to ensure that citizens have access to social welfare benefits and to promote economic stability. Examples of social welfare funds include the Social Security Trust Fund in the United States, which manages and invests contributions to the country's Social Security program, and the Government Pension Fund in Japan, which manages the country's public pension system.

Conclusion

Sovereign wealth funds are an important and growing force in global financial markets. These funds play a significant role in the global economy by investing in various asset classes and promoting economic development. There are different types of sovereign wealth funds, each with their own unique characteristics and objectives. Some of these funds are established to save for future generations, while others focus on promoting sustainable development, investing in infrastructure projects, or providing social welfare benefits to citizens. Despite the controversies and criticisms surrounding sovereign wealth funds, they are likely to continue to grow in importance and influence in the global financial system.

Role of sovereign wealth funds in managing the assets of governments

Sovereign wealth funds (SWFs) have become a key player in managing the assets of governments around the world. As governments accumulate large amounts of wealth, SWFs provide a means to diversify investments, maximize returns, and manage risks. In this section, we will explore the role of SWFs in managing the assets of governments, including their investment strategies, risk management practices, and impact on the global financial system.

Investment Strategies of SWFs

SWFs are unique in their investment strategies, which often differ from traditional asset managers. They typically have long investment horizons and are less focused on short-term gains. This allows them to invest in less liquid assets, such as real estate, infrastructure, private equity, and venture capital. SWFs are also known for their large stakes in public equities, bonds, and other traditional asset classes.

The investment strategies of SWFs vary depending on their objectives and mandates. For example, stabilization funds tend to have a conservative approach, with a focus on preserving capital and providing a buffer against economic shocks. Meanwhile, growth-oriented funds may take on more risk and pursue higher returns, often by investing in emerging markets and alternative asset classes.

One notable trend among SWFs in recent years has been a shift towards sustainability and socially responsible investing. This reflects a growing awareness of environmental, social, and governance (ESG) issues and the impact they can have on investment performance. Many SWFs have implemented ESG screening criteria and are actively seeking out investments that align with their sustainability goals.

Risk Management Practices of SWFs

Given their size and importance, SWFs are subject to intense scrutiny and face significant risks. Risk management is therefore a critical aspect of their operations. SWFs employ a range of risk management practices to ensure they can fulfill their objectives and protect their investments, including:

Diversification: SWFs aim to spread their investments across different asset classes, geographies, and sectors to minimize risks.

Asset-liability management: SWFs take into account their future liabilities, such as pension obligations or future spending needs, when making investment decisions.

Stress testing: SWFs use scenario analysis and stress testing to assess the potential impact of different market scenarios on their portfolios.

Due diligence: SWFs conduct rigorous due diligence before making investments, including financial analysis, legal reviews, and ESG assessments.

Active management: Many SWFs take an active approach to managing their portfolios, rather than simply holding passive index funds.

Impact on the Global Financial System

SWFs have grown rapidly in recent years and have become a significant force in global financial markets. Their impact on the financial system has been the subject of much debate, with some concerned about their potential to disrupt markets and influence national policies. Some of the key issues surrounding SWFs and their impact on the global financial system include:

Transparency: As discussed earlier, SWFs have faced criticism for their lack of transparency, with concerns raised about the potential for insider trading, market manipulation, and political influence.

Investment concentration: SWFs are often large shareholders in major companies, which can give them significant influence over corporate governance and strategic decision-making. This has led to concerns about their potential to disrupt markets and create conflicts of interest.

Sovereignty: Some have argued that SWFs represent a form of economic imperialism, allowing governments to exert influence over other countries' economies and assets. This has led to calls for greater regulation and oversight of SWFs.

Conclusion

SWFs have emerged as an important player in global financial markets, with assets under management of around $8 trillion. They play a critical role in managing the assets of governments, providing a means to diversify investments, maximize returns, and manage risks. Their investment strategies, risk management practices, and impact on the global financial system have been the subject of much debate, with concerns raised about transparency and political influence.

Despite the controversies surrounding SWFs, they continue to grow in size and importance. As governments seek to diversify their investments and generate higher returns, SWFs offer an attractive solution. The growth of

SWFs also reflects the changing nature of global finance, as emerging markets play a larger role in the global economy.

As SWFs continue to expand their investments and influence, it will be important to monitor their activities and ensure transparency and accountability. While SWFs can bring significant benefits to countries, they can also pose risks to global financial stability if their investment activities are not well managed.

In conclusion, sovereign wealth funds are state-owned investment funds that are designed to manage a country's surplus wealth. These funds have emerged as an important player in global financial markets, with assets under management of around $8 trillion. There are several types of SWFs, including stabilization funds, pension reserve funds, strategic development funds, and future generations funds. Each type of fund has a unique purpose and investment strategy.

SWFs play a critical role in managing the assets of governments, providing a means to diversify investments, maximize returns, and manage risks. They can also play a significant role in promoting economic growth and development in their home countries. However, there are concerns about their lack of transparency, potential for political influence, and impact on global financial stability.

As the global economy continues to evolve, it is likely that SWFs will continue to grow in importance. It will be important to monitor their activities and ensure transparency and accountability to minimize the risks that they pose to the global financial system.

Risks and benefits of investing in sovereign wealth funds

Sovereign wealth funds (SWFs) have become significant players in global financial markets, managing assets worth around $8 trillion. SWFs have a unique position, as they are established and managed by national governments and central banks. These funds are a critical tool for governments to manage their wealth and diversify their investments, but they also come with risks. In this section, we will discuss the risks and benefits of investing in SWFs.

Benefits of Investing in SWFs:

Diversification of Investments

SWFs are established to diversify the investments of national governments and central banks. Investing in a SWF allows for diversification across asset classes, regions, and sectors. This diversification helps reduce risk and can lead to higher returns.

Long-term Investment Horizon

SWFs are typically long-term investors, with investment horizons ranging from several years to decades. This long-term investment horizon enables SWFs to invest in illiquid assets such as infrastructure, real estate, and private equity. These investments can generate higher returns than traditional public market investments.

Access to Unexplored Investment Opportunities

SWFs have the ability to invest in opportunities that are not available to other investors. For example, some SWFs have invested in innovative technology startups or emerging markets that are not yet accessible to other investors.

Stabilizing Force in Financial Markets

SWFs can act as a stabilizing force in financial markets during times of economic instability. During the global financial crisis of 2008, SWFs invested in distressed assets and provided liquidity to financial markets, helping to prevent a complete market collapse.

Risks of Investing in SWFs:

Geopolitical Risk

SWFs are often established by national governments, and as such, they are subject to geopolitical risk. Political instability, regulatory changes, or conflicts can affect the investment decisions of SWFs.

Lack of Transparency

SWFs are not always transparent in their investment decisions and operations. This lack of transparency can make it difficult for investors to assess the risks and returns of investing in a SWF.

Concentration Risk

SWFs often have significant holdings in certain companies or sectors, which can lead to concentration risk. A significant downturn in a particular sector or company can result in significant losses for the SWF.

Lack of Control over Investment Decisions

Investors in SWFs do not have control over the investment decisions of the fund. This lack of control can result in investments that do not align with the investor's objectives or risk tolerance.

Reputational Risk

SWFs are often subject to scrutiny from the media and public due to their association with national governments. Any negative news or controversy surrounding a SWF can harm the reputation of the investor.

Conclusion:

SWFs have benefits and risks associated with investing in them. While SWFs can provide access to unique investment opportunities, diversification, and stable long-term returns, they also have geopolitical, concentration, transparency, and reputational risks. Investors must carefully consider these risks and benefits before investing in a SWF. Furthermore, SWFs need to be transparent in their investment decisions and operations, and they must follow ethical investment practices to ensure the long-term stability and success of the fund.

Performance of sovereign wealth funds compared to other investments

Sovereign wealth funds (SWFs) have become a significant player in the global financial markets, with assets under management (AUM) of around $8 trillion. SWFs have a unique mandate to invest on behalf of their respective governments and aim to maximize returns while minimizing risks. However, the performance of SWFs has been a subject of debate and scrutiny, with questions raised about their investment strategies, transparency, and impact on global financial markets. In this section, we will examine the performance of SWFs compared to other investments and explore the reasons behind their performance.

Overview of SWFs' performance

SWFs' performance can be measured using various metrics, such as returns, risk-adjusted returns, and volatility. According to data from the Sovereign Wealth Fund Institute, the median annualized return of SWFs between 2000 and 2021 was 6.1%, compared to 7.5% for the MSCI World Index. However, SWFs' performance varied widely depending on their investment strategies, asset allocation, and risk management practices.

Factors affecting SWFs' performance

Investment strategies: SWFs' investment strategies vary widely, ranging from passive to active, and from traditional to alternative investments. Some SWFs invest heavily in equities, while others focus on fixed income, real estate, or private equity. The choice of investment strategy depends on the SWFs' risk appetite, return expectations, and market conditions. However, SWFs that rely heavily on a single asset class or a narrow range of investments may be exposed to concentration risk, market volatility, and liquidity risk.

Asset allocation: SWFs' asset allocation is influenced by their investment objectives, risk tolerance, and external factors such as economic growth, inflation, and political stability. SWFs' asset allocation typically includes a mix of domestic and international investments, including equities, fixed income, real estate, and alternative investments. However, SWFs' asset allocation can also be affected by macroeconomic factors, such as changes in interest rates, currency fluctuations, and commodity prices.

Risk management: SWFs' risk management practices are critical to their performance, as they aim to minimize losses and protect their capital. SWFs use various risk management tools, such as diversification, hedging, and active management, to manage their risks. However, SWFs' risk management practices can also be affected by external factors, such as changes in regulations, geopolitical risks, and natural disasters.

Comparing SWFs' performance to other investments

Public equities: Public equities, such as stocks, have been a popular investment for SWFs due to their liquidity, diversification, and potential for long-term returns. However, the performance of public equities is subject to market volatility, economic cycles, and geopolitical risks. According to a report by Preqin, SWFs' public equity portfolios returned an average of 8.4% in 2020, compared to 8.2% for the MSCI World Index. However, SWFs' public equity portfolios have underperformed the MSCI World Index over the long term, with a median annualized return of 5.6% between 2000 and 2021, compared to 7.5% for the MSCI World Index.

Fixed income: Fixed income investments, such as bonds, are a popular investment for SWFs due to their stability, income generation, and diversification benefits. However, the performance of fixed income investments is subject to changes in interest rates, credit ratings, and inflation. According to a report by the Sovereign Wealth Fund Institute, SWFs' fixed income portfolios returned an average of 4.6% in 2020, compared to 4.4% for the Bloomberg Barclays Global Aggregate Index. However, SWFs' fixed income portfolios have underperformed the Bloomberg Barclays Global Aggregate Index over the long term, with a median annualized return of 3.3% between 2000 and 2021, compared to 4.8% for the Bloomberg Barclays Global Aggregate Index.

Real estate: Real estate is a popular investment for SWFs due to its potential for long-term capital appreciation, stable income streams, and diversification benefits. However, the performance of real estate investments is subject to changes in market conditions, interest rates, and tenant demand. According to a report by the Sovereign Wealth Fund Institute, SWFs' real estate portfolios returned an average of 3.2% in 2020, compared to 3.7% for the MSCI All Property Index. SWFs' real estate portfolios have outperformed the MSCI All Property Index over the long term, with a median annualized return of 7.2% between 2000 and 2021, compared to 5.6% for the MSCI All Property Index.

Alternative investments: Alternative investments, such as private equity, hedge funds, and infrastructure, are a popular investment for SWFs due to their potential for high returns, low correlation with public markets, and diversification benefits. However, the performance of alternative investments is subject to changes in market conditions, operational risks, and regulatory risks. According to a report by the Sovereign Wealth Fund Institute, SWFs' alternative investments returned an average of 7.2% in 2020, compared to 4.4% for public equity and 4.6% for fixed income. However, SWFs' alternative investments have underperformed public equities over the long term, with a median annualized return of 7.2% between 2000 and 2021, compared to 10.7% for the MSCI World Index.

Overall, SWFs have generally performed well compared to other investments, with solid returns across asset classes. However, the performance of SWFs is subject to market conditions, geopolitical risks, and the investment decisions of their managers. Additionally, SWFs may face unique challenges, such as political pressure, transparency concerns, and public perception issues, which may impact their ability to achieve their investment objectives. As such, investors should carefully consider the risks and benefits of investing in SWFs, and conduct thorough due diligence before making investment decisions.

Conclusion

In this chapter, we have explored the world of alternative investment funds, including hedge funds, pension funds, mutual funds, and sovereign wealth funds. We have discussed their history, investment strategies, performance, risks, and benefits. Here are the key points that we have covered in this chapter:

Key Points:

Hedge funds are private investment funds that use a variety of strategies, such as long-short, global macro, and event-driven, to generate high returns for their investors.

Pension funds are retirement savings plans that are sponsored by employers or unions and are designed to provide retirement benefits to employees.

Mutual funds are investment vehicles that pool money from individual investors to invest in a diversified portfolio of stocks, bonds, and other securities.

Sovereign wealth funds are investment funds that are owned by governments and are designed to invest in a diversified portfolio of assets, including stocks, bonds, real estate, and alternative investments.

Alternative investment funds offer several benefits, such as diversification, risk management, and potential for high returns.

However, alternative investment funds also carry several risks, such as liquidity risk, leverage risk, and concentration risk.

Hedge funds have historically outperformed traditional investments, but their high fees and lack of transparency have been the subject of much criticism.

Pension funds are subject to regulatory oversight and are designed to provide long-term returns for their members, but their performance is influenced by factors such as interest rates and market volatility.

Mutual funds are popular among retail investors due to their accessibility, diversification, and professional management, but their fees can be high, and their performance is subject to market volatility.

Sovereign wealth funds have emerged as an important player in global financial markets, with assets under management of around $8 trillion. They play a critical role in managing the assets of governments, providing a means to diversify investments, maximize returns, and manage risks.

Alternative investment funds are likely to continue to play an important role in the financial industry, as investors seek diversification and new sources of returns.

Future of alternative investment funds in the financial industry:

The future of alternative investment funds in the financial industry is likely to be shaped by several trends, including:

Increased focus on ESG investing: Environmental, social, and governance (ESG) investing has gained momentum in recent years, as investors seek to align their investments with their values and promote sustainable practices.

Technology and data-driven investing: The use of technology, such as artificial intelligence and machine learning, is likely to continue to transform the investment industry, enabling investors to make better-informed decisions and optimize their portfolios.

Regulatory oversight: Alternative investment funds are subject to varying degrees of regulatory oversight, and the regulatory landscape is likely to continue to evolve, with an emphasis on transparency, investor protection, and systemic risk management.

Demographic shifts: Changes in demographics, such as aging populations and increasing wealth inequality, are likely to influence the demand for alternative investment funds, as investors seek to manage risk and generate income in a changing economic environment.

Final thoughts and recommendations:

Alternative investment funds offer investors the potential for high returns and diversification, but they also carry risks, such as liquidity risk, leverage risk, and concentration risk. Therefore, investors should carefully consider their investment goals, risk tolerance, and financial situation before investing in alternative investment funds.

Some recommendations for investors considering alternative investment funds include:

Conduct thorough due diligence: Investors should carefully research alternative investment funds before investing, including analyzing their investment strategies, performance history, fees, and risks.

Consider working with a financial advisor: A financial advisor can provide guidance and expertise in selecting and managing alternative investment funds, as well as help investors navigate the regulatory landscape and manage risk.

Diversify investments: It is important for investors to diversify their portfolio by investing in a variety of alternative investment funds, as well as traditional investments such as stocks and bonds. This can help to minimize risk and optimize returns.

Stay informed and up-to-date: Investors should stay informed about market trends, regulatory changes, and performance of their alternative investment funds. Regularly reviewing investment portfolios and conducting due diligence can help investors make informed decisions and adjust their investments as needed.

Conclusion

Alternative investment funds, including hedge funds, pension funds, mutual funds, and sovereign wealth funds, have become increasingly popular in the financial industry. These funds offer a range of investment strategies and opportunities, including higher potential returns and diversification benefits.

However, alternative investment funds also come with risks, including high fees, illiquidity, and potential for market volatility. It is important for investors to conduct thorough due diligence, diversify their investments, and stay informed about market trends and regulatory changes.

Despite the risks, alternative investment funds are likely to continue to play a significant role in the financial industry, as investors seek to optimize their returns and manage risk in a changing market landscape. By carefully selecting and managing alternative investment funds, investors can achieve their financial goals and build a strong and diversified investment portfolio.

CHAPTER 12: FINANCIAL REGULATIONS

Introduction

Financial regulations refer to the laws, policies, and rules that govern the operation of financial systems and institutions, with the goal of ensuring stability, fairness, and transparency in the financial industry. These regulations cover a wide range of areas, including banking, securities, insurance, and investments, and are enforced by government agencies, such as the Securities and Exchange Commission (SEC) in the United States, the Financial Conduct Authority (FCA) in the United Kingdom, and the European Securities and Markets Authority (ESMA) in the European Union.

Financial regulations are essential for protecting investors, maintaining financial stability, and promoting economic growth. They provide a framework for market participants to operate within, and ensure that financial institutions and products are safe and sound. Without financial regulations, the financial industry would be vulnerable to fraud, manipulation, and instability, which could lead to severe economic consequences.

The history of financial regulations dates back to ancient times, with the first recorded financial regulations appearing in ancient Babylon, where the Code of Hammurabi established rules for lending and borrowing. Since then, financial regulations have evolved and expanded to keep pace with the changing financial landscape, including the growth of modern banking, securities markets, and global financial systems.

This chapter provides an in-depth examination of financial regulations, including their definition, importance, and history. It explores the different types of financial regulations, the regulatory bodies responsible for enforcing them, and the challenges and controversies surrounding financial regulations in the modern era. By the end of this chapter, readers will have a comprehensive understanding of financial regulations and their impact on the financial industry.

Types of financial regulations

Financial regulations are a crucial aspect of the global financial system. These regulations are designed to maintain the stability of the financial system, protect consumers, and prevent financial crises. There are several types of financial regulations, each with its own specific purpose and focus. In this section, we will examine three broad categories of financial regulations: market regulations, prudential regulations, and consumer protection regulations.

Market Regulations

Market regulations are designed to ensure that financial markets are efficient, transparent, and fair. These regulations are typically aimed at preventing market manipulation, fraud, and other forms of misconduct. Some examples of market regulations include:

Securities Regulations: These regulations govern the issuance and trading of securities, such as stocks, bonds, and other investment products. Securities regulations typically require companies to disclose certain financial information to the public, and to adhere to specific rules and standards when issuing or trading securities.

Exchange Regulations: These regulations govern the operations of stock exchanges and other financial marketplaces. Exchange regulations typically set rules for trading, including price limits, trading hours, and other parameters.

Market Conduct Regulations: These regulations are designed to ensure that market participants behave in a fair and ethical manner. Market conduct regulations may prohibit insider trading, market manipulation, or other forms of misconduct.

Prudential Regulations

Prudential regulations are designed to ensure the safety and soundness of financial institutions. These regulations are typically aimed at preventing institutions from taking excessive risks or engaging in activities that could undermine their financial stability. Some examples of prudential regulations include:

Capital Requirements: These regulations require financial institutions to maintain a minimum level of capital relative to their assets. Capital requirements are designed to ensure that institutions have a buffer against losses and can absorb financial shocks.

Liquidity Requirements: These regulations require financial institutions to maintain a certain level of liquid assets to ensure that they can meet their obligations in the event of a liquidity crisis.

Risk Management Requirements: These regulations require financial institutions to have robust risk management systems in place to identify and mitigate risks. Risk management requirements may include stress testing, scenario analysis, and other measures.

Consumer Protection Regulations

Consumer protection regulations are designed to protect consumers from financial fraud, abuse, and other forms of misconduct. These regulations are typically aimed at ensuring that consumers have access to accurate information about financial products and services, and that they are treated fairly by financial institutions. Some examples of consumer protection regulations include:

Disclosure Requirements: These regulations require financial institutions to disclose certain information to consumers, such as fees, interest rates, and other terms and conditions.

Consumer Complaint Mechanisms: These regulations require financial institutions to have systems in place for handling consumer complaints and resolving disputes.

Consumer Education Programs: These regulations may require financial institutions to provide educational materials or other resources to help consumers understand financial products and services.

Conclusion

Financial regulations are essential for maintaining the stability and integrity of the global financial system. Market regulations, prudential regulations, and consumer protection regulations all play an important role in ensuring that financial markets are efficient, transparent, and fair, that financial institutions are sound and stable, and that consumers are protected from financial fraud and abuse. While financial regulations can sometimes be complex and difficult to navigate, they are a necessary component of a healthy and functioning financial system.

Market regulations

In the United States, market regulations are overseen by a variety of government agencies, including the Securities and Exchange Commission (SEC) and the Commodities Futures Trading Commission (CFTC). Internationally, the International Organization of Securities Commissions (IOSCO) is a key regulatory body that works to develop and implement global standards for securities regulation. In this section, we will provide an overview of market regulations and these three key regulatory bodies.

Securities and Exchange Commission (SEC)

The Securities and Exchange Commission (SEC) is a U.S. government agency that was created in 1934 in response to the stock market crash of 1929. The SEC's mission is to protect investors, maintain fair, orderly, and efficient markets, and facilitate capital formation. The SEC regulates securities markets and the companies that issue securities, including stocks, bonds, and mutual funds.

The SEC has a wide range of regulatory powers and responsibilities, including:

Registering and regulating securities exchanges, such as the New York Stock Exchange and Nasdaq
Enforcing federal securities laws, such as the Securities Act of 1933 and the Securities Exchange Act of 1934
Regulating securities brokers and dealers
Requiring companies to disclose certain financial and other information to investors
Investigating and prosecuting securities fraud and other violations of securities laws
One of the key ways the SEC carries out its regulatory duties is through the review and approval of registration statements and prospectuses for new securities offerings. These documents must contain detailed information about the issuer, the securities being offered, and the risks involved. The SEC also monitors trading activity and can halt trading in a security if it believes there is manipulation or other illegal activity.

Commodities Futures Trading Commission (CFTC)

The Commodities Futures Trading Commission (CFTC) is another U.S. government agency that regulates the futures and options markets. The CFTC was created in 1974 in response to concerns about price manipulation and other abuses in the commodities markets. The CFTC's mission is to protect market participants and the public from fraud, manipulation, and abusive practices related to derivatives and other financial products.

The CFTC has a broad range of regulatory responsibilities, including:

Registering and regulating futures exchanges, such as the Chicago Mercantile Exchange and the New York Mercantile Exchange
Regulating futures brokers and dealers
Enforcing federal commodities laws, such as the Commodity Exchange Act
Reviewing and approving new futures contracts and trading rules
Investigating and prosecuting fraud and other violations of commodities laws
One of the key functions of the CFTC is to ensure that futures and options contracts are traded in a fair and transparent manner. To this end, the CFTC requires market participants to report their positions and trading activity, and it conducts regular audits of exchanges and clearinghouses.

International Organization of Securities Commissions (IOSCO)

The International Organization of Securities Commissions (IOSCO) is a global regulatory body that was established in 1983 to promote high standards of regulation in the securities markets. IOSCO's membership includes securities regulators from more than 120 countries, and its mission is to protect investors, ensure fair and efficient markets, and reduce systemic risk.

IOSCO has a wide range of responsibilities, including:

Developing and promoting global standards for securities regulation
Conducting research on securities markets and regulatory issues
Providing guidance to member regulators on regulatory best practices
Coordinating regulatory activities among its members
Promoting cross-border cooperation and information sharing
One of the key initiatives that IOSCO has undertaken in recent years is the development of principles for the regulation of hedge funds and other alternative investment funds. IOSCO has also worked to develop guidelines for the regulation of credit rating agencies, which play a crucial role in

financial markets by providing assessments of the creditworthiness of various entities, including corporations and governments.

Another important market regulator is the Securities and Exchange Commission (SEC), which is responsible for regulating securities markets in the United States. The SEC has a broad mandate to protect investors, maintain fair, orderly, and efficient markets, and facilitate capital formation. Some of the key areas that the SEC regulates include:

Disclosure: The SEC requires companies to provide investors with accurate and timely information about their financial performance, operations, and risks through periodic filings, such as annual and quarterly reports, and other disclosures.

Insider trading: The SEC prohibits insiders, such as company executives and directors, from trading on material nonpublic information that they obtain through their positions.

Fraud: The SEC investigates and prosecutes fraudulent activities in the securities markets, such as Ponzi schemes, accounting fraud, and market manipulation.

Market structure: The SEC regulates the structure and operation of securities markets, including exchanges, alternative trading systems, and clearing and settlement systems.

The Commodities Futures Trading Commission (CFTC) is another important market regulator in the United States. The CFTC oversees the trading of futures, options, and swaps contracts on commodities, such as agricultural products, energy, and metals. The CFTC's mandate includes promoting transparency, preventing fraud and manipulation, and ensuring the financial integrity of the futures and swaps markets. Some of the key areas that the CFTC regulates include:

Market surveillance: The CFTC monitors trading activity in the futures and swaps markets to detect and prevent fraud, manipulation, and other abusive practices.

Clearing and settlement: The CFTC oversees the clearing and settlement of futures and swaps contracts to ensure that they are settled in a timely and efficient manner and that the risks associated with these contracts are appropriately managed.

Registration: The CFTC requires certain market participants, such as commodity pool operators and commodity trading advisors, to register with the agency and comply with certain rules and regulations.

Enforcement: The CFTC investigates and prosecutes violations of its rules and regulations, including fraud, manipulation, and other illegal activities in the futures and swaps markets.

Overall, market regulations play a critical role in ensuring the stability and integrity of financial markets, promoting transparency and accountability, protecting investors, and fostering economic growth and innovation. By setting standards and guidelines for market participants and enforcing compliance with these standards, market regulators help to create a level playing field for all participants and reduce the potential for market failures and systemic risks.

Prudential regulations

In addition to market regulations and consumer protection regulations, prudential regulations form an important part of the regulatory framework governing the financial industry. Prudential regulations aim to ensure the stability and safety of financial institutions by imposing various requirements and standards on banks and other financial institutions. These regulations are typically overseen by specialized regulatory agencies, such as the Federal Reserve System (Fed), the Office of the Comptroller of the Currency (OCC), and the Federal Deposit Insurance Corporation (FDIC) in the United States. In this section, we will provide an overview of prudential regulations and discuss the role of each of these regulatory agencies.

Federal Reserve System (Fed)

The Federal Reserve System (Fed) is the central bank of the United States and plays a key role in the regulation of banks and other financial institutions. The Fed was established in 1913 with the passage of the Federal Reserve Act and has since been responsible for implementing monetary policy, supervising and regulating banks, and providing financial services to the government.

The Fed's supervisory responsibilities involve overseeing the operations of state-chartered banks that are members of the Federal Reserve System, as well as bank holding companies and foreign banks operating in the United States. The Fed is also responsible for supervising and regulating the operations of U.S. branches and agencies of foreign banks.

To fulfill its supervisory responsibilities, the Fed conducts regular examinations of banks and other financial institutions to ensure that they are complying with prudential regulations and are operating in a safe and sound manner. The Fed also has the authority to take enforcement actions against banks and other financial institutions that are found to be in violation of prudential regulations.

Office of the Comptroller of the Currency (OCC)

The Office of the Comptroller of the Currency (OCC) is an independent bureau within the U.S. Department of the Treasury that is responsible for regulating and supervising national banks and federal savings associations. The OCC was established in 1863 as part of the National Currency Act and has since been responsible for ensuring the safety and soundness of the national banking system.

The OCC's supervisory responsibilities involve overseeing the operations of national banks and federal savings associations, which together comprise approximately 70% of all U.S. banking assets. The OCC conducts regular examinations of these institutions to ensure that they are complying with prudential regulations and are operating in a safe and sound manner.

Like the Fed, the OCC has the authority to take enforcement actions against banks and other financial institutions that are found to be in violation of prudential regulations. The OCC also has the authority to charter new national banks and to approve the establishment of new branches and subsidiaries by national banks.

Federal Deposit Insurance Corporation (FDIC)

The Federal Deposit Insurance Corporation (FDIC) is an independent U.S. government agency that is responsible for insuring deposits in banks and savings associations. The FDIC was established in 1933 as part of the Banking Act and has since been responsible for maintaining public confidence in the U.S. banking system.

The FDIC's primary responsibility is to insure deposits in banks and savings associations up to a certain amount, which is currently $250,000 per depositor per insured bank. The FDIC also has the authority to supervise and regulate state-chartered banks that are not members of the Federal Reserve System.

To fulfill its supervisory responsibilities, the FDIC conducts regular examinations of insured banks and savings associations to ensure that they are complying with prudential regulations and are operating in a safe and sound manner. The FDIC also has the authority to take enforcement actions against insured banks and savings associations that are found to be in violation of prudential regulations.

Conclusion:

In conclusion, prudential regulations are designed to ensure that financial institutions operate in a safe and sound manner, and to protect consumers and the overall financial system from the risks associated with financial intermediation. These regulations include a variety of requirements and restrictions aimed at promoting stability, transparency, and accountability in the financial sector.

The Federal Reserve System, the Office of the Comptroller of the Currency, and the Federal Deposit Insurance Corporation are the main regulators responsible for enforcing prudential regulations in the United States. These agencies oversee a range of institutions, from large banks to small savings and loans associations, and work to promote safety and soundness in the financial system.

While prudential regulations have been effective in promoting financial stability, they also have their limitations. For example, some argue that prudential regulations can be overly burdensome, leading to increased compliance costs for financial institutions and potentially reducing the availability of credit. Others argue that prudential regulations can create moral hazard by providing a safety net for financial institutions, leading to excessive risk-taking.

Despite these criticisms, prudential regulations remain a critical component of the regulatory framework governing the financial industry. As the financial landscape continues to evolve and new risks emerge, it is likely that prudential regulations will continue to play an important role in promoting financial stability and protecting consumers and the broader financial system.

Overall, prudential regulations are an essential tool for promoting a safe and stable financial system. By setting standards for financial institutions and imposing restrictions on their activities, prudential regulations help to prevent excessive risk-taking and promote transparency and accountability in the financial sector. As such, they are an important part of the regulatory framework that governs the financial industry, and will likely continue to play a critical role in promoting financial stability and protecting consumers in the years to come.

Consumer protection regulations

Consumer protection regulations aim to protect consumers from financial fraud, deception, and other unethical practices by financial institutions. These regulations exist to ensure that consumers are well-informed and can make informed decisions when taking out loans, opening bank accounts, and engaging in other financial transactions. In the United States, the Consumer Financial Protection Bureau (CFPB) is the primary federal agency responsible for enforcing consumer protection regulations. In this section, we will discuss the CFPB, as well as two key consumer protection regulations, the Truth in Lending Act (TILA) and the Fair Credit Reporting Act (FCRA).

Consumer Financial Protection Bureau (CFPB)

The Consumer Financial Protection Bureau (CFPB) is a federal agency established in 2011 under the Dodd-Frank Wall Street Reform and Consumer Protection Act. The CFPB's mission is to protect consumers by regulating financial institutions and enforcing consumer protection laws. The CFPB has the authority to issue regulations, conduct investigations and bring enforcement actions against financial institutions that violate consumer protection laws. It also provides consumer education and handles consumer complaints.

The CFPB has the power to regulate a wide range of financial products and services, including mortgages, credit cards, and student loans. It also has the authority to investigate and enforce regulations related to debt collection, payday loans, and other financial products.

Truth in Lending Act (TILA)

The Truth in Lending Act (TILA) is a federal law that requires lenders to disclose the terms and conditions of a loan to the borrower before the borrower agrees to the loan. TILA is designed to ensure that consumers are informed about the true cost of credit and are not misled by lenders.

TILA requires lenders to provide the following information to consumers:

The annual percentage rate (APR) of the loan
The total amount of interest to be paid over the life of the loan

The total amount of fees and charges associated with the loan
The total amount of the loan
The repayment schedule for the loan
Lenders are required to disclose this information in a clear and understandable manner. TILA also gives consumers the right to cancel certain types of loans within three days of signing the agreement.

Fair Credit Reporting Act (FCRA)

The Fair Credit Reporting Act (FCRA) is a federal law that regulates how credit reporting agencies collect, use, and share consumer credit information. The FCRA is designed to ensure that credit reporting agencies maintain accurate and fair credit reports and that consumers have the right to access and dispute inaccurate information.

The FCRA requires credit reporting agencies to:

Provide consumers with a copy of their credit report once a year for free
Investigate disputed information within 30 days
Remove inaccurate information from credit reports
Notify consumers if negative information is added to their credit report
The FCRA also gives consumers the right to sue credit reporting agencies and other entities that violate their rights under the law.

Conclusion

Consumer protection regulations are an essential component of the regulatory framework governing the financial industry. These regulations exist to ensure that consumers are well-informed and protected from fraudulent and deceptive practices by financial institutions. The CFPB is the primary federal agency responsible for enforcing consumer protection regulations, and the Truth in Lending Act (TILA) and the Fair Credit Reporting Act (FCRA) are two key regulations that aim to protect consumers from unfair and misleading practices. By promoting transparency and accountability in the financial industry, consumer protection regulations help to maintain a healthy and stable financial system that benefits both consumers and financial institutions.

Impact of financial regulations on the financial industry

Financial regulations play a critical role in the financial industry, affecting both financial institutions and the consumers who use their services.

Regulations can have both positive and negative impacts on the industry, and can result in a variety of responses from financial institutions.

Positive and Negative Effects of Financial Regulations

Financial regulations are designed to protect consumers, prevent fraud, and maintain the stability of financial institutions. These regulations can have positive effects on the financial industry, such as:

Increased Stability: Regulations can help prevent financial institutions from engaging in risky activities that could destabilize the industry. For example, regulations requiring higher capital requirements and limits on leverage can help ensure that financial institutions have the resources to weather economic downturns.

Consumer Protection: Regulations can help protect consumers from unfair practices, such as predatory lending or deceptive marketing. For example, the Truth in Lending Act (TILA) requires lenders to disclose the terms and conditions of a loan to the borrower, giving consumers the information they need to make informed decisions.

Confidence in the Financial System: Regulations can help build confidence in the financial system by providing a clear framework for the industry to operate within. This can help investors and consumers feel more secure in their financial dealings.

However, financial regulations can also have negative effects on the financial industry, such as:

Increased Costs: Regulations can require financial institutions to incur additional costs, such as compliance costs or fees. These costs can make it more difficult for smaller institutions to compete with larger ones.

Reduced Innovation: Regulations can limit the ability of financial institutions to innovate and offer new products and services. This can make it more difficult for the industry to adapt to changing market conditions.

Reduced Availability of Credit: Regulations can make it more difficult for consumers and businesses to obtain credit. For example, regulations requiring higher capital requirements can limit the amount of credit that financial institutions are able to provide.

How Financial Institutions Comply with Regulations

Financial institutions are required to comply with a wide range of regulations, and compliance can be a complex and costly process. Financial institutions must implement policies and procedures to ensure compliance with regulations, and must monitor their activities to ensure that they remain in compliance.

Financial institutions may respond to regulations in a variety of ways, depending on the nature of the regulation and the institution's business model. Some common responses include:

Increased Compliance Staff: Financial institutions may hire additional staff to help manage the compliance process. This can help ensure that the institution is able to meet its regulatory obligations, but can also increase costs.

Changes to Business Practices: Financial institutions may need to make changes to their business practices in order to comply with regulations. For example, a regulation requiring lenders to disclose certain information to borrowers may require changes to the institution's loan origination process.

Reductions in Risky Activities: Financial institutions may reduce or eliminate risky activities in order to comply with regulations. For example, regulations requiring higher capital requirements may make it more difficult for institutions to engage in highly-leveraged activities.

Conclusion

Financial regulations play a critical role in the financial industry, affecting both financial institutions and the consumers who use their services. Regulations can have both positive and negative impacts on the industry, and can result in a variety of responses from financial institutions. While regulations can help promote stability and protect consumers, they can also increase costs and limit innovation. Financial institutions must implement policies and procedures to ensure compliance with regulations, and may need to make changes to their business practices in order to comply.

Recent and upcoming changes to financial regulations

The financial industry has undergone significant changes in the past decade, with the introduction of new regulations aimed at protecting consumers and promoting financial stability. The global financial crisis of 2008 highlighted the need for stronger regulatory oversight, resulting in a wave of new regulations in the years that followed. In this section, we will explore the current state of financial regulations, recent legislative changes, and upcoming regulatory changes that are likely to shape the financial industry in the years ahead.

Current State of Financial Regulations

Financial regulations can be broadly divided into two categories: prudential regulations, which are designed to promote financial stability by regulating the activities of financial institutions, and consumer protection regulations, which are designed to protect consumers from unfair or deceptive practices by financial institutions.

In the United States, financial regulations are overseen by a number of regulatory bodies, including the Federal Reserve System (Fed), the Office of the Comptroller of the Currency (OCC), and the Securities and Exchange Commission (SEC), among others. These agencies are responsible for implementing and enforcing regulations that govern the activities of banks, investment firms, and other financial institutions.

Recent Legislative Changes

In recent years, there have been a number of significant legislative changes that have impacted the financial industry. Some of the most notable include:

Dodd-Frank Wall Street Reform and Consumer Protection Act: This legislation, which was passed in 2010 in response to the global financial crisis, established a number of new regulations aimed at promoting financial stability and protecting consumers. Some of the key provisions of the law include the creation of the Consumer Financial Protection Bureau (CFPB), which is tasked with enforcing consumer protection regulations, and the Volcker Rule, which limits the ability of banks to engage in certain types of speculative trading.

Economic Growth, Regulatory Relief, and Consumer Protection Act: This legislation, which was passed in 2018, aimed to roll back some of the more onerous provisions of the Dodd-Frank Act. Among other things, the law raised the asset threshold for banks that are subject to enhanced regulatory scrutiny, and exempted some small banks from certain reporting requirements.

Tax Cuts and Jobs Act: This legislation, which was passed in 2017, included a number of provisions that impacted the financial industry. Among other things, the law lowered the corporate tax rate from 35% to 21%, which had a significant impact on the profitability of banks and other financial institutions.

Upcoming Regulatory Changes

Looking ahead, there are several regulatory changes that are currently in the works that are likely to impact the financial industry. Some of the most significant include:

Regulation Best Interest: This new regulation, which was adopted by the SEC in 2019, imposes a new standard of conduct on brokers and investment advisers who provide investment advice to retail customers. The rule requires these professionals to act in the best interest of their clients when recommending investment products.

Current Expected Credit Losses (CECL): This new accounting standard, which was adopted by the Financial Accounting Standards Board (FASB) in 2016, requires banks and other financial institutions to estimate their expected credit losses over the life of a loan, rather than just over the next 12 months. This change is expected to result in higher loan-loss reserves for many banks, which could impact their profitability.

Cybersecurity Regulations: There has been a growing concern in recent years about the threat of cyber attacks on financial institutions. As a result, there has been a push to strengthen cybersecurity regulations in order to protect against these threats. The Federal Financial Institutions Examination Council (FFIEC) has issued guidelines for banks and other financial institutions to follow in order to protect against cyber attacks, and there is likely to be additional regulatory action in this area in the years to come.

Conclusion

Financial regulations are constantly evolving, as regulators work to keep pace with changes in the industry and to ensure the stability and safety of the financial system. The regulatory framework is complex and can be difficult to navigate, but it serves an important role in protecting consumers and the broader economy.

As we have seen in this discussion, there are a variety of different types of financial regulations, including those related to prudential standards, consumer protection, impact on the financial industry, and recent and upcoming changes. Each of these areas is important in its own right and affects different stakeholders in the financial system.

Overall, the regulatory landscape is likely to continue to evolve in response to ongoing technological advancements, changing market conditions, and political considerations. It is important for financial institutions to stay up-to-date with changes in regulations and to ensure compliance in order to avoid potential legal and financial consequences.

At the same time, it is also important for policymakers to strike a balance between protecting consumers and promoting innovation and growth in the financial sector. This requires careful consideration of the potential costs and benefits of different regulatory approaches, as well as an understanding of the complex interplay between financial institutions, markets, and the broader economy.

In conclusion, financial regulations play a critical role in ensuring the safety and stability of the financial system, but they must be carefully designed and implemented in order to achieve their intended goals. As the financial industry continues to evolve, it is likely that regulations will also continue to change in order to address new challenges and opportunities.

Conclusion

In conclusion, financial regulations play a critical role in ensuring the stability and integrity of the financial system. The primary goal of financial regulations is to protect consumers and investors, maintain the safety and soundness of financial institutions, and promote market efficiency and transparency. Financial regulations can take many forms, including laws, rules, and standards that are imposed by government agencies and other regulatory bodies.

Throughout this chapter, we have explored the various types of financial regulations, including prudential regulations, consumer protection regulations, and cybersecurity regulations. We have discussed the positive and negative effects of financial regulations on the financial industry, as well as the challenges that financial institutions face in complying with these regulations.

Summary of Key Points

Financial regulations are rules and standards imposed by government agencies and other regulatory bodies to protect consumers and investors, maintain the safety and soundness of financial institutions, and promote market efficiency and transparency.

Prudential regulations aim to ensure the stability and soundness of financial institutions, while consumer protection regulations are designed to protect consumers from abusive or deceptive practices.

Cybersecurity regulations have become increasingly important in recent years due to the growing threat of cyber attacks on financial institutions.

Financial regulations can have both positive and negative effects on the financial industry. While they can increase stability and protect consumers, they can also increase costs and reduce innovation.

Financial institutions face many challenges in complying with regulations, including the costs of compliance and the potential for unintended consequences.

The future of financial regulations is likely to include continued evolution and adaptation to new technologies and market developments.

Future of Financial Regulations

The financial industry is constantly evolving, and financial regulations must keep up with these changes in order to remain effective. In the future, we can expect to see several trends that will shape the future of financial regulations:

Technological innovation: Financial regulations will need to adapt to new technologies such as blockchain, artificial intelligence, and machine learning.

Globalization: As financial markets become more interconnected, financial regulations will need to be coordinated across different jurisdictions to ensure consistency and effectiveness.

Climate change: Financial regulations will need to address the risks posed by climate change, including the potential for physical damage to financial institutions and the impact of climate-related events on the broader economy.

Consumer protection: There is likely to be continued focus on protecting consumers from abusive or deceptive practices, particularly in areas such as consumer lending and debt collection.

Final Thoughts and Recommendations

In conclusion, financial regulations are essential for maintaining the stability and integrity of the financial system. While regulations can have both positive and negative effects on the financial industry, they are necessary to protect consumers and investors and ensure that financial institutions operate in a safe and sound manner.

As financial regulations continue to evolve, it is important for policymakers and regulators to balance the need for stability and safety with the need for innovation and efficiency. Financial institutions must also play a role in complying with regulations and working to mitigate any unintended consequences.

In order to ensure the effectiveness of financial regulations, it is important for policymakers and regulators to engage in ongoing dialogue with industry stakeholders and to monitor and evaluate the impact of regulations over time. By doing so, we can continue to improve the financial regulatory framework and ensure that it remains effective and efficient in the years to come.

CHAPTER 13: ETHICAL ISSUES IN FINANCE

Introduction

Ethics plays a vital role in the finance industry. The financial sector is a complex web of institutions and individuals that interact with each other in various ways to achieve their goals. The decisions made by financial institutions and their employees have far-reaching consequences that affect individuals, businesses, and the economy as a whole. Therefore, it is crucial for the industry to operate with a high degree of integrity and ethical standards. This chapter will provide an overview of ethics in finance, the importance of ethical behavior in the industry, and a discussion of some of the ethical issues that arise in finance.

Definition of Ethics in Finance

Ethics can be defined as a set of moral principles or values that guide behavior. In finance, ethics refers to the moral principles and standards that govern the behavior of financial professionals and institutions. Ethical behavior in finance involves acting with integrity, honesty, and transparency and adhering to ethical standards and codes of conduct.

The Importance of Ethics in the Finance Industry

Ethics is critical to the success of the finance industry for several reasons:

Trust: The financial industry relies heavily on trust. Investors, lenders, and borrowers all need to trust that financial institutions and professionals will act in their best interests. Ethical behavior helps build and maintain trust, which is essential for the smooth functioning of the financial system.

Reputation: Reputation is essential in the finance industry. A good reputation can help financial institutions attract new customers and investors, while a bad reputation can lead to a loss of business and legal action. Ethical behavior helps maintain a good reputation and can help institutions avoid legal and regulatory problems.

Legal and Regulatory Compliance: Financial institutions and professionals must comply with a wide range of laws and regulations. Ethical behavior helps ensure compliance with these laws and regulations and helps prevent legal and regulatory problems.

Overview of Ethical Issues in Finance

The finance industry is subject to a wide range of ethical issues. Some of the key ethical issues in finance include:

Insider Trading: Insider trading involves using confidential information to gain an advantage in the financial markets. This unethical practice is illegal and can lead to fines and even imprisonment.

Conflicts of Interest: Conflicts of interest can arise when financial professionals have competing interests that may interfere with their ability to act in the best interests of their clients. For example, a financial advisor may recommend an investment that benefits them more than their client.

Corporate Social Responsibility: Corporate social responsibility involves the ethical and social obligations of corporations to stakeholders, including shareholders, employees, customers, and the wider community. Financial institutions have a responsibility to operate in a socially responsible manner and to consider the impact of their actions on the environment and society.

Pay and Bonuses: The pay and bonuses of financial professionals have come under scrutiny in recent years. There is a concern that excessive pay and bonuses can lead to unethical behavior, such as taking excessive risks.

Conclusion

Ethics is a critical aspect of the finance industry. Ethical behavior is essential for building and maintaining trust, maintaining a good reputation, and complying with legal and regulatory requirements. The financial industry is subject to a wide range of ethical issues, including insider trading, conflicts of interest, corporate social responsibility, and pay and bonuses. In the following chapters, we will explore these ethical issues in more detail and examine ways to address them.

Insider Trading

Insider trading is a term that is used to describe the practice of buying or selling securities by individuals who possess material, non-public information about a company. This type of trading is considered illegal in most countries, including the United States, as it can give an unfair advantage to those with access to privileged information. In this chapter, we will explore the different types of insider trading, the ethical concerns surrounding this practice, and some notable examples of insider trading cases.

Definition of Insider Trading

Insider trading is a type of trading activity that occurs when an individual or entity buys or sells securities in a company based on information that is not available to the public. This information is considered "material," which means that it could impact the price of the securities if it were widely known. Examples of material information may include earnings reports, merger announcements, and other news that could significantly impact the value of a company's stock.

Types of Insider Trading

There are two main types of insider trading: legal and illegal.

Legal insider trading occurs when insiders, such as directors or executives of a company, purchase or sell shares of their company's stock based on public information. For example, if a director of a company purchases shares of the company's stock based on the fact that the company is performing well, this would be considered legal insider trading.

Illegal insider trading, on the other hand, occurs when insiders trade securities based on material, non-public information. This type of insider trading is considered illegal because it can give an unfair advantage to those with access to privileged information. For example, if an executive of a company purchases shares of the company's stock based on the knowledge of an upcoming merger that has not been publicly announced, this would be considered illegal insider trading.

Ethical Concerns Surrounding Insider Trading

Insider trading is often considered unethical because it can give an unfair advantage to those with access to privileged information. This can be particularly harmful to small investors who do not have access to this type of information. Additionally, insider trading can erode public trust in the stock market and in the companies that are being traded.

Another ethical concern surrounding insider trading is the potential for conflicts of interest. For example, if an executive of a company sells shares of the company's stock before a negative announcement, they may be seen as putting their own interests ahead of the company's and its shareholders.

Examples of Insider Trading Cases

There have been many high-profile cases of insider trading over the years, including the following:

Martha Stewart: In 2001, Martha Stewart, a well-known television personality, sold shares of ImClone Systems after receiving information from the CEO of the company that the stock was going to decline. She was found guilty of insider trading and served five months in prison.

Raj Rajaratnam: In 2011, Raj Rajaratnam, a hedge fund manager, was found guilty of insider trading and sentenced to 11 years in prison. He was accused of receiving information about companies such as Google and Goldman Sachs from insiders and using that information to make trades.

Michael Milken: In the 1980s, Michael Milken, a prominent financier, was accused of insider trading in connection with the junk bond market. He was fined hundreds of millions of dollars and served time in prison.

Conclusion

Insider trading is a complex issue that involves the use of privileged information to make trades in the stock market. While legal insider trading is allowed, illegal insider trading can have serious consequences and is considered unethical. As the examples above show, insider trading is a serious crime that can result in significant fines and prison time. It is important for investors to be aware of these issues and to understand the ethical concerns surrounding insider trading.

Conflicts of Interest

Conflicts of interest are a common ethical issue in finance that arise when a financial professional's personal interests or biases conflict with their professional obligations to act in their client's best interest. Such conflicts can arise in a variety of financial activities, such as investment management, banking, and securities trading, and can lead to serious consequences for both the financial professional and their clients.

In this section, we will first define conflicts of interest and describe the different types of conflicts of interest that can occur in finance. We will then discuss the ethical concerns associated with conflicts of interest and explore real-world examples of conflicts of interest in finance.

Definition of Conflicts of Interest

A conflict of interest occurs when a financial professional's personal interests or biases interfere with their professional duties to act in their client's best interest. In finance, conflicts of interest can occur in various ways, such as when a financial professional:

Receives personal financial gain from a financial transaction with a client
Has a personal relationship with a client that may influence their decision-making
Represents two parties with opposing interests in a transaction
Acts on behalf of a client while also having a financial interest in the outcome of the transaction
Types of Conflicts of Interest in Finance

There are several types of conflicts of interest that can arise in finance. The most common types include:

Self-Dealing
Self-dealing occurs when a financial professional uses their position to benefit themselves financially at the expense of their clients. For example, a financial advisor may recommend high-commission products to their clients, even if these products are not in the clients' best interest but generate significant commissions for the advisor.

Personal Relationships
Personal relationships can create conflicts of interest when a financial professional allows their personal relationships to influence their professional decisions. For example, a banker may give preferential treatment to their family members or close friends when approving loans or offering investment opportunities.

Dual Representation
Dual representation occurs when a financial professional represents two parties with opposing interests in a transaction. For example, a real estate

agent may represent both the buyer and seller in a transaction, potentially leading to a conflict of interest.

Financial Interest

A financial interest conflict arises when a financial professional has a financial interest in the outcome of a transaction. For example, an investment banker may recommend a merger or acquisition to a client because it would result in a large fee for the investment bank, rather than because it is the best decision for the client.

Ethical Concerns Surrounding Conflicts of Interest

Conflicts of interest in finance raise several ethical concerns, including:

Fairness and Equity

Conflicts of interest can result in unequal treatment of clients, where some clients receive preferential treatment at the expense of others. This can erode trust in financial professionals and the financial industry as a whole.

Misaligned Incentives

When a financial professional's personal interests are not aligned with their client's interests, the financial professional may act in ways that are not in the client's best interest. This can result in financial harm to the client and damage to the financial professional's reputation.

Lack of Transparency

Conflicts of interest can often be hidden from clients, making it difficult for them to make informed decisions about their finances. This lack of transparency can also contribute to mistrust and undermine the integrity of the financial industry.

Examples of Conflicts of Interest in Finance

There have been several high-profile examples of conflicts of interest in finance. Here are a few:

Wells Fargo Account Opening Scandal

In 2016, it was revealed that Wells Fargo employees had opened millions of fake bank accounts in order to meet sales targets and earn bonuses. This was a clear example of self-dealing, where employees prioritized their own financial interests over the interests of their clients and the reputation of the bank. The scandal resulted in a $185 million fine and the resignation of several top executives.

Goldman Sachs Abacus Deal

In 2010, the US Securities and Exchange Commission (SEC) accused Goldman Sachs of misleading investors in the sale of a mortgage-backed security called Abacus. The SEC alleged that Goldman had created the security in collaboration with hedge fund manager John Paulson, who had taken a short position against it, without disclosing this fact to investors. This created a conflict of interest, as Goldman had a financial incentive to sell the security even though it was unlikely to perform well. Goldman eventually settled the case for $550 million.

JPMorgan Chase London Whale

In 2012, JPMorgan Chase suffered massive losses on a portfolio of complex derivatives trades made by a London-based trader known as the "London Whale." The trades had been made with the bank's own funds, and the trader had reportedly been able to bypass the bank's risk controls. The scandal led to a $6.2 billion loss for JPMorgan Chase and raised questions about conflicts of interest within the bank.

Conclusion

Conflicts of interest are a pervasive problem in finance, and can have serious consequences for individuals, companies, and the economy as a whole. It is important for financial professionals to be aware of the types of conflicts of interest that can arise in their work, and to take steps to mitigate them. This may involve implementing policies and procedures to ensure that employees act in the best interests of their clients, avoiding situations where personal financial interests could conflict with professional obligations, and being transparent about potential conflicts of interest. By addressing conflicts of interest proactively and ethically, the finance industry can help to build trust and confidence among investors and the public.

Corporate Social Responsibility

Corporate social responsibility (CSR) is a concept that has gained a significant amount of attention in the business world in recent years. The term refers to the responsibility of corporations to consider the interests of their stakeholders, including customers, employees, suppliers, shareholders, and the wider community, in their decision-making processes. In the finance industry, CSR is particularly important, as financial institutions have a significant impact on the economy and society as a whole. This section will explore the definition of CSR, its importance in finance, ethical concerns surrounding CSR, and examples of CSR in finance.

Definition of Corporate Social Responsibility

Corporate social responsibility (CSR) is a concept that refers to the responsibility of corporations to operate in a way that is beneficial to society as a whole. This includes taking into account the interests of all stakeholders, including customers, employees, suppliers, shareholders, and the wider community, in their decision-making processes. CSR involves companies taking an active role in addressing social and environmental issues, such as poverty, inequality, and climate change, through their operations, policies, and practices.

Importance of Corporate Social Responsibility in Finance

In the finance industry, CSR is particularly important due to the significant impact that financial institutions have on the economy and society as a whole. Financial institutions have a responsibility to ensure that their actions contribute to the well-being of society and the environment, rather than just the bottom line. Here are a few reasons why CSR is important in finance:

Reputation: A strong reputation is vital for financial institutions to attract and retain clients. CSR can help to enhance a company's reputation by demonstrating its commitment to social and environmental issues.

Regulatory compliance: Financial institutions are subject to numerous regulations, and CSR can help them to comply with these regulations by ensuring that they operate in a socially responsible and ethical manner.

Risk management: CSR can also help financial institutions to manage risk by identifying potential social and environmental risks associated with their operations and implementing strategies to mitigate them.

Long-term sustainability: CSR is essential for the long-term sustainability of financial institutions. By operating in a socially responsible and sustainable manner, financial institutions can ensure that they remain profitable in the long-term and contribute to the well-being of society.

Ethical Concerns Surrounding Corporate Social Responsibility

Despite the many benefits of CSR, there are also ethical concerns associated with the concept. Some of the main ethical concerns surrounding CSR include:

Greenwashing: This refers to companies engaging in CSR activities solely for the purpose of improving their image, rather than out of a genuine commitment to social and environmental issues.

Conflicts of interest: Financial institutions may prioritize their own financial interests over their CSR commitments, leading to conflicts of interest.

Lack of accountability: There is often a lack of accountability and transparency in CSR practices, making it difficult for stakeholders to evaluate the true impact of a company's CSR initiatives.

Resource allocation: Financial institutions may allocate resources to CSR activities that are not aligned with the interests of their stakeholders, leading to inefficiencies and waste.

Examples of Corporate Social Responsibility in Finance

Despite the ethical concerns associated with CSR, there are many examples of financial institutions engaging in socially responsible practices. Here are a few examples:

Environmental sustainability: Many financial institutions are taking steps to reduce their environmental footprint, such as investing in renewable energy and implementing energy-efficient practices.

Social impact investing: Some financial institutions are investing in social impact initiatives, such as affordable housing and community development projects.

Ethical investing: Financial institutions are increasingly offering ethical investment options that allow clients to invest in companies that align with their values.

Corporate philanthropy: Financial institutions often engage in corporate philanthropy, such as donating to charities and community organizations.

Conclusion

Corporate social responsibility (CSR) is a concept that is becoming increasingly important in the finance industry. As businesses become more aware of their impact on society and the environment, the need for ethical and responsible behavior is becoming more pressing. By incorporating CSR into their operations, companies can not only benefit society and the environment but also improve their reputation and financial performance in the long run.

However, there are also ethical concerns surrounding CSR. Some critics argue that it can be used as a way for companies to appear ethical and socially responsible without actually making meaningful changes to their operations. Additionally, the focus on CSR can sometimes detract from other important ethical considerations, such as fair labor practices and avoiding conflicts of interest.

Despite these concerns, the trend towards incorporating CSR into the finance industry is likely to continue, driven by consumer demand and the need to address pressing social and environmental issues. As such, it is important for finance professionals to remain aware of the ethical considerations involved in CSR and to work towards making meaningful changes that benefit society as a whole.

Overall, ethical considerations are a critical part of the finance industry. As businesses and financial professionals navigate complex financial transactions and decisions, it is important to keep in mind the potential impact on all stakeholders involved, including investors, clients, employees, and the broader community. By prioritizing ethical behavior and decision-making, finance professionals can not only avoid legal and reputational risks but also contribute to a more just and sustainable financial system.

Ethical Decision Making

In the world of finance, ethical decision making is a critical component of ensuring that individuals and organizations act in a responsible and trustworthy manner. It involves considering the implications of one's actions and decisions on stakeholders, including clients, shareholders, employees, and society as a whole. This section will explore the factors that influence ethical decision making in finance, the steps involved in making ethical decisions, and a case study of ethical decision making in finance.

Factors Influencing Ethical Decision Making in Finance

There are several factors that can influence ethical decision making in finance. These include:

Personal values and beliefs: Personal values and beliefs can play a significant role in ethical decision making. Individuals who have strong ethical beliefs are more likely to make ethical decisions.

Organizational culture: The culture of an organization can influence ethical decision making. Organizations that prioritize ethical behavior are more likely to have employees who make ethical decisions.

Incentives and rewards: Incentives and rewards can also influence ethical decision making. For example, if an organization rewards employees for meeting sales targets, employees may be more likely to engage in unethical behavior to meet those targets.

Legal and regulatory requirements: Legal and regulatory requirements can also influence ethical decision making. Individuals and organizations must comply with the law and regulations, and failure to do so can have significant consequences.

Social norms: Social norms can influence ethical decision making. If unethical behavior is widely accepted in a particular industry or society, individuals may be more likely to engage in such behavior.

Steps for Making Ethical Decisions in Finance

Making ethical decisions in finance involves several steps. The following are the key steps that individuals and organizations can take to make ethical decisions:

Identify the ethical dilemma: The first step in making an ethical decision is to identify the ethical dilemma. This involves understanding the issue at hand and recognizing the potential consequences of different courses of action.

Gather information: Once the ethical dilemma has been identified, the next step is to gather information about the issue. This involves researching the relevant laws and regulations, consulting with experts, and gathering all relevant data.

Identify alternatives: After gathering information, the next step is to identify alternative courses of action. This involves considering all possible options and weighing the potential benefits and drawbacks of each.

Evaluate the alternatives: Once alternatives have been identified, the next step is to evaluate them. This involves assessing the potential consequences of each option and determining which course of action is most likely to result in the best outcome.

Make a decision: After evaluating the alternatives, the next step is to make a decision. This involves choosing the course of action that is most likely to result in the best outcome while also taking into account ethical considerations.

Implement the decision: The final step is to implement the decision. This involves putting the chosen course of action into practice and monitoring the outcome to ensure that it aligns with ethical considerations.

Case Study of Ethical Decision Making in Finance

One example of ethical decision making in finance is the case of Goldman Sachs and the 1MDB scandal. In this case, Goldman Sachs was accused of playing a key role in the 1MDB scandal, which involved the embezzlement of billions of dollars from a Malaysian government investment fund. Goldman Sachs helped to raise $6.5 billion for the fund, and received $600 million in fees for its work. However, the funds were allegedly misused, and Goldman Sachs was accused of ignoring warning signs and failing to conduct proper due diligence.

The ethical dilemma in this case involved whether Goldman Sachs should have raised funds for the 1MDB fund, given the potential for fraud and misconduct. The steps involved in making an ethical decision in this case could have included:

Identifying the ethical dilemma The first step in making an ethical decision in this case would be to identify the ethical dilemma. In this case, the ethical dilemma was whether or not Goldman Sachs should have raised funds for the 1MDB fund, given the potential for fraud and misconduct.

Gathering information
Once the ethical dilemma has been identified, the next step is to gather all relevant information related to the situation. This would include

understanding the goals of the 1MDB fund, the potential risks associated with the fund, and the regulatory requirements and guidelines for raising funds for such a project.

Analyzing the situation

After gathering all relevant information, the next step is to analyze the situation and assess the potential consequences of the different courses of action. This would involve considering the potential benefits and risks associated with raising funds for the 1MDB fund, as well as the potential impact on stakeholders such as investors, regulators, and the public.

Considering ethical principles

The next step in making an ethical decision is to consider ethical principles and values that are relevant to the situation. This would involve considering principles such as honesty, integrity, and accountability, as well as the potential impact on stakeholders such as investors, regulators, and the public.

Making a decision

After analyzing the situation and considering ethical principles, the next step is to make a decision. In this case, the decision would involve whether or not to raise funds for the 1MDB fund, given the potential risks and ethical concerns.

Taking action

Once a decision has been made, the final step is to take action. This would involve implementing the decision and monitoring the situation to ensure that the ethical principles are upheld and that the potential risks are minimized.

In the case of Goldman Sachs and the 1MDB scandal, it is clear that the ethical decision-making process was not followed. Goldman Sachs was accused of ignoring warning signs and failing to conduct proper due diligence before raising funds for the 1MDB fund. This highlights the importance of ethical decision making in finance, and the need for financial institutions to prioritize ethical principles and values in their business practices.

Regulation and Enforcement

The financial sector is heavily regulated by various regulatory agencies to ensure that ethical standards are upheld. Some of the key regulatory agencies involved in ethical issues in finance include:

Securities and Exchange Commission (SEC): The SEC is a federal agency responsible for regulating the securities industry, which includes stocks, bonds, and other financial instruments. The SEC is responsible for enforcing the Securities Act of 1933 and the Securities Exchange Act of 1934, which require companies to disclose important financial information and prohibit fraudulent and manipulative practices in the securities market.

Financial Industry Regulatory Authority (FINRA): FINRA is a self-regulatory organization (SRO) that regulates the brokerage industry. FINRA sets ethical standards for brokers and brokerage firms and enforces those standards through disciplinary actions, fines, and suspensions.

Federal Reserve System (the Fed): The Fed is responsible for regulating and supervising banks and other financial institutions. It oversees the safety and soundness of the banking system and ensures that banks comply with federal laws and regulations.

Consumer Financial Protection Bureau (CFPB): The CFPB is a federal agency responsible for protecting consumers from unfair, deceptive, or abusive practices in the financial industry. The CFPB regulates a wide range of financial products and services, including mortgages, credit cards, and student loans.

Enforcement of Ethical Regulations in Finance

Regulatory agencies play a critical role in enforcing ethical regulations in finance. Some of the key enforcement mechanisms used by regulatory agencies include:

Inspections and audits: Regulatory agencies conduct inspections and audits of financial firms to ensure that they are complying with ethical regulations. These inspections may involve reviewing financial records, interviewing employees, and examining business practices.

Investigations: Regulatory agencies have the authority to investigate potential violations of ethical regulations. Investigations may involve collecting evidence, interviewing witnesses, and analyzing financial data.

Disciplinary actions: If a financial firm is found to have violated ethical regulations, regulatory agencies can take disciplinary actions, such as fines, suspensions, or revoking licenses. These actions are intended to deter future violations and hold firms accountable for their actions.

Effectiveness of Regulatory Agencies in Addressing Ethical Issues in Finance

While regulatory agencies play a critical role in upholding ethical standards in finance, there is ongoing debate about their effectiveness. Some argue that regulatory agencies are too slow to respond to emerging ethical issues and that their enforcement mechanisms are too weak to deter bad actors. Others argue that regulatory agencies are too heavy-handed and impose unnecessary burdens on financial firms, which can stifle innovation and growth.

There are several factors that can influence the effectiveness of regulatory agencies in addressing ethical issues in finance, including:

Regulatory capture: Regulatory capture occurs when regulatory agencies become too closely aligned with the industries they regulate, leading to a reluctance to enforce regulations or a bias towards industry interests.

Lack of resources: Regulatory agencies may not have sufficient resources, such as funding and staff, to effectively enforce ethical regulations.

Complexity of regulations: The financial sector is highly complex, and regulations can be difficult to interpret and enforce. This can make it challenging for regulatory agencies to keep up with emerging ethical issues.

Political pressure: Regulatory agencies may be subject to political pressure from elected officials, which can influence their decision-making and enforcement actions.

Overall, while regulatory agencies play an important role in upholding ethical standards in finance, there are ongoing challenges in ensuring their effectiveness.

Conclusion

Regulation and enforcement are critical components of ensuring ethical standards in finance. Regulatory agencies play a critical role in setting ethical standards, enforcing regulations, and holding financial firms accountable for their actions. However, there are ongoing challenges to ensuring the effectiveness of regulatory agencies, including regulatory capture, lack of resources, complexity of regulations, and the constant evolution of the financial industry.

Despite these challenges, there are steps that can be taken to improve regulation and enforcement in finance. These include:

Increasing transparency: One of the most effective ways to prevent ethical violations is to increase transparency in financial transactions. This can be accomplished through more thorough reporting requirements, standardized accounting practices, and public disclosures of financial information.

Strengthening regulatory agencies: Regulatory agencies must have the resources, expertise, and independence necessary to effectively regulate the financial industry. This includes recruiting and retaining top talent, investing in technology and data analysis tools, and creating a culture of accountability and transparency.

Encouraging industry self-regulation: In addition to government regulation, financial firms can also take a more active role in regulating themselves. This can be accomplished through the development of industry-wide standards and codes of conduct, as well as the establishment of independent monitoring bodies.

Addressing regulatory capture: Regulatory capture occurs when regulatory agencies become too closely aligned with the interests of the industries they regulate. To address this, regulators must remain independent and vigilant in monitoring the industry, and should be subject to oversight and accountability measures.

Fostering a culture of ethics: Ultimately, the most effective way to prevent ethical violations in finance is to foster a culture of ethics within the industry. This requires a commitment to ethical behavior from all stakeholders, including financial firms, regulators, investors, and the general public.

In conclusion, regulation and enforcement are critical components of ensuring ethical standards in finance. While there are ongoing challenges to effective regulation and enforcement, there are also steps that can be taken to improve the effectiveness of regulatory agencies and promote ethical behavior within the financial industry. By working together, stakeholders can help to create a financial system that is more transparent, accountable, and ethical.

Future of Ethical Issues in Finance

Ethical issues in finance have been a concern for many years, and despite efforts to address them, they continue to pose a challenge to the industry. As the financial landscape evolves and new technologies are introduced, it is important to consider potential future ethical issues that may arise, as well as potential solutions to address these issues. In this section, we will explore some potential future ethical issues in finance, potential solutions to address these issues, and the impact of technology on ethical issues in finance.

Potential Future Ethical Issues in Finance

Artificial Intelligence and Bias
Artificial intelligence (AI) is becoming increasingly prevalent in the finance industry, and while it has the potential to improve efficiency and accuracy, it also poses ethical concerns. One such concern is the potential for bias in AI systems. If AI systems are trained on biased data, they may perpetuate and amplify existing biases. For example, if an AI system is trained on historical loan data that contains bias against certain groups of people, the system may unfairly deny loans to those groups in the future.

Cybersecurity and Data Privacy
As more financial transactions take place online, cybersecurity and data privacy become more critical. Cyber attacks can lead to the theft of sensitive financial information, which can be used for fraud or identity theft. Additionally, the collection and use of personal financial data raises concerns about privacy and data protection.

Climate Change and Environmental Risk
Climate change poses a significant risk to the financial system, and as such, it is becoming an increasingly important issue for financial institutions to address. Financial institutions may be exposed to environmental risks, such as physical risks (e.g., damage to property from extreme weather events) or transition risks (e.g., changes in regulation or technology that could lead to stranded assets).

Social Responsibility and Impact Investing
Social responsibility and impact investing are becoming increasingly important to investors, particularly younger generations. Investors are increasingly looking for ways to align their investments with their values and promote positive social and environmental impact. However, there is a risk that these investments may be used for greenwashing or other forms of deception.

Potential Solutions to Address Future Ethical Issues in Finance

Ethical AI

To address potential bias in AI systems, financial institutions can take steps to ensure that their systems are trained on unbiased data and that they are regularly audited for bias. Additionally, they can implement processes to ensure that AI systems are transparent and explainable, so that users can understand how decisions are being made.

Stronger Cybersecurity and Data Privacy Measures

To address cybersecurity and data privacy concerns, financial institutions can implement strong security measures, such as two-factor authentication and encryption, and regularly test their systems for vulnerabilities. Additionally, they can be transparent with customers about how their data is being used and provide them with the ability to control their data.

Climate Risk Assessment and Disclosure

To address environmental risks, financial institutions can conduct climate risk assessments and disclose their exposure to environmental risks. They can also work to develop products and services that promote sustainability and support the transition to a low-carbon economy.

Ethical Investing Standards

To address concerns about social responsibility and impact investing, financial institutions can develop and adhere to ethical investing standards, such as the United Nations Principles for Responsible Investment. They can also be transparent with investors about the impact of their investments and ensure that their investments align with their stated values.

Impact of Technology on Ethical Issues in Finance

Technology has the potential to both exacerbate and address ethical issues in finance. On the one hand, as we have seen, AI and cybersecurity pose ethical concerns. On the other hand, technology can also be used to address these concerns. For example, blockchain technology can be used to enhance transparency and reduce the risk of fraud in financial transactions. Additionally, machine learning can be used to improve risk management and compliance, thereby reducing the potential for unethical behavior.

However, there are also concerns that technology may amplify existing inequalities in the financial industry, as access to advanced technology and data analytics may give some firms an unfair advantage over others. This could lead to market distortions and potentially unethical practices. Additionally, the increasing use of automated decision-making algorithms raises concerns about bias and discrimination.

To address these concerns, it will be important for regulatory agencies to keep pace with technological advancements and ensure that ethical standards are upheld in the use of new technologies in finance. It will also be important for financial firms to prioritize ethical considerations in their use of technology, and to work to mitigate any potential negative impacts.

Overall, the future of ethical issues in finance will depend on the ability of regulatory agencies, financial firms, and other stakeholders to adapt to new challenges and prioritize ethical considerations in decision-making. By remaining vigilant and proactive in addressing emerging ethical issues, we can work towards a more ethical and sustainable financial system.

Conclusion

Ethical issues in finance are complex and multifaceted, and they require a comprehensive approach to address them effectively. In this chapter, we have discussed various ethical issues in finance, including conflicts of interest, insider trading, and the use of AI and other technologies in finance. We have also discussed the importance of regulatory agencies in promoting ethical behavior and enforcing regulations, as well as the potential impact of technology on ethical issues in finance.

Summary of Key Points

Conflicts of interest can arise when financial professionals have personal or financial interests that conflict with the interests of their clients.

Insider trading involves the use of non-public information to make trades or other financial transactions, which can harm investors and undermine market integrity.

AI and other technologies pose ethical concerns in finance, including issues related to data privacy, bias, and cybersecurity.

Regulatory agencies play a critical role in setting ethical standards, enforcing regulations, and holding financial firms accountable for their actions.

There are ongoing challenges to ensuring the effectiveness of regulatory agencies, including regulatory capture, lack of resources, and complexity of regulations.

Technology has the potential to both exacerbate and address ethical issues in finance.

Final Thoughts and Recommendations

In order to promote ethics in finance, it is important to take a comprehensive approach that addresses the underlying causes of ethical issues. This includes addressing conflicts of interest, improving transparency and accountability, and promoting ethical behavior and culture within financial firms.

Some specific recommendations for promoting ethics in finance include:

Improving regulatory oversight: Regulatory agencies should be given the resources and authority necessary to effectively enforce regulations and hold financial firms accountable for their actions.

Enhancing transparency and accountability: Financial firms should be required to disclose conflicts of interest and other potential ethical issues, and should be held accountable for any unethical behavior.

Promoting ethical culture: Financial firms should develop and promote a culture of ethics and integrity, with clear policies and procedures for addressing ethical issues.

Encouraging ethical behavior: Financial professionals should be incentivized to act in the best interests of their clients, and should be held accountable for any unethical behavior.

Embracing technology: While technology can pose ethical concerns, it also has the potential to address ethical issues in finance. Financial firms should embrace technology that enhances transparency and accountability, while also taking steps to mitigate potential risks.

In conclusion, promoting ethics in finance is critical for maintaining trust in financial markets and protecting investors. While there are ongoing challenges to ensuring ethical behavior, there are also many opportunities for improvement through regulatory oversight, transparency and accountability, ethical culture, and technology. By taking a comprehensive approach to addressing ethical issues, we can help ensure that financial markets operate in a fair and ethical manner for the benefit of all stakeholders.

CHAPTER 14 MICROFINANCE

Introduction to Microfinance

Microfinance is a term that refers to the provision of financial services to people who are typically excluded from traditional banking systems. It has become an important tool for promoting financial inclusion and reducing poverty in developing countries. In this section, we will explore what microfinance is, its history, the types of microfinance institutions, and the benefits and challenges of microfinance.

What is Microfinance?

Microfinance is the provision of financial services to low-income individuals or groups who do not have access to traditional banking services. These services can include small loans, savings accounts, insurance, and money transfers. The goal of microfinance is to empower people to improve their economic well-being and reduce poverty.

Microfinance institutions (MFIs) provide financial services to clients who do not have collateral or a credit history, and who may be considered high-risk borrowers by traditional banks. MFIs use alternative methods to assess borrowers' creditworthiness, such as peer group lending or social collateral. These methods can be effective in reducing the risks associated with lending to people without collateral or a credit history.

History of Microfinance

The origins of microfinance can be traced back to the 19th century when savings and credit cooperatives were established in Germany, Italy, and France. However, the modern microfinance movement began in the 1970s when Professor Muhammad Yunus, a Bangladeshi economist, started providing small loans to poor women in rural Bangladesh.

Professor Yunus founded the Grameen Bank in 1983 to provide microcredit to the poor. The Grameen Bank model uses peer group lending, where borrowers form groups and guarantee each other's loans. This model has been replicated in many countries around the world and has become the most well-known and successful microfinance model.

Types of Microfinance Institutions

There are different types of microfinance institutions that provide financial services to the poor. These institutions include:

Non-Governmental Organizations (NGOs): These organizations are typically involved in community development and provide microfinance services as part of their overall mission.

Cooperatives: These are member-owned financial institutions that provide financial services to their members. They are typically focused on a particular community or region.

Commercial Banks: Some commercial banks have started providing microfinance services to low-income clients. However, these banks may not be as effective as specialized microfinance institutions in serving the needs of the poor.

Benefits of Microfinance

Microfinance has many potential benefits for both individuals and society. Some of these benefits include:

Poverty reduction: Microfinance can help reduce poverty by providing people with the means to start or expand their own businesses, generate income, and improve their standard of living.

Financial inclusion: Microfinance can promote financial inclusion by providing financial services to people who are excluded from traditional banking systems.

Empowerment: Microfinance can empower women and other marginalized groups by providing them with access to financial resources and the ability to make their own economic decisions.

Social capital: Microfinance can promote the formation of social capital by encouraging borrowers to form groups and work together to achieve their economic goals.

Challenges of Microfinance

While microfinance has the potential to bring many benefits, there are also several challenges that must be addressed. Some of these challenges include:

Sustainability: Microfinance institutions must be financially sustainable in order to continue providing services to the poor. Many institutions struggle to achieve financial sustainability due to the high costs associated with serving low-income clients.

Over-indebtedness: Microfinance can lead to over-indebtedness if borrowers take on too much debt and are unable to repay their loans.

Lack of regulation: The lack of regulation in some countries has led to the proliferation of unregulated microfinance institutions that may engage in predatory lending practices or charge exorbitant interest rates, leading to borrower exploitation and financial distress.

Gender disparities: Women are often disproportionately affected by poverty and have limited access to financial services, including microfinance. However, microfinance has also been shown to empower women and promote gender equality.

Limited impact: Microfinance alone is not a panacea for poverty and may have limited impact in addressing the root causes of poverty, such as lack of education, healthcare, and infrastructure.

Lack of financial literacy: Microfinance clients may have limited financial literacy, which can lead to poor financial decision-making and increased vulnerability to financial shocks.

Cultural barriers: In some cultures, there may be social and cultural barriers to accepting loans or participating in financial activities, particularly for women.

The challenges faced by microfinance institutions vary depending on the context, and there is no one-size-fits-all solution to addressing these challenges. However, there are several strategies that can be employed to promote sustainable and responsible microfinance practices.

Strategies for Promoting Responsible Microfinance

Financial inclusion is a critical component of poverty reduction, and microfinance has the potential to play an important role in promoting financial inclusion. However, to ensure that microfinance is effective and responsible, several strategies can be employed, including:

Regulation: Regulatory frameworks can help ensure that microfinance institutions operate in a responsible and sustainable manner. Regulations can also protect borrowers from exploitation and promote fair lending practices. However, regulations must be balanced to avoid stifling innovation and restricting access to finance.

Financial education: Providing financial education to microfinance clients can help promote financial literacy and responsible financial decision-making. This can include basic financial education, such as budgeting and saving, as well as education on financial products and services.

Technology: The use of technology, such as mobile banking and digital payments, can help reduce the costs associated with serving low-income clients and promote financial inclusion. However, technology must be implemented responsibly and ethically to ensure that it does not exacerbate existing inequalities.

Collaboration: Collaboration between microfinance institutions, governments, and other stakeholders can help promote responsible microfinance practices and improve the effectiveness of microfinance in reducing poverty.

Impact assessment: Measuring the impact of microfinance on poverty reduction is critical to ensuring that microfinance is effective and responsible. Impact assessments can help identify areas for improvement and promote best practices.

Conclusion

Microfinance has the potential to promote financial inclusion and poverty reduction, but it also faces several challenges, including sustainability, over-indebtedness, lack of regulation, gender disparities, limited impact, lack of financial literacy, and cultural barriers. To promote responsible microfinance practices, several strategies can be employed, including regulation, financial education, technology, collaboration, and impact assessment. By implementing these strategies, microfinance can be an effective tool for promoting financial inclusion and reducing poverty.

Importance of Microfinance

Microfinance has become an increasingly popular tool for alleviating poverty in low-income communities around the world. This financial service is designed to provide access to financial products, such as loans and savings accounts, to individuals and small businesses who may not have access to traditional banking services. The importance of microfinance lies in its ability to empower people, stimulate economic growth, and reduce poverty.

Providing Access to Financial Services:

One of the key benefits of microfinance is its ability to provide access to financial services for individuals and small businesses who would otherwise be excluded from traditional banking services. In many low-income communities, traditional banks do not provide services to people who lack collateral, credit history, or a stable income. Microfinance institutions (MFIs) are specifically designed to provide financial services to these underserved communities.

Empowering Low-Income Individuals and Small Businesses:

Microfinance is an important tool for empowering low-income individuals and small businesses. By providing access to financial services, MFIs help people to become more self-reliant and independent. This, in turn, helps to reduce their dependence on welfare programs and other forms of assistance.

Microfinance also helps to empower small businesses by providing them with the necessary funding to start or expand their businesses. Small businesses are often the engines of economic growth in low-income communities, and microfinance can help to support their growth and development.

Economic Growth and Poverty Reduction:

Microfinance can stimulate economic growth in low-income communities by providing access to funding for small businesses. By supporting small businesses, microfinance can help to create jobs, increase incomes, and improve living standards.

In addition to promoting economic growth, microfinance can also help to reduce poverty. Studies have shown that access to financial services can help to improve household incomes and reduce poverty. This is because access to financial services can help people to build assets, start businesses, and manage financial risks.

Challenges and Criticisms of Microfinance:

While microfinance has many benefits, it also faces several challenges and criticisms. Some of these include:

Sustainability: Many MFIs struggle to achieve financial sustainability due to the high costs associated with serving low-income clients. In order to remain sustainable, MFIs must find ways to reduce costs and generate revenue.

Over-indebtedness: Microfinance can lead to over-indebtedness if borrowers take on too much debt and are unable to repay their loans. This can lead to a cycle of debt and poverty, which can be difficult to break.

Lack of regulation: The lack of regulation in some countries has led to the proliferation of unregulated microfinance institutions that may engage in predatory lending practices.

Conclusion:

Despite the challenges and criticisms, microfinance has proven to be an effective tool for promoting economic growth and reducing poverty in low-income communities. By providing access to financial services, microfinance institutions empower low-income individuals and small businesses, promote economic growth, and reduce poverty. While there is still much work to be done to address the challenges and criticisms of microfinance, its potential for positive impact on the lives of the poor cannot be ignored.

Types of Microfinance Institutions

Microfinance institutions (MFIs) are organizations that provide financial services to low-income individuals and small businesses. There are several types of microfinance institutions, each with its own unique characteristics and advantages. In this section, we will discuss four types of microfinance institutions: microfinance banks, non-governmental organizations (NGOs), credit unions, and cooperatives.

Microfinance Banks

Microfinance banks are financial institutions that specialize in providing financial services to low-income individuals and small businesses. They are similar to traditional banks, but with a focus on serving low-income clients. Microfinance banks offer a range of financial products and services, including savings accounts, loans, and insurance.

One advantage of microfinance banks is that they are often better equipped to handle the needs of low-income clients than traditional banks. For example, microfinance banks may offer smaller loans than traditional banks, which are more manageable for low-income clients. Additionally, microfinance banks may have more flexible loan terms, such as lower interest rates or longer repayment periods, which can make loans more accessible for low-income clients.

Non-Governmental Organizations (NGOs)

Non-governmental organizations (NGOs) are organizations that are independent of government control and are typically funded by donations from individuals, corporations, or governments. NGOs may provide a range of services, including healthcare, education, and social services. Some NGOs also provide microfinance services to low-income individuals and small businesses.

One advantage of NGOs is that they often have a strong focus on social responsibility and are committed to helping disadvantaged communities. As a result, NGOs may be more willing to work with individuals and businesses that traditional banks would consider too high-risk. Additionally, NGOs may offer more personalized service than other microfinance institutions, as they may have a smaller client base and a more local focus.

Credit Unions

Credit unions are member-owned financial cooperatives that provide financial services to their members. They are similar to banks, but instead of being owned by shareholders, they are owned by their members. Credit unions offer a range of financial products and services, including savings accounts, loans, and insurance.

One advantage of credit unions is that they are typically more accessible to low-income clients than traditional banks. Credit unions often have lower fees and interest rates than traditional banks, which can make financial services more affordable for low-income clients. Additionally, credit unions may offer more flexible loan terms than traditional banks, which can make loans more accessible to low-income clients.

Cooperatives

Cooperatives are member-owned organizations that provide a range of services to their members, including financial services. Cooperatives may be formed for a variety of reasons, including to provide financial services to low-income individuals and small businesses.

One advantage of cooperatives is that they are typically more responsive to the needs of their members than traditional banks. Cooperatives are owned and operated by their members, which means that they have a vested interest in providing services that meet the needs of their members. Additionally, cooperatives may offer more flexible loan terms than traditional banks, which can make loans more accessible to low-income clients.

Conclusion

In conclusion, microfinance institutions play an important role in providing financial services to low-income individuals and small businesses. There are several types of microfinance institutions, each with its own unique characteristics and advantages. Microfinance banks, NGOs, credit unions, and cooperatives all have a role to play in promoting financial inclusion and reducing poverty. By providing access to financial services and empowering low-income individuals and small businesses, microfinance institutions can help to promote economic growth and reduce poverty around the world.

Microfinance Products and Services

Microfinance institutions offer a variety of financial products and services to help low-income individuals and small businesses gain access to capital and improve their economic situations. In this section, we will discuss the four primary microfinance products and services: microcredit, microsavings, microinsurance, and microleasing.

Microcredit

Microcredit is perhaps the most well-known microfinance product, and it involves providing small loans to low-income individuals who are typically unable to access traditional banking services. Microcredit loans are usually used to start or expand a small business or to meet other financial needs, such as paying for education or healthcare expenses.

Microcredit loans are generally small, ranging from a few hundred dollars to a few thousand dollars. They are also typically short-term loans, with repayment periods of a few weeks to a few months. Microcredit loans often come with higher interest rates than traditional bank loans, as they are riskier for the lender due to the lack of collateral and credit history of the borrower.

While microcredit has been successful in helping many low-income individuals and small businesses access capital and grow their businesses, it is not without its challenges. One of the primary challenges of microcredit is over-indebtedness, which occurs when borrowers take on too much debt and are unable to repay their loans. This can lead to financial distress for both the borrower and the lender, and it can also harm the overall microfinance industry.

Microsavings

Microsavings is another important microfinance product, which involves providing low-income individuals with a safe and convenient place to save their money. Microsavings accounts are designed to be accessible and affordable, with low minimum balances and no or low fees.

Microsavings accounts can help low-income individuals build up their savings and improve their financial security. This can be especially important in times of economic instability or unexpected expenses, such as healthcare or education costs.

In addition to helping individuals save money, microsavings can also be an important source of funding for microfinance institutions. By mobilizing savings from their clients, microfinance institutions can reduce their dependence on external funding sources and increase their financial sustainability.

Microinsurance

Microinsurance is a relatively new microfinance product, which involves providing low-income individuals with insurance products designed to protect against financial shocks. Microinsurance products may include health insurance, life insurance, crop insurance, or other types of insurance tailored to the needs of the target population.

Microinsurance can help protect low-income individuals from financial risks and improve their overall economic security. For example, health insurance can help cover the costs of unexpected medical expenses, while crop insurance can protect farmers from losses due to weather or other factors outside of their control.

One of the challenges of microinsurance is designing products that are both affordable and effective. Microinsurance products must be priced in a way that is accessible to low-income individuals, while also providing adequate coverage to protect against financial shocks. This can be a delicate balance, and it requires careful product design and pricing.

Microleasing

Microleasing is another microfinance product that is designed to help small businesses access capital. Microleasing involves leasing equipment or other assets to small businesses, which allows them to access the assets they need without having to make a large upfront investment.

Microleasing can be especially important for businesses that require expensive equipment or other assets to operate, such as agricultural businesses or manufacturing businesses. By leasing the assets they need, these businesses can avoid the high upfront costs of purchasing the assets outright, which can be a significant barrier to entry.

One of the challenges of microleasing is ensuring that the leased assets are well-maintained and that the leasing arrangements are transparent and fair. Microleasing can be more complex than other microfinance products, as it requires the microfinance institution to manage and maintain the assets being leased.

Conclusion

Microfinance products and services have the potential to improve the lives of low-income individuals and small businesses by providing access to financial services, empowering them to invest in their future and improve their economic well-being. Microcredit, microsavings, microinsurance, and microleasing are all essential components of microfinance, each with their own unique features and benefits.

While microfinance has many potential benefits, there are also challenges that must be addressed. Sustainability, over-indebtedness, lack of regulation, and ensuring transparency and fairness in microleasing arrangements are just a few of the challenges that must be navigated to ensure that microfinance products and services are effective in helping the poor.

Despite these challenges, microfinance has proven to be a powerful tool in promoting economic growth and poverty reduction. Microfinance institutions have played a critical role in expanding access to financial services for low-income individuals and small businesses, empowering them to achieve their goals and aspirations. As the field of microfinance continues to evolve and mature, it will be important to continue to address these challenges and ensure that microfinance products and services are effective, sustainable, and accessible to all who need them.

Challenges in Microfinance

Microfinance has been hailed as a tool for poverty reduction and economic empowerment for low-income individuals and small businesses. However, despite its potential, microfinance faces several challenges that limit its impact and effectiveness. In this section, we will explore some of the challenges that microfinance institutions encounter and how they can be addressed.

High Costs and Limited Resources

One of the biggest challenges facing microfinance institutions is the high costs associated with delivering financial services to low-income individuals and small businesses. This is due to several factors, including the need for personalized service, the cost of delivering services in rural or remote areas, and the cost of training and capacity building for staff and clients. In addition, many microfinance institutions operate on limited budgets and resources, which further exacerbates the challenge of high costs.

To address this challenge, microfinance institutions can consider the following strategies:

Embracing technology: Microfinance institutions can leverage technology to reduce the cost of delivering financial services. For example, digital platforms can be used to offer mobile banking, online loan applications, and other services that reduce the need for face-to-face interactions.

Building partnerships: Microfinance institutions can build partnerships with other organizations, such as banks, NGOs, and government agencies, to share resources and expertise. This can help to reduce the costs associated with delivering financial services.

Default and Credit Risk

Another challenge facing microfinance institutions is the risk of default and credit risk. Microfinance institutions often lend to individuals and small businesses with little or no credit history, which increases the risk of default. In addition, many microfinance institutions operate in high-risk environments, such as conflict-affected or disaster-prone areas, which further increases the risk of default.

To address this challenge, microfinance institutions can consider the following strategies:

Implementing strong risk management practices: Microfinance institutions can implement strong risk management practices, such as conducting credit assessments, developing risk models, and monitoring loan portfolios. This can help to reduce the risk of default and credit risk.

Diversifying loan portfolios: Microfinance institutions can diversify their loan portfolios to reduce the risk of default. For example, they can offer loans to individuals and small businesses in different sectors or industries, which spreads the risk across different borrowers.

Regulatory Issues and Government Support

Regulatory issues and government support are also major challenges facing microfinance institutions. Many microfinance institutions operate in countries with weak or inadequate regulatory frameworks, which can limit their ability to operate effectively. In addition, government support for microfinance institutions is often limited or non-existent, which can hinder their growth and sustainability.

To address this challenge, microfinance institutions can consider the following strategies:

Advocating for regulatory reform: Microfinance institutions can advocate for regulatory reform to improve the regulatory environment in which they operate. This can include lobbying for the adoption of regulations that support microfinance institutions and the clients they serve.

Building relationships with government agencies: Microfinance institutions can build relationships with government agencies to increase their visibility and access to government support. This can include collaborating on projects and programs that support the growth and sustainability of microfinance institutions.

Limited Access to Capital Markets

Limited access to capital markets is another challenge facing microfinance institutions. Many microfinance institutions operate on limited budgets and rely on donor funding or government grants to finance their operations. This limits their ability to scale their operations and reach more clients.

To address this challenge, microfinance institutions can consider the following strategies:

Attracting investment: Microfinance institutions can attract investment from private investors or capital markets to finance their operations. This can include issuing bonds, establishing investment funds, or attracting equity investors.

Developing innovative financing models: Microfinance institutions can develop innovative financing models, such as revenue-sharing agreements or social impact bonds, to attract investment and finance their operations.

Conclusion

Microfinance has emerged as a critical tool in poverty alleviation and economic development efforts worldwide, providing financial services to those who are traditionally underserved by formal financial institutions. However, microfinance is not without its challenges, and microfinance institutions must navigate complex financial and regulatory landscapes to ensure their sustainability and effectiveness.

The high costs and limited resources of microfinance institutions can limit their reach and impact, while default and credit risk can threaten their financial stability. Regulatory issues and limited government support can also pose significant challenges, as can limited access to capital markets.

To overcome these challenges, microfinance institutions can employ a variety of strategies, such as partnering with other organizations, developing innovative financing models, and attracting investment from private investors or capital markets.

Overall, the challenges facing microfinance institutions require careful consideration and management to ensure that they are able to continue providing critical financial services to those in need. By taking a proactive and strategic approach to addressing these challenges, microfinance institutions can help ensure that they are able to make a meaningful and lasting impact in the lives of the individuals and communities they serve.

Criticisms of Microfinance

Microfinance has been widely promoted as an effective tool for poverty alleviation and economic development, especially in developing countries. However, it has also been subject to criticism from various quarters, including academics, policymakers, and practitioners. In this section, we will examine some of the criticisms of microfinance and explore their validity.

High Interest Rates and Over-indebtedness

One of the most common criticisms of microfinance is that it charges high-interest rates that can lead to over-indebtedness among borrowers. While microfinance institutions often charge interest rates higher than those of commercial banks, this is primarily due to the high costs associated with serving low-income borrowers.

Counterargument:

Some proponents of microfinance argue that these interest rates are necessary to cover the high costs of microfinance operations, including the costs of loan administration, risk assessment, and borrower education. Additionally, microfinance institutions may have limited access to cheaper sources of funding due to their size and risk profile.

Lack of Sustainability and Scalability

Another criticism of microfinance is that it may not be sustainable or scalable in the long run. Many microfinance institutions have struggled to achieve financial sustainability, relying on donor funding or subsidies to continue their operations.

Counterargument:

However, some argue that the lack of financial sustainability can be attributed to factors beyond the control of microfinance institutions, such as unfavorable regulatory environments, limited access to capital markets, and the challenging socioeconomic conditions in which they operate. Microfinance institutions have been working to address these challenges, developing innovative business models and leveraging technology to improve their efficiency and scalability.

Limited Impact on Poverty Reduction

Another criticism of microfinance is that it has limited impact on poverty reduction. Some studies have found that microfinance has not significantly improved the livelihoods of poor households, particularly in terms of income and asset ownership.

Counterargument:

However, other studies have found that microfinance has had a positive impact on the welfare of poor households, including improvements in health, education, and social capital. Moreover, microfinance can be seen as just one component of a broader development strategy that includes access to education, healthcare, and other basic services.

Cultural and Social Challenges

A further criticism of microfinance is that it can perpetuate cultural and social norms that discriminate against women and other marginalized groups. For example, some microfinance programs require that loans be guaranteed by male family members, effectively excluding women from access to credit.

Counterargument:

However, many microfinance institutions have recognized these challenges and have implemented strategies to address them. For example, some institutions have developed programs specifically targeted at women and other marginalized groups, while others have worked to raise awareness of gender and social issues among their staff and clients.

Conclusion

While microfinance has been lauded as an effective tool for poverty alleviation and economic development, it is not without its critics. However, many of these criticisms can be addressed through innovative business models, improved access to capital markets, and a greater focus on social and gender issues. Overall, microfinance remains a promising approach to addressing the challenges of poverty and economic inequality in developing countries.

Future of Microfinance

Microfinance has come a long way since its inception, with a growing number of microfinance institutions and organizations working to provide financial services to individuals and small businesses around the world. While microfinance has faced its share of criticisms, it has also demonstrated the potential to empower individuals, promote economic growth, and reduce poverty. Looking ahead, there are several key trends and developments shaping the future of microfinance.

Technological Innovations and Digital Finance

One of the most significant developments in the world of microfinance is the rise of technological innovations and digital finance. With the advent of mobile banking, digital wallets, and other forms of electronic payment systems, microfinance institutions are now able to offer their services to customers in remote and underserved areas more easily and efficiently than ever before.

Digital finance also enables microfinance institutions to reach a wider customer base by lowering transaction costs and simplifying the lending process. For example, a borrower can apply for a loan online, with the entire process taking only a few minutes, rather than having to visit a physical location and wait for approval. In addition, digital finance allows for faster disbursement of funds and easier tracking of loan repayments, reducing the risk of default and credit risk.

Integration with Traditional Financial Institutions

Another trend shaping the future of microfinance is the integration of microfinance institutions with traditional financial institutions. Microfinance institutions are increasingly partnering with banks, credit unions, and other financial institutions to expand their reach and offer a wider range of financial products and services.

For example, microfinance institutions may partner with banks to offer microcredit, while banks may partner with microfinance institutions to offer savings accounts and other financial products to underserved populations. This collaboration between microfinance and traditional financial institutions can help to expand financial inclusion and improve access to credit and other financial services.

Expansion of Microfinance Services to New Markets

As microfinance institutions continue to grow and evolve, there is a growing focus on expanding microfinance services to new markets. For example, microfinance institutions are increasingly targeting women entrepreneurs, who often face significant barriers to accessing credit and financial services. Microfinance institutions are also expanding their services to rural areas, where access to financial services is often limited.

In addition, microfinance institutions are exploring new business models to serve previously underserved markets, such as migrant workers, refugees, and smallholder farmers. These new markets represent significant potential for growth in the microfinance industry and can help to promote financial inclusion and economic development.

Collaboration and Partnerships

Finally, collaboration and partnerships will continue to be critical for the future of microfinance. Microfinance institutions will need to work closely with governments, NGOs, and other organizations to address the challenges facing the industry and to expand financial inclusion.

Collaboration and partnerships can also help to improve the sustainability of microfinance institutions by providing access to resources and expertise that may be lacking within the organization. For example, partnerships with universities and research institutions can help to promote innovation and the development of new microfinance products and services.

Conclusion

In conclusion, the future of microfinance is promising, with technological innovations, integration with traditional financial institutions, expansion into new markets, and collaboration and partnerships all shaping the industry's growth and development. While microfinance has faced criticism, it has also demonstrated the potential to promote financial inclusion and reduce poverty, and it will continue to play a vital role in promoting economic development around the world.

CHAPTER 15: FINANCIAL TECHNOLOGY (FINTECH)

Introduction

The global financial landscape has been undergoing a transformational shift in recent years, with the advent of innovative financial technologies, commonly referred to as Fintech, and an increased focus on sustainable and responsible investment (SRI). These two concepts have become increasingly relevant in the financial industry, and the study of their interplay has become an area of growing interest.

This section will provide an overview of Fintech and SRI, their definitions, and why studying them is essential in today's financial landscape.

Definition of Fintech

Fintech refers to the use of technology to improve financial services and systems. It involves the application of innovative technology to the delivery of financial services, products, and solutions. Fintech companies are disrupting traditional financial institutions and have been at the forefront of providing financial services in a more efficient and cost-effective manner.

Fintech has been transforming the way we conduct financial transactions, including payments, investments, and lending. Mobile banking and payment systems, digital wallets, and online investment platforms are examples of Fintech products that have gained widespread adoption.

Definition of SRI

SRI is an investment strategy that seeks to achieve both financial returns and social and environmental objectives. It involves investing in companies that meet specific social and environmental criteria, such as those that have a positive impact on climate change, promote gender equality, or have good labor practices.

SRI investors use a variety of methods to assess a company's social and environmental performance, including negative screening (excluding companies with poor records), positive screening (including companies with good records), and engagement (actively engaging with companies to improve their social and environmental practices).

Importance of Studying Fintech and SRI

The study of Fintech and SRI is critical for several reasons.

Firstly, Fintech is rapidly transforming the financial landscape, and it is essential to understand its impact on financial markets, institutions, and consumers. The widespread adoption of digital financial services has led to significant changes in the way we manage our finances, and these changes have implications for financial stability, consumer protection, and access to financial services.

Secondly, SRI has become increasingly important as investors look for ways to achieve both financial returns and positive social and environmental impacts. As sustainability and responsible investing become more mainstream, understanding the principles and methods of SRI is crucial for financial professionals, policymakers, and investors.

Finally, the intersection of Fintech and SRI presents an exciting opportunity to develop innovative financial products and services that promote sustainable and responsible investing. By leveraging Fintech tools and technology, financial institutions can develop innovative investment products that not only deliver financial returns but also contribute to a more sustainable and equitable world.

In conclusion, the study of Fintech and SRI is essential in today's financial landscape, and it presents an opportunity to develop innovative financial products and services that promote sustainable and responsible investing. Understanding the principles and methods of these two concepts is critical for financial professionals, policymakers, and investors alike.

Financial Technology (Fintech)

Financial Technology (Fintech) is a term used to describe innovative digital solutions that have emerged in the financial sector over the past few decades. Fintech companies have been able to leverage technological advancements to create new financial services and products that are faster, more efficient, and more convenient than traditional financial services. In this section, we will provide an overview of Fintech, its history, examples of

Fintech services and products, advantages and disadvantages of Fintech, and the impact of Fintech on traditional financial institutions.

Overview of Fintech and Its History

Fintech refers to the use of technology to deliver financial services and products to consumers. Fintech companies use software and digital platforms to provide banking, investment, insurance, and other financial services. Fintech companies have been able to disrupt traditional financial services by offering faster, more convenient, and more cost-effective services. They have been able to achieve this by leveraging technological advancements such as artificial intelligence, blockchain, and machine learning.

The history of Fintech can be traced back to the emergence of the internet in the 1990s. The internet provided a platform for businesses to connect with customers without the need for a physical presence. This led to the emergence of online banking, online stock trading, and online insurance services. In the 2000s, the emergence of mobile devices and mobile apps led to the development of mobile banking, mobile payments, and mobile wallets. More recently, technological advancements in artificial intelligence and blockchain have enabled the development of new financial services such as robo-advisory services and cryptocurrency trading platforms.

Examples of Fintech Services and Products

Fintech services and products can be classified into various categories, including banking, investment, insurance, and payments. Here are some examples of Fintech services and products:

Banking: Fintech companies have developed online and mobile banking platforms that allow customers to manage their accounts, deposit and withdraw funds, and pay bills. Some examples of online banks include Ally Bank, Chime, and Marcus by Goldman Sachs.

Investment: Fintech companies have developed investment platforms that allow customers to buy and sell stocks, bonds, and other securities. Some examples of investment platforms include Robinhood, Acorns, and Betterment.

Insurance: Fintech companies have developed online insurance platforms that allow customers to purchase insurance policies, file claims, and manage their policies. Some examples of online insurance platforms include Lemonade, Metromile, and Policygenius.

Payments: Fintech companies have developed mobile payment platforms that allow customers to make payments using their smartphones. Some examples of mobile payment platforms include Apple Pay, Google Pay, and Venmo.

Advantages and Disadvantages of Fintech

Advantages:

Convenience: Fintech services are available 24/7, allowing customers to access financial services at their convenience.

Cost-effectiveness: Fintech services are generally cheaper than traditional financial services, as they do not require a physical presence and have lower overhead costs.

Accessibility: Fintech services are accessible to anyone with an internet connection and a smartphone, making financial services more inclusive.

Speed: Fintech services are faster than traditional financial services, as they use digital platforms that can process transactions in real-time.

Disadvantages:

Cybersecurity risks: Fintech services are vulnerable to cyber attacks, which can compromise customers' personal and financial information.

Lack of human interaction: Fintech services do not offer the same level of human interaction as traditional financial services, which can be a disadvantage for customers who prefer face-to-face interaction.

Reliance on technology: Fintech services are dependent on technology, which can be a disadvantage if there are technological disruptions or failures. This can result in service outages or delays, which can negatively impact customers.

Regulatory challenges: Fintech companies are subject to various regulatory requirements, which can be a significant barrier to entry for startups. Furthermore, regulatory requirements can differ across countries, making it difficult for Fintech companies to expand globally.

Limited access to financial services: Despite the growing popularity of Fintech, there are still many people who do not have access to these services due to factors such as lack of internet access, limited financial literacy, or being excluded from traditional financial services.

Potential for unethical or fraudulent practices: The rapid development and deployment of Fintech services can create opportunities for unethical or fraudulent practices, such as unauthorized account access or fraudulent loan applications. This can damage the reputation of Fintech companies and undermine customer trust.

Impact of Fintech on Traditional Financial Institutions

Fintech has had a significant impact on traditional financial institutions. Some of the key ways in which Fintech has disrupted the financial industry include:

Increased competition: Fintech companies have introduced new and innovative products and services that have disrupted the traditional banking model. This has resulted in increased competition in the financial industry, with traditional financial institutions now competing with Fintech startups for market share.

Changes in customer behavior: Fintech has changed the way that customers interact with financial institutions. Customers now expect a more personalized and streamlined experience, with a focus on convenience and speed.

Pressure to innovate: Fintech has put pressure on traditional financial institutions to innovate and adapt to changing customer demands. In order to stay competitive, traditional financial institutions are now investing heavily in technology and developing new products and services.

New partnerships and collaborations: Fintech has also led to new partnerships and collaborations between traditional financial institutions and Fintech startups. Many traditional financial institutions are now partnering with Fintech companies in order to access new technologies and reach new customers.

Conclusion

Fintech has transformed the financial industry, introducing new products and services that have disrupted traditional financial institutions. While there are many advantages to Fintech, there are also some disadvantages, including cybersecurity risks, lack of human interaction, and regulatory challenges. Fintech has also had a significant impact on traditional financial institutions, with increased competition, changes in customer behavior, and pressure to innovate. As Fintech continues to evolve, it will be important for both Fintech companies and traditional financial institutions to adapt and stay competitive in a rapidly changing landscape.

Socially Responsible Investing (SRI)

approach is to use a customized investment strategy that aligns with an investor's specific values and goals. This may involve working with a financial advisor or investment firm that specializes in SRI to create a personalized portfolio that meets the investor's criteria for socially responsible investing.

It is also possible to incorporate SRI principles into traditional investment strategies. For example, an investor may choose to avoid companies that have a history of negative social or environmental impacts, or invest in companies that have a strong record of corporate social responsibility.

Investors who are interested in SRI should carefully research their options and consider their own values and investment goals when making decisions about how to incorporate socially responsible investing into their portfolio. It is important to understand that SRI may involve trade-offs, such as lower returns or limited investment options, and to weigh these factors against the potential social and environmental benefits of investing in a socially responsible way.

Conclusion

Socially responsible investing has become increasingly popular in recent years as investors have become more aware of the social and environmental impacts of their investments. SRI involves investing in companies that meet certain social and environmental criteria, such as those that have a strong track record of corporate social responsibility or that operate in sustainable industries.

While SRI offers potential benefits, such as the opportunity to align investments with personal values and contribute to positive social and environmental change, there are also potential drawbacks, such as lower returns and limited investment options. It is important for investors to carefully consider their options and weigh the potential benefits and trade-offs of socially responsible investing when making investment decisions.

Fintech and SRI: Intersections and Potential Synergies

to intersect and potentially create synergies.

Overall, it is clear that the integration of Fintech and SRI can offer several advantages, including greater transparency, increased accessibility, and better alignment with investors' values. However, it is important to note that these benefits are not without their limitations and challenges.

As the industry continues to develop and evolve, it will be important for stakeholders to work together to address these challenges and ensure that Fintech and SRI can continue to intersect and create synergies. With the right approaches and strategies, the intersection of these two fields has the potential to create significant value for investors, as well as for society and the environment as a whole.

Future of Fintech and SRI

Fintech and SRI are rapidly evolving fields, and there are several trends and innovations that are shaping their future.

Artificial intelligence and machine learning: AI and machine learning are being used to analyze and interpret large volumes of financial and environmental data, which can help investors make more informed decisions. For example, some fintech companies are using machine learning algorithms to analyze satellite imagery and weather data to assess the impact of climate change on crop yields, which can inform investment decisions in agricultural commodities.

Blockchain and distributed ledger technology: Blockchain and distributed ledger technology (DLT) are being used to develop new investment platforms that are more transparent, efficient, and secure. For example, some fintech companies are using blockchain to create digital tokens that represent ownership in real estate or infrastructure projects, which can provide investors with access to alternative assets that were previously inaccessible.

Mobile and digital platforms: Mobile and digital platforms are becoming increasingly popular among investors, particularly millennials and Gen Zers, who are more likely to use their smartphones to manage their finances. Fintech companies are developing new mobile apps and digital platforms that provide users with access to investment advice, portfolio management tools, and other financial services.

Impact investing: Impact investing is a growing trend in the SRI space, and involves investing in companies and funds that have a positive social or environmental impact. Fintech companies are developing new impact investing platforms that use AI and machine learning to identify and evaluate potential investments based on their impact.

Potential impact on financial industry and society

The convergence of fintech and SRI has the potential to disrupt the financial industry and have a positive impact on society in several ways.

Increased transparency and accessibility: Fintech solutions can make investing more transparent and accessible to a wider range of investors. For example, digital platforms can provide users with real-time data and analysis, which can help them make more informed investment decisions. Additionally, fintech solutions can reduce the costs and minimum investment requirements associated with traditional investment products, making investing more accessible to a wider range of investors.

Alignment with investor values: SRI investing allows investors to align their financial goals with their personal values, which can have a positive impact on society. By using fintech solutions to facilitate SRI investing, investors can more easily identify and invest in companies that align with their values and beliefs, which can help drive positive change in the world.

Improved efficiency and effectiveness: Fintech solutions can improve the efficiency and effectiveness of SRI investing by providing investors with more accurate and timely data, and by automating certain investment processes. For example, fintech solutions can use machine learning algorithms to identify and evaluate potential investments based on their social and environmental impact, which can save investors time and improve the accuracy of investment decisions.

Challenges and opportunities for investors, regulators, and policymakers

While the convergence of fintech and SRI presents many opportunities, there are also several challenges that must be addressed by investors, regulators, and policymakers.

Data quality and standardization: One of the biggest challenges facing the fintech and SRI industries is the quality and standardization of data. While there is a growing amount of environmental, social, and governance (ESG) data available, there is still a lack of standardization and transparency, which can make it difficult for investors to make informed decisions. Regulators and policymakers need to work with the industry to establish standards for ESG data, and to ensure that the data is accurate and reliable.

Regulatory challenges: The fintech and SRI industries are subject to a complex web of regulations and compliance requirements, which can vary by jurisdiction. Regulators and policymakers need to work together to create a regulatory framework that supports innovation and growth in the industry, while also protecting investors and ensuring that companies are operating ethically and transparently.

Opportunities for Investors, Regulators, and Policymakers

Despite the challenges that Fintech and SRI face, there are also numerous opportunities for investors, regulators, and policymakers to leverage the potential of these industries for positive impact.

For Investors

One of the key opportunities for investors is to leverage Fintech and SRI to drive positive social and environmental outcomes while generating financial returns. With the increasing demand for responsible investing, investors can use innovative digital platforms to identify and invest in companies that align with their values, and use data and analytics to measure and track the impact of their investments. This can help to drive positive social and environmental change while generating financial returns.

For Regulators

Regulators can also benefit from the potential of Fintech and SRI to drive positive social and environmental outcomes. By supporting innovation in the industry and creating a regulatory framework that encourages responsible investing, regulators can help to promote greater transparency, accountability, and ethical behavior in the financial industry. This can help to build trust with investors, and support the growth of the industry over the long term.

For Policymakers

Policymakers also have an important role to play in promoting the future of Fintech and SRI. By supporting the development of innovative technologies and creating policies that encourage responsible investing, policymakers can help to drive positive social and environmental outcomes, and promote sustainable economic growth. This can also help to create new jobs and stimulate innovation, supporting economic growth and prosperity.

Conclusion

The future of Fintech and SRI is bright, with numerous opportunities for innovation and growth in both industries. As investors continue to demand responsible investing options, and Fintech continues to disrupt traditional financial services, the potential for these two industries to intersect and create synergies is significant. However, there are also significant challenges and limitations that must be addressed, including data quality, regulatory challenges, limited investment options, higher costs, and limited market demand.

Overall, the future of Fintech and SRI will depend on the ability of investors, regulators, and policymakers to work together to leverage the potential of these industries for positive social and environmental outcomes, while also generating financial returns. As the investment industry continues to evolve, it will be interesting to see how Fintech and SRI continue to intersect and shape the future of responsible investing.

CHAPTER 16 VENTURE CAPITAL

Introduction

of venture capital investing typically involves several stages, each with its own unique characteristics and challenges. The stages include:

Seed Stage: At this stage, the company is still in its early stages of development, and the investment is typically used to fund research and development, market testing, and early product development. The investment amount is relatively small, typically ranging from $100,000 to $2 million.

Early Stage: At this stage, the company has developed a product or service that is in the early stages of commercialization. The investment is typically used to fund product development, market expansion, and initial scaling. The investment amount is typically between $2 million and $10 million.

Growth Stage: At this stage, the company has established a market presence and is generating significant revenue. The investment is typically used to fund further expansion, increase market share, and further product development. The investment amount is typically between $10 million and $50 million.

Late Stage: At this stage, the company is approaching maturity, and the investment is typically used to fund major expansion or acquisition opportunities. The investment amount is typically above $50 million.

Each stage of the venture capital process comes with its own set of challenges and opportunities. Early-stage investments are typically high-risk, high-reward, while later-stage investments are lower-risk, lower-reward. Regardless of the stage, venture capitalists aim to identify high-potential companies with the potential to generate significant returns.

Characteristics of Successful Venture Capital Firms

Successful venture capital firms share several common characteristics that contribute to their ability to identify high-potential companies and generate significant returns. These characteristics include:

Experience: Successful venture capitalists typically have extensive experience in the industry, as well as a deep understanding of the market and the competitive landscape. They have a track record of successful investments and a reputation for identifying high-potential companies.

Network: Successful venture capitalists have a broad network of contacts within the industry, including entrepreneurs, executives, and investors. This network allows them to identify high-potential opportunities early on and to leverage their contacts to support the growth of their portfolio companies.

Financial acumen: Successful venture capitalists have a deep understanding of financial markets, including trends, risk management, and portfolio management. They are able to evaluate investment opportunities based on their potential for generating returns and are skilled at managing risk.

Patience: Successful venture capitalists are patient and have a long-term perspective. They understand that building a successful company takes time and are willing to support their portfolio companies through the ups and downs of the market.

Challenges and Risks of Venture Capital Investing

Venture capital investing comes with several unique challenges and risks, including:

High risk: Venture capital investments are inherently risky, as many startups fail to generate significant returns. Venture capitalists must be comfortable taking on high levels of risk and have the expertise to evaluate investment opportunities based on their potential for generating returns.

Illiquid investments: Venture capital investments are typically illiquid, meaning that it may be difficult to sell the investment if needed. This illiquidity can create challenges for investors who need to access their funds quickly.

Limited diversification: Venture capital investments are typically highly concentrated, with investments focused on a small number of companies. This limited diversification can increase risk, as the failure of one or two investments can have a significant impact on the overall portfolio.

Regulatory and compliance risks: Venture capital investing is subject to a complex web of regulations and compliance requirements. Failure to comply with these regulations can result in fines, penalties, and reputational damage.

Conclusion

Venture capital investing plays an important role in driving innovation and supporting the growth of high-potential companies. Successful venture capitalists possess a unique combination of experience, network, and investment acumen that allows them to identify and support promising entrepreneurs and businesses.

As the venture capital industry continues to evolve, it will be interesting to see how new technologies and changing market conditions impact the industry. From the rise of fintech and blockchain to the growing demand for impact investing, venture capitalists will need to adapt to changing trends and innovate in order to stay competitive.

Despite the challenges and risks associated with venture capital investing, many investors and entrepreneurs see it as an exciting opportunity to be at the forefront of innovation and growth. Whether it is a new technology that has the potential to disrupt an entire industry, or a social enterprise that is tackling a pressing social or environmental issue, venture capital has the potential to support some of the most promising and impactful ventures.

Aspiring venture capitalists should be prepared to work hard, take risks, and be comfortable with uncertainty. By developing a deep understanding of the industry and building a strong network of contacts, they can position themselves for success and contribute to the growth and innovation of the economy.

Venture Capital Industry

The venture capital (VC) industry is an important source of funding for high-potential startup companies. Venture capital firms invest in companies with the potential to grow quickly and become major players in their respective markets. VC firms typically provide funding to companies that are in the early stages of development, and as such, are often seen as a high-risk, high-reward investment opportunity. In this section, we will provide an overview of the venture capital industry, including the types of investors and funds that are involved.

Types of Investors in Venture Capital

There are several types of investors that are involved in the venture capital industry, including institutional investors, family offices, and high net worth individuals.

Institutional Investors: Institutional investors are typically large organizations that invest on behalf of their clients, such as pension funds, endowments, and foundations. These investors often have significant resources and expertise in identifying and evaluating investment opportunities.

Family Offices: Family offices are private wealth management firms that provide investment management services to high net worth families. These firms often have a long-term investment horizon and can provide significant capital to early-stage companies.

High Net Worth Individuals: High net worth individuals are wealthy individuals who invest their personal funds in startup companies. These investors can provide capital, as well as industry expertise and connections.

Types of Funds in Venture Capital

Venture capital firms typically raise funds from institutional investors, family offices, and high net worth individuals, which are then used to invest in early-stage companies. There are several types of funds that venture capital firms can raise, including:

Seed Funds: Seed funds are typically the first stage of investment in a startup company. These funds are used to support the initial development of a product or service, as well as to build out the team and establish a business plan.

Early-Stage Funds: Early-stage funds are used to support companies that have already developed a product or service and are beginning to generate revenue. These funds are used to help the company scale their operations and expand their market reach.

Late-Stage Funds: Late-stage funds are used to support companies that have already established a significant market presence and are generating significant revenue. These funds are used to help the company continue to grow and expand, as well as to provide liquidity to early investors and employees.

Mezzanine Funds: Mezzanine funds are used to support companies that are in the later stages of development and are preparing for an initial public offering (IPO) or acquisition. These funds are used to provide additional capital to support the company's growth and to help prepare for the transition to a public company.

Conclusion

The venture capital industry plays an important role in supporting the growth of high-potential startup companies. Venture capital firms provide capital, expertise, and connections that can help early-stage companies develop and expand their business. The industry is made up of a variety of investors and funds, each with their own unique characteristics and investment strategies. By understanding the different types of investors and funds involved in the venture capital industry, entrepreneurs can better position themselves to secure funding and support for their startup companies.

The Venture Capital Process

Venture capital (VC) firms play a critical role in funding and supporting high-growth startups, providing the necessary capital and expertise to help entrepreneurs turn their ideas into successful businesses. However, the process of raising venture capital can be complex and challenging for both entrepreneurs and investors. In this section, we will explore the different stages of the venture capital process, including raising capital, evaluating and selecting companies, and negotiating the terms of the deal.

Raising Venture Capital

The first step in the venture capital process is for entrepreneurs to identify potential investors and pitch their ideas to them. This typically involves creating a pitch deck, a concise and compelling presentation that outlines the business idea, target market, competitive landscape, and financial projections. Entrepreneurs may also need to create a business plan, which provides a more detailed overview of the company's goals, strategies, and operations.

Once the pitch deck and business plan are ready, entrepreneurs can begin reaching out to potential investors. This may involve attending networking events, contacting venture capitalists (VCs) directly, or seeking referrals from industry contacts. It is important to note that not all VCs are a good fit for every company, and entrepreneurs should focus on identifying investors who have experience in their industry and are likely to be interested in their business model.

If a VC expresses interest in a company, the next step is usually to schedule a meeting or call to discuss the opportunity in more detail. This may involve answering questions about the business model, market opportunity, competition, and financial projections. If the VC is still interested after this initial meeting, they may request additional information, such as detailed financial statements, customer data, or market research reports.

Evaluating and Selecting Companies

After reviewing the information provided by the entrepreneur, the VC will typically conduct a more thorough evaluation of the company to determine whether it is a good fit for their investment portfolio. This evaluation process may involve the following steps:

Due Diligence: VCs will typically conduct extensive due diligence on a company before making an investment. This may include reviewing financial statements, customer data, market research, and legal documents, as well as interviewing key employees and conducting background checks on the founders.

Market Analysis: VCs will also analyze the market opportunity for the company, including the size of the market, the potential for growth, and the competitive landscape. They will also consider macroeconomic trends, industry dynamics, and other factors that may affect the company's prospects.

Team Assessment: VCs will evaluate the experience and track record of the management team, as well as their ability to execute on the business plan and navigate challenges as they arise.

Financial Analysis: VCs will analyze the company's financial projections to assess its revenue potential, profitability, and cash flow. They will also consider the company's burn rate (the rate at which it is using up its cash reserves) and its funding needs over the next several years.

Fit with Portfolio: VCs will also consider how the company fits into their overall investment portfolio. They may evaluate factors such as sector diversification, risk tolerance, and return expectations.

Negotiating Terms and Closing the Deal

If the VC decides to move forward with an investment, the next step is to negotiate the terms of the deal. This may involve negotiating the valuation of the company, the amount of capital to be invested, the rights and responsibilities of the investor and the entrepreneur, and the conditions for future funding rounds.

Common terms that may be included in a venture capital deal include:

Valuation: The valuation of the company is the amount of money the investor is willing to pay for a certain percentage of ownership in the company. This can be a contentious issue, as the entrepreneur will typically want a higher valuation, while the investorwill want a lower one.

Liquidation preference: This is the amount of money that the investor will receive in the event that the company is sold or goes public. Typically, the investor will have a preference over the common shareholders and will receive a multiple of their original investment before the remaining proceeds are divided among other shareholders.

Anti-dilution protection: This provision protects the investor from having their ownership percentage in the company reduced in the event that the company issues new shares at a lower price than the investor paid. There are two main types of anti-dilution protection: full ratchet and weighted average.

Board seats: Investors may negotiate for one or more seats on the company's board of directors in exchange for their investment. This gives them a say in important decisions and allows them to monitor the company's progress.

Vesting: Vesting refers to the process by which the entrepreneur's ownership in the company becomes fully vested over time. This means that if the entrepreneur leaves the company before the vesting period is complete, they may forfeit some or all of their ownership in the company.

Exit strategy: Investors will want to know how they can eventually exit their investment and realize a return. This may include an IPO, a merger or acquisition, or a buyout.

Due diligence: Before making an investment, venture capitalists will typically conduct extensive due diligence to evaluate the company's financial health, market potential, management team, and other factors. This can involve reviewing financial statements, interviewing key personnel, and conducting market research.

The term sheet: If the investor is interested in making an investment, they will typically provide the entrepreneur with a term sheet outlining the proposed terms of the deal. The term sheet is non-binding and serves as a starting point for negotiations between the entrepreneur and the investor.

Negotiating the terms: Once the term sheet has been issued, the entrepreneur and the investor will negotiate the specific terms of the deal. This can involve multiple rounds of negotiations and may take several weeks or months.

Closing the deal: Once the terms of the deal have been agreed upon, the parties will sign a binding agreement and the investor will provide the agreed-upon funding to the company. This marks the beginning of the partnership between the entrepreneur and the investor, and the start of the next phase of the company's growth.

Risks and Returns

Venture capital investing is a high-risk, high-reward activity. While there is the potential for significant returns, there is also the possibility of substantial losses. In this section, we will examine the risks and returns associated with venture capital investing, the importance of diversification in mitigating risk, and the various exit strategies that venture capitalists use to realize returns on their investments.

Risks and Returns Associated with Venture Capital Investing
Venture capital investing involves a significant amount of risk. Startups are inherently risky investments due to their early-stage status and the uncertainty surrounding their future prospects. Some of the risks associated with venture capital investing include:

Business risk: This is the risk that the startup will fail to execute its business plan and generate the expected revenue and profits.

Market risk: This is the risk that the startup's products or services will not find a market or will not be able to compete effectively in their target market.

Technology risk: This is the risk that the startup's technology will not work as intended or will become obsolete due to advances made by competitors or changes in the market.

Management risk: This is the risk that the startup's management team will be unable to execute the business plan effectively or make poor decisions that lead to the failure of the company.

Despite these risks, venture capital investing can also offer the potential for significant returns. The returns from venture capital investments are typically higher than those from traditional investments, such as stocks or bonds. However, the returns are also more volatile and uncertain.

Portfolio Theory and Diversification

Given the high level of risk associated with venture capital investing, it is important for venture capitalists to diversify their portfolios to minimize the impact of any single investment's failure. This is known as portfolio theory, which holds that investors can reduce their overall risk by spreading their investments across multiple assets.

Diversification is a key strategy for mitigating risk in venture capital investing. By investing in a diversified portfolio of startups, venture capitalists can minimize the impact of any single investment's failure on their overall returns. The diversification strategy involves investing in a range of startups across different industries, stages of development, and geographic regions.

Exit Strategies for Venture Capitalists

Venture capitalists invest in startups with the intention of realizing a return on their investment within a certain period of time. There are several exit strategies that venture capitalists can use to realize returns on their investments, including:

Initial public offering (IPO): This is when a company goes public by offering shares of its stock to the public for the first time. An IPO can be a lucrative exit strategy for venture capitalists, as they can sell their shares at a premium price.

Merger or acquisition: This is when a company is acquired by another company or merges with another company. In a merger or acquisition, the acquiring company typically pays a premium price for the startup, providing a return on investment for the venture capitalists.

Secondary sale: This is when the venture capitalists sell their shares to another investor. This can be a quick way for venture capitalists to realize returns on their investment, but the returns may be lower than those from an IPO or merger.

Recapitalization: This is when the startup issues new shares of stock, diluting the ownership percentage of the venture capitalists. The venture capitalists can then sell their shares to new investors, realizing a return on their investment.

Conclusion

Venture capital investing is a high-risk, high-reward activity that requires careful consideration of the risks and returns associated with each investment. Diversification is a key strategy for mitigating risk in venture capital investing, as it allows investors to spread their investments across multiple assets. Additionally, venture capitalists use a range of exit strategies to realize returns on their investments, including IPOs, mergers and acquisitions, and secondary offerings.

While venture capital investing can be a lucrative investment opportunity for those willing to take on high risk, it is important to note that not all venture capital investments will be successful. In fact, the majority of startups fail, and as a result, the majority of venture capital investments will not yield positive returns. As a result, it is important for investors to carefully evaluate potential investments and to work closely with portfolio companies to help maximize their chances of success.

Furthermore, the venture capital industry itself is not immune to risks. Changes in market conditions, regulatory environments, and shifts in investor sentiment can all impact the industry and the returns that investors can expect to receive. However, despite these risks, the potential for significant returns has led many investors to continue to allocate a portion of their portfolios to venture capital investments.

In conclusion, venture capital investing plays an important role in driving innovation and supporting the growth of high-potential companies. While it is a high-risk, high-reward activity, the potential for significant returns has led many investors to seek out venture capital opportunities. By carefully evaluating potential investments, diversifying their portfolios, and working closely with portfolio companies to help maximize their chances of success, investors can mitigate risk and increase their chances of achieving positive returns in the venture capital market.

The Role of Venture Capital in Innovation

Venture capital has been an important driver of innovation and entrepreneurship for several decades. Venture capitalists (VCs) invest in companies with high growth potential, typically in the technology and life sciences sectors, with the aim of realizing substantial returns on their investments. In return, VCs provide not only funding, but also expertise, guidance, and access to networks that can help companies grow and succeed. This section will explore the role of venture capital in driving innovation, its impact on economic growth, and some examples of successful companies that received venture capital funding.

The relationship between venture capital and innovation:

Venture capital is often associated with innovation, as VCs are willing to invest in companies with novel technologies, products, or services that have the potential to disrupt existing markets or create new ones. VCs seek out companies that have a competitive advantage, such as proprietary technology or intellectual property, and are led by experienced and capable management teams. In addition, VCs often provide strategic guidance and operational support to help companies overcome obstacles and achieve their goals.

Venture capital is particularly important for companies that are too risky or unconventional to attract traditional sources of financing, such as bank loans or public offerings. VCs are willing to take on more risk than other investors, as they are looking for high returns on their investments. This willingness to take risks has enabled many innovative companies to get off the ground and succeed, where they might otherwise have failed.

The impact of venture capital on economic growth:

Venture capital has a significant impact on economic growth, as it enables the development and commercialization of new technologies and products that can create jobs, generate wealth, and enhance productivity. In particular, venture-backed companies have been responsible for many of the most important technological innovations of the past few decades, including the internet, biotechnology, and renewable energy.

Venture-backed companies also tend to grow more quickly than other types of companies, which can have a positive impact on local and national economies. These companies create jobs, attract talent, and stimulate the formation of new businesses and industries. In addition, successful venture-backed companies often become acquisition targets or go public, creating wealth for their founders, employees, and investors.

Examples of successful companies that received venture capital funding:

There are many examples of successful companies that received venture capital funding and went on to become industry leaders. Here are a few notable examples:

Google: Google was founded in 1998 by Larry Page and Sergey Brin, who received $100,000 in seed funding from Andy Bechtolsheim, a co-founder of Sun Microsystems. The company went on to become the world's most popular search engine, with a market capitalization of over $1 trillion as of 2021.

Facebook: Facebook was founded in 2004 by Mark Zuckerberg, who received $500,000 in seed funding from Peter Thiel, a co-founder of PayPal. The company went public in 2012, and as of 2021, has a market capitalization of over $800 billion.

Tesla: Tesla was founded in 2003 by Elon Musk, who received $7.5 million in funding from several venture capital firms, including Draper Fisher Jurvetson and Valor Equity Partners. The company is now the leading producer of electric vehicles and has a market capitalization of over $800 billion as of 2021.

Airbnb: Airbnb was founded in 2008 by Brian Chesky, Joe Gebbia, and Nathan Blecharczyk, who received $20,000 in seed funding from Y Combinator. The company has revolutionized the hospitality industry, allowing individuals to rent out their homes to travelers, and has a market capitalization of over $100 billion as of 2021.

Moderna: Moderna was founded in 2010 by a group of entrepreneurs, including CEO Stéphane Bancel, who received early funding from venture capital firms Flagship Pioneering and Polaris Partners. The company's focus on mRNA technology has led to the development of the COVID-19 vaccine, which has been highly effective in preventing illness and reducing transmission of the virus.

These companies are just a few examples of the many successful ventures that have been fueled by venture capital funding. Without the capital and support of venture capitalists, it is likely that these companies would not have been able to achieve the level of success they have today. In addition to providing funding, venture capitalists often provide guidance, expertise, and access to networks that can help startups grow and thrive.

The impact of venture capital on economic growth

Venture capital has also been shown to have a significant impact on economic growth. By providing funding to innovative startups, venture capitalists help to drive technological advances and create new industries, which in turn create jobs and stimulate economic growth. Studies have shown that venture capital-backed companies tend to grow more quickly and create more jobs than non-venture-backed companies.

One study by the National Bureau of Economic Research found that venture capital has a positive effect on economic growth, with each dollar of venture capital investment leading to an increase in real GDP of $5.00 within five years. The study also found that venture-backed companies were more likely to go public, acquire other companies, and introduce new products and services than non-venture-backed companies.

Another study by the Ewing Marion Kauffman Foundation found that companies that received venture capital funding accounted for 20% of all new jobs created in the US between 1980 and 2005, despite representing only 1% of all companies.

The relationship between venture capital and innovation

Venture capital is often seen as a key driver of innovation, as it provides funding to startups that are working on cutting-edge technologies and ideas. Without venture capital, many of these startups would struggle to get off the ground, as they often require significant upfront investment to develop and bring their products to market.

Additionally, venture capitalists often bring expertise and connections to the table, which can help startups navigate the challenges of developing and commercializing new technologies. This support can be particularly important for startups working in fields with high levels of regulatory or market uncertainty.

However, there are some who argue that venture capital may actually hinder innovation by promoting a "unicorn" culture, where startups are encouraged to pursue rapid growth and large valuations at the expense of long-term sustainability and innovation. This can lead to a focus on short-term gains and a reluctance to invest in risky, but potentially groundbreaking, technologies.

Conclusion

In conclusion, venture capital plays an important role in driving innovation and economic growth by providing funding, guidance, and expertise to startups. Successful companies such as Google, Facebook, Tesla, Airbnb, and Moderna are just a few examples of the impact that venture capital can have on a company's success. However, it is important to be aware of the potential downsides of venture capital, including the pressure to pursue rapid growth and the potential to stifle long-term innovation. Ultimately, venture capital is a tool that can be used to help startups achieve their goals, but it is not a one-size-fits-all solution, and careful consideration should be given to the risks and benefits of venture capital before pursuing it as a funding source.

Challenges and Criticisms

on sectors that have historically shown promising growth potential, such as technology, healthcare, and energy. It can also involve diversification of the investor base, including seeking out new sources of capital from different regions or types of investors, such as family offices or sovereign wealth funds.

Additionally, diversification can also be applied at the portfolio level, where venture capital firms can spread their investments across a larger number of companies and sectors to mitigate risks associated with individual investments. This strategy can help mitigate the potential losses that come with a single failed investment, and can increase the likelihood of success across a range of investments.

Increased Transparency

Another potential solution to challenges faced by the venture capital industry is to increase transparency. Currently, venture capital firms are not required to disclose their performance metrics, making it difficult for investors to evaluate the performance of these firms. However, increased transparency can help investors make more informed decisions about their investments, and can also help the industry as a whole by promoting best practices and encouraging more efficient allocation of capital.

To this end, some venture capital firms have begun to voluntarily disclose more information about their performance, including the types of companies they invest in, their returns, and their investment strategies. Others have started to use technology to provide greater transparency and data analysis, such as using machine learning algorithms to identify potential investment opportunities.

Social and Environmental Impact Investing

Another potential solution to challenges faced by the venture capital industry is to focus on social and environmental impact investing. This involves investing in companies that are working to solve important social and environmental challenges, such as poverty, climate change, and inequality.

Impact investing can help to address criticisms of venture capital as a purely profit-driven industry, by promoting investments that align with broader social and environmental goals. Impact investing can also help to create a positive reputation for venture capital firms, making them more attractive to investors who are interested in both financial returns and social impact.

Conclusion

Despite the challenges and criticisms facing the venture capital industry, it remains a key driver of innovation and economic growth. Venture capital firms provide critical funding and support to startups and entrepreneurs, helping to turn innovative ideas into successful companies that create jobs and drive economic growth.

While there are certainly challenges facing the industry, including concerns around risk, performance, and diversity, there are also potential solutions to these challenges, including diversification, increased transparency, and impact investing.

As the venture capital industry continues to evolve and adapt to changing market conditions and societal expectations, it will be critical for firms to remain focused on their core mission of supporting innovation and economic growth, while also addressing the concerns of investors and other stakeholders. By doing so, the industry can continue to thrive and make a positive impact on the world.

CHAPTER 17
CROWDFUNDING

Introduction

Crowdfunding is a relatively new method of raising capital that has gained popularity in recent years. It involves raising small amounts of money from a large number of individuals, typically through online platforms. Crowdfunding has been used to fund a wide range of projects, including new businesses, creative projects, and charitable causes.

The rise of crowdfunding can be attributed to several factors, including advancements in technology and changes in the regulatory landscape. With the advent of social media and other online communication tools, it has become easier than ever to reach out to potential investors and supporters. Additionally, changes in securities laws have made it easier for small businesses and startups to raise funds from non-accredited investors.

This chapter will explore the concept of crowdfunding in detail, including its different types, benefits, and challenges. We will also examine the regulatory framework governing crowdfunding, as well as the potential risks and rewards for investors and entrepreneurs. Finally, we will discuss the future of crowdfunding and its potential to transform the way we think about investing and funding innovation.

Types of Crowdfunding

There are several different types of crowdfunding, each with its own unique characteristics and benefits. These include:

Equity crowdfunding: This involves raising capital by selling shares of ownership in a business or project. Investors receive a stake in the company in exchange for their investment, and may also receive dividends or other forms of compensation.

Reward-based crowdfunding: This involves offering rewards, such as products or services, to individuals who contribute to a project. The rewards are typically tiered, with more valuable rewards offered to those who contribute larger amounts.

Donation-based crowdfunding: This involves soliciting donations from individuals who support a particular cause or project. Donors may not receive any tangible benefits in return for their contributions, other than the satisfaction of supporting a cause they believe in.

Debt crowdfunding: This involves raising capital by offering debt securities, such as bonds or notes, to investors. The company or project agrees to repay the debt with interest over a specified period of time.

Benefits of Crowdfunding

Crowdfunding offers several benefits for both entrepreneurs and investors, including:

Access to capital: Crowdfunding allows entrepreneurs to raise capital from a large number of individuals, often without the need for collateral or a strong credit history.

Market validation: By presenting their idea or product to potential investors and supporters, entrepreneurs can gain valuable feedback and market validation before launching their venture.

Community engagement: Crowdfunding allows entrepreneurs to build a community of supporters who are invested in the success of their venture. This can lead to greater brand loyalty and customer engagement.

Challenges and Risks of Crowdfunding

While crowdfunding offers several benefits, it also poses several challenges and risks for entrepreneurs and investors. These include:

Regulatory compliance: Crowdfunding is subject to a complex regulatory framework that can be difficult to navigate. Entrepreneurs and investors must ensure that they comply with all applicable laws and regulations.

Lack of investor protections: Crowdfunding is a relatively new and untested investment model, and there is a risk that investors may not fully understand the risks involved. Additionally, there are few protections in place to ensure that investors receive accurate information and that their investments are protected.

Crowding out: As crowdfunding becomes more popular, there is a risk that it may crowd out other sources of funding, such as traditional bank loans or venture capital. This could limit the availability of capital for certain types of ventures.

Types of Crowdfunding

Crowdfunding is a relatively new phenomenon that has emerged in response to the changing landscape of financing. While traditional funding sources, such as venture capital and angel investing, have been around for decades, crowdfunding provides a new option for entrepreneurs to access capital. Crowdfunding involves raising money from a large number of people through an online platform. There are several types of crowdfunding, including donation-based crowdfunding, rewards-based crowdfunding, equity-based crowdfunding, and debt-based crowdfunding.

Donation-based crowdfunding
Donation-based crowdfunding is a type of crowdfunding in which individuals or organizations donate money to support a cause or project. This type of crowdfunding is often used for charitable causes, such as disaster relief or medical bills. Donors do not receive anything in return for their contribution, other than the satisfaction of helping a cause they believe in. Donations can range from small amounts to large sums, and the crowdfunding platform typically takes a percentage of the funds raised as a fee.

Rewards-based crowdfunding
Rewards-based crowdfunding is a type of crowdfunding in which individuals contribute money in exchange for a reward. This type of crowdfunding is often used by entrepreneurs and artists to fund creative projects, such as a new album or film. Contributors receive a reward for their contribution, such as a copy of the album or a DVD of the film. The reward can range from small items, such as stickers or T-shirts, to more significant rewards, such as a personal meeting with the creator. The crowdfunding platform typically takes a percentage of the funds raised as a fee.

Equity-based crowdfunding

Equity-based crowdfunding is a type of crowdfunding in which individuals invest money in exchange for equity in a company. This type of crowdfunding is often used by early-stage companies that are seeking capital to grow their business. Investors receive a share of ownership in the company and are entitled to a portion of the profits. This type of crowdfunding is regulated by the Securities and Exchange Commission (SEC) in the United States, and the crowdfunding platform typically takes a percentage of the funds raised as a fee.

Debt-based crowdfunding

Debt-based crowdfunding is a type of crowdfunding in which individuals lend money to a company in exchange for a return on their investment. This type of crowdfunding is often used by companies that need to raise capital but do not want to give up equity in their company. Investors receive a fixed interest rate on their investment and are repaid over time, typically with interest. This type of crowdfunding is also regulated by the SEC in the United States, and the crowdfunding platform typically takes a percentage of the funds raised as a fee.

Overall, crowdfunding provides a new way for entrepreneurs to access capital and for individuals to support causes and projects they believe in. While each type of crowdfunding has its own benefits and drawbacks, it is important for entrepreneurs to carefully consider which type of crowdfunding is best suited for their needs. Additionally, investors should carefully consider the risks and potential returns of investing in a crowdfunding campaign before making a decision.

Advantages of Crowdfunding

Access to funding for small businesses and startups is a critical factor in their success. However, traditional methods of securing funding, such as bank loans or venture capital, can be difficult to obtain for many small businesses and startups, particularly those in the early stages of development. Crowdfunding has emerged as a viable alternative to these traditional methods, providing small businesses and startups with access to funding and a range of other benefits.

Increased exposure and market validation

One of the primary benefits of crowdfunding for small businesses and startups is increased exposure and market validation. By launching a crowdfunding campaign, businesses can showcase their products or services to a wider audience than would be possible through traditional marketing methods. This exposure can help to generate interest and buzz around a business and its offerings, which can ultimately lead to increased sales.

In addition to increased exposure, crowdfunding can also provide small businesses and startups with valuable market validation. By launching a campaign and receiving funding from investors, businesses can demonstrate that there is a demand for their products or services in the market. This can be particularly valuable for businesses that are in the early stages of development and may not yet have a proven track record or established customer base.

Potential for early customer feedback and engagement

Crowdfunding can also provide small businesses and startups with an opportunity to engage with potential customers and receive early feedback on their products or services. By launching a crowdfunding campaign, businesses can solicit feedback from investors and potential customers, which can help to refine their offerings and improve their chances of success.

This early feedback can also help businesses to identify potential challenges or areas for improvement before they launch their products or services to the wider market. By addressing these challenges early on, businesses can improve their chances of success and avoid potential pitfalls down the road.

Low barriers to entry for investors

Another key benefit of crowdfunding for small businesses and startups is the low barriers to entry for investors. Traditional methods of investing, such as venture capital or private equity, typically require investors to have significant capital or a high net worth. Crowdfunding, on the other hand, allows investors to invest smaller amounts of money, making it more accessible to a wider range of individuals.

This accessibility can be particularly valuable for small businesses and startups that may not have a large network of high-net-worth individuals or institutional investors. By opening up their fundraising efforts to a wider audience, businesses can increase their chances of success and secure the funding they need to grow and scale.

Challenges of crowdfunding for small businesses and startups

While crowdfunding can provide small businesses and startups with a range of benefits, it is not without its challenges. Some of the key challenges of crowdfunding include:

Difficulty standing out in a crowded market
Limited control over the fundraising process
Potential for negative publicity or backlash

Difficulty standing out in a crowded market

One of the primary challenges of crowdfunding for small businesses and startups is the difficulty of standing out in a crowded market. With so many campaigns vying for the attention of investors, it can be challenging to create a campaign that truly resonates with potential backers.

To overcome this challenge, businesses must create compelling campaigns that effectively communicate the value of their products or services. This can involve leveraging social media, creating engaging video content, and providing detailed information about the business and its offerings.

Limited control over the fundraising process

Another challenge of crowdfunding for small businesses and startups is the limited control they have over the fundraising process. When launching a crowdfunding campaign, businesses must rely on the platform they are using to handle the fundraising and payment processing.

This can be challenging for businesses that are accustomed to having more control over their fundraising efforts. To overcome this challenge, businesses must carefully research and select a crowdfunding platform that aligns with their needs and priorities.

Potential for negative publicity or backlash

Finally, crowdfunding can also come with the potential for negative publicity or backlash. If a campaign fails to meet its goal or is criticized for any reason, it can lead to negative press and a damaged reputation. For example, in 2014, a company called Coolest Cooler launched a crowdfunding campaign on Kickstarter and raised over $13 million in funding. However, after numerous delays in delivering the product and additional costs for backers, the company faced backlash and negative publicity.

Furthermore, crowdfunding campaigns that fail to deliver on their promises or produce a low-quality product can also lead to negative reviews and damage to the company's reputation. This can have long-lasting effects on the business, making it difficult to secure future funding or retain customers.

Despite these potential drawbacks, crowdfunding remains a valuable option for small businesses and startups that may not have access to traditional funding sources. With the ability to gain exposure, validation, and early customer feedback, as well as the low barriers to entry for investors, crowdfunding can provide a much-needed boost for companies looking to grow and expand.

Disadvantages of Crowdfunding

While crowdfunding has many benefits, it also has some potential drawbacks that entrepreneurs and investors should be aware of before deciding to participate in a crowdfunding campaign. In this section, we will discuss some of the main disadvantages of crowdfunding, including the potential for fraud and scams, lack of investor control and influence, limited investment amounts, and high risk of failure for projects.

Potential for Fraud and Scams

One of the main disadvantages of crowdfunding is the potential for fraud and scams. While most crowdfunding platforms have measures in place to prevent fraudulent campaigns, it can still be difficult to verify the legitimacy of some projects. This is especially true for donation-based and rewards-based crowdfunding campaigns, where there is often little or no oversight of how the funds are being used.

In some cases, individuals or groups may create fake crowdfunding campaigns to scam investors out of their money. This can be particularly damaging for investors who may have invested a significant amount of money in a project, only to find out later that the campaign was a scam.

To avoid falling victim to fraud or scams, investors should do their due diligence before investing in a crowdfunding campaign. This can include researching the project and the individuals behind it, reading reviews and feedback from other investors, and verifying that the campaign is being run by a legitimate organization or individual.

Lack of Investor Control and Influence

Another disadvantage of crowdfunding is the lack of control and influence that investors have over the projects they invest in. Unlike traditional venture capital or angel investing, crowdfunding investors typically have little or no say in how the funds are used or how the project is managed.

This lack of control can be frustrating for investors who want to have a more hands-on role in the projects they invest in. It can also lead to conflicts between investors and project managers if there are disagreements about how the funds should be used.

Limited Investment Amounts

One limitation of crowdfunding is the relatively small investment amounts that are typically allowed. While this can be an advantage for entrepreneurs who only need a small amount of funding to get started, it can be a disadvantage for investors who want to invest larger sums of money.

In addition, the limited investment amounts can make it difficult for entrepreneurs to raise the amount of funding they need to launch a successful project. This is particularly true for equity-based crowdfunding campaigns, where entrepreneurs may need to raise a significant amount of funding to attract institutional investors or achieve their goals.

High Risk of Failure for Projects

Finally, one of the biggest disadvantages of crowdfunding is the high risk of failure for projects. While many crowdfunding campaigns are successful, there is always a risk that a project will fail to meet its funding goals or that the project itself will fail to deliver on its promises.

This risk is particularly high for early-stage startups and entrepreneurs who may not have a proven track record of success. In addition, even successful crowdfunding campaigns can still face significant challenges in delivering on their promises, such as delays in product development or unexpected costs.

Conclusion

In conclusion, while crowdfunding has many benefits, it also has some potential drawbacks that entrepreneurs and investors should be aware of before deciding to participate in a crowdfunding campaign. These disadvantages include the potential for fraud and scams, lack of investor control and influence, limited investment amounts, and high risk of failure for projects. However, with careful research and due diligence, investors can minimize these risks and take advantage of the many benefits of crowdfunding to support innovative startups and entrepreneurs.

Crowdfunding Platforms

Crowdfunding platforms have revolutionized the way that individuals and organizations raise money for their projects, products, and ideas. These platforms allow people to access funding from a variety of sources, including individuals, businesses, and institutional investors. Crowdfunding platforms vary in terms of their focus, the types of projects they support, and the fees and costs associated with their services. In this section, we will explore popular crowdfunding platforms, compare their features, and examine the fees and costs associated with using these platforms.

Popular Crowdfunding Platforms

There are a number of crowdfunding platforms available to individuals and organizations looking to raise money for their projects. Each platform has its own strengths and weaknesses, and choosing the right platform for your project is an important decision. Some of the most popular crowdfunding platforms include:

Kickstarter: Kickstarter is one of the most well-known crowdfunding platforms, and has helped to fund over 200,000 projects. The platform is primarily focused on creative projects, including art, music, film, and technology. Kickstarter operates on an all-or-nothing funding model, which means that projects must reach their funding goals in order to receive any money. Kickstarter takes a 5% fee from successful projects, in addition to payment processing fees.

Indiegogo: Indiegogo is another popular crowdfunding platform, and is focused on a wider range of projects than Kickstarter. The platform has helped to fund everything from films and music albums to new products and inventions. Indiegogo offers both fixed and flexible funding options, and takes a 5% fee from successful projects, in addition to payment processing fees.

GoFundMe: GoFundMe is a crowdfunding platform that is primarily focused on personal fundraising campaigns, such as medical expenses, emergency situations, and charitable causes. Unlike Kickstarter and Indiegogo, GoFundMe does not have an all-or-nothing funding model. The platform takes a 2.9% fee, in addition to payment processing fees.

Patreon: Patreon is a crowdfunding platform that is focused on ongoing support for artists and creators. The platform allows fans to pledge a monthly amount to support their favorite creators, and offers a variety of benefits and rewards for different pledge levels. Patreon takes a 5-12% fee from creators, in addition to payment processing fees.

These are just a few examples of popular crowdfunding platforms, and there are many others available depending on your project and funding needs.

Comparison of Crowdfunding Platforms

When deciding which crowdfunding platform to use, it's important to consider a number of factors, including the types of projects the platform supports, the funding models available, and the fees and costs associated with using the platform. Some key differences between popular crowdfunding platforms include:

Project focus: Some platforms are focused on specific types of projects, such as creative projects or personal fundraising campaigns, while others are more open to a wide range of projects.

Funding models: Platforms may offer different funding models, such as all-or-nothing or flexible funding, which can impact how funding is received and how projects are managed.

Fees and costs: Crowdfunding platforms may charge different fees for their services, including fees for successful projects, payment processing fees, and fees for additional services like marketing and promotion.

Ease of use: The ease of use of a crowdfunding platform can vary, depending on factors such as the platform's user interface and the level of support provided to project creators.

By considering these factors and comparing the features of different crowdfunding platforms, project creators can choose the platform that best meets their needs.

Fees and Costs Associated with Crowdfunding

In addition to considering the features of different crowdfunding platforms, project creators must also consider the fees and costs associated with using these platforms. Crowdfunding platforms typically charge a fee for their services, which can impact the amount of funding that project creators receive. Some common fees and costs associated with crowdfunding include:

Platform fees: These are fees charged by the crowdfunding platform for hosting the campaign and providing other services such as payment processing, customer support, and campaign management. Platform fees can range from 2% to 10% of the total funds raised, depending on the platform and the type of crowdfunding campaign.

Payment processing fees: These are fees charged by payment processors such as PayPal or Stripe for processing payments made by backers. Payment processing fees can vary depending on the payment method used and can range from 1.5% to 3.5% of the total amount raised.

Transaction fees: These are fees charged by banks or financial institutions for transferring funds from the crowdfunding platform to the project creator's account. Transaction fees can vary depending on the bank and the amount of money being transferred.

Currency conversion fees: If the crowdfunding campaign is run in a currency different from the project creator's local currency, the platform or payment processor may charge a currency conversion fee. These fees can be significant, and project creators should factor them into their budget when planning their campaign.

Tax implications: Crowdfunding can have tax implications for both the project creator and the backers. Project creators may be required to pay income tax on the funds raised, while backers may be subject to gift tax if they contribute more than a certain amount. Project creators should consult with a tax professional to understand their tax obligations and factor these costs into their budget.

It is important for project creators to carefully review the fees and costs associated with each crowdfunding platform they are considering, as these can significantly impact the amount of funding they receive. They should also factor these costs into their budget when planning their campaign to ensure that they are able to meet their funding goals.

Overall, crowdfunding platforms have made it easier for individuals and organizations to raise funds for their projects and initiatives. However, with the increasing number of platforms available, it is important for project creators to carefully consider their options and choose the platform that best fits their needs and goals. By understanding the advantages and disadvantages of crowdfunding, as well as the features and fees associated with different platforms, project creators can make informed decisions and increase their chances of success.

Future of Crowdfunding

The future of crowdfunding is shaped by the trends, technology, opportunities, and challenges that will emerge in the coming years. As an alternative form of financing, crowdfunding has already established itself as a viable option for entrepreneurs, artists, and other individuals seeking to fund their projects. However, with the continued growth and evolution of the crowdfunding industry, new opportunities and challenges are expected to arise. In this section, we will explore the trends, potential impact of technology, and opportunities and challenges for crowdfunding in the future.

Trends in Crowdfunding
Crowdfunding has seen significant growth since its inception, and this trend is expected to continue in the future. According to a report by Transparency Market Research, the global crowdfunding market is expected to grow at a CAGR of 16.8% from 2021 to 2028, reaching $28.8 billion by the end of 2028. This growth is attributed to the following trends:

Increased adoption of crowdfunding by non-profit organizations and social causes
Expansion of crowdfunding into emerging markets
The growth of equity crowdfunding, which allows investors to own a stake in a company
Integration of blockchain technology, which enables greater transparency and security in crowdfunding transactions
Potential Impact of Technology on Crowdfunding
Technology is expected to play a significant role in the future of crowdfunding, with the following areas having the potential to impact the industry:

Blockchain Technology: As mentioned above, blockchain technology offers increased transparency and security in crowdfunding transactions, which can help to reduce fraud and increase investor confidence. Additionally, blockchain-based crowdfunding platforms can offer greater flexibility and accessibility to investors and project creators.

Artificial Intelligence: AI has the potential to improve the efficiency and accuracy of crowdfunding campaigns by analyzing data on investor behavior and preferences. This can help project creators to tailor their campaigns to their target audience and increase the likelihood of success.

Virtual Reality: Virtual reality can provide a more immersive and engaging experience for investors and project creators, allowing them to better visualize and showcase their projects. This can help to increase the appeal of crowdfunding campaigns and attract more investors.

Opportunities and Challenges for Crowdfunding
While crowdfunding offers many opportunities for project creators and investors, it also presents several challenges that must be addressed to ensure its continued success. Some of these challenges include:

Increased competition: With the growing popularity of crowdfunding, there is a risk of increased competition among project creators, making it more difficult to attract funding.

Regulatory challenges: As discussed earlier, crowdfunding is subject to regulatory requirements that vary by jurisdiction. Compliance with these regulations can be challenging and may limit the growth of crowdfunding.

Risk of fraud: As with any form of investment, there is a risk of fraud in crowdfunding campaigns. This can lead to a loss of funds for investors and damage to the reputation of crowdfunding platforms.

Sustainability of projects: Some crowdfunding campaigns may be successful in raising funds but fail to deliver on their promised outcomes. This can lead to a loss of investor confidence and damage to the reputation of crowdfunding platforms.

Investor education: Many investors may not fully understand the risks and rewards associated with crowdfunding, which can lead to unrealistic expectations and disappointment.

Despite these challenges, there are also many opportunities for crowdfunding in the future, including:

Greater democratization of financing: Crowdfunding can provide access to financing for a wider range of individuals and projects, reducing the reliance on traditional sources of funding.

Increased social impact: Crowdfunding can be used to fund social causes and non-profit organizations, which can have a positive impact on society.

Innovation and entrepreneurship: Crowdfunding can support innovative and entrepreneurial projects that may not have access to traditional sources of funding.

Community building: Crowdfunding can help to build communities around projects, creating a sense of belonging and shared Expanding into new markets: Crowdfunding has the potential to reach new markets and demographics, such as emerging economies or underrepresented groups, providing opportunities for growth and expansion.

Integration with other technologies: Crowdfunding can be integrated with other emerging technologies, such as blockchain, to increase transparency, security, and efficiency.

However, in order to fully realize these opportunities, the crowdfunding industry will also need to address a number of challenges.

Regulatory uncertainty: As discussed earlier, regulations around crowdfunding can be complex and vary by jurisdiction. This can create uncertainty for both project creators and backers, and may limit the growth of the industry.

Crowding out of smaller projects: As the crowdfunding industry continues to grow, there is a risk that larger, more established projects will crowd out smaller, less well-known projects. This could limit the diversity and innovation within the industry.

Risk of fraud: Crowdfunding can also be vulnerable to fraud and scams, which can damage the reputation of the industry and undermine trust among backers.

Competition from traditional sources of funding: Although crowdfunding has the potential to democratize financing, traditional sources of funding such as banks and venture capitalists are still dominant players in the industry. Crowdfunding will need to continue to demonstrate its value and effectiveness in order to compete with these established sources of funding.

Conclusion

In conclusion, crowdfunding has emerged as a popular and effective way to finance a wide range of projects, from creative endeavors to social causes to innovative startups. While the industry faces a number of challenges, such as regulatory complexity and the risk of fraud, there are also many opportunities for growth and expansion in the future. As the industry continues to evolve and mature, it will be important to strike a balance between innovation and regulation, and to continue to build trust and confidence among backers and project creators alike.

CHAPTER 18 DERIVATIVES

Derivatives are financial instruments whose value is based on an underlying asset or set of assets. They can be used to manage risk or speculate on price movements, and they have become an important part of modern finance. This chapter will provide an in-depth analysis of derivatives, including their purpose in finance, their history, and their potential risks and benefits.

Explanation of Derivatives

Derivatives are contracts between two parties that are based on an underlying asset or set of assets. The value of the contract is based on the value of the underlying asset, and the contract specifies the terms of the transaction. There are many different types of derivatives, including options, futures, swaps, and forwards.

Derivatives are used for a variety of purposes, including hedging and speculation. Hedging is the process of using derivatives to reduce risk, while speculation involves taking a position in a derivative in order to profit from price movements.

History of Derivatives

The use of derivatives dates back to ancient times, when farmers would use forward contracts to sell their crops in advance of the harvest. In the modern era, derivatives have become more complex and sophisticated, and they are now used by a wide range of financial institutions and investors.

The modern derivatives market began to develop in the 1970s, when the Chicago Board Options Exchange was founded. This led to the development of new types of derivatives, including futures contracts and options. The growth of the derivatives market accelerated in the 1980s and 1990s, as financial institutions began to use derivatives to manage risk and speculate on price movements.

Types of Derivatives

There are many different types of derivatives, including options, futures, swaps, and forwards. Each type of derivative has its own unique characteristics and uses.

Options are contracts that give the holder the right, but not the obligation, to buy or sell an underlying asset at a specified price within a specified time period. Options can be used for hedging or speculation.

Futures are contracts that obligate the buyer or seller to buy or sell an underlying asset at a specified price and date in the future. Futures are often used to hedge against price movements in the underlying asset.

Swaps are contracts in which two parties agree to exchange cash flows based on the value of an underlying asset. Swaps can be used to manage risk or to speculate on price movements.

Forwards are contracts in which two parties agree to buy or sell an underlying asset at a specified price at a specified time in the future. Forwards are often used in commodity markets to lock in prices.

Benefits and Risks of Derivatives

Derivatives have many potential benefits, including the ability to manage risk, increase liquidity, and provide price discovery. However, they also carry significant risks, including the potential for large losses and systemic risk.

One of the main benefits of derivatives is their ability to manage risk. For example, a farmer could use a forward contract to sell their crops in advance of the harvest, reducing their exposure to price fluctuations. Derivatives can also increase liquidity in markets, making it easier for buyers and sellers to find each other.

However, derivatives can also be used for speculative purposes, which can lead to large losses. For example, a hedge fund might use options to bet on the price of a stock, and if the bet goes wrong, the fund could lose a significant amount of money.

Derivatives also carry systemic risk, which means that a failure of one institution or market participant could have a ripple effect on the entire financial system. This was evident during the 2008 financial crisis, when the failure of Lehman Brothers, a major derivatives dealer, had a significant impact on the global financial system

Types of Derivatives

Explanation of different types of derivatives, including

Derivatives are financial instruments that derive their value from an underlying asset or group of assets. The value of derivatives is based on the price of the underlying asset or assets, but they allow investors to speculate or hedge against the future price movements of the asset without actually owning the underlying asset. Derivatives can be traded on organized exchanges or over-the-counter (OTC) markets.

There are various types of derivatives, but some of the most common types include futures contracts, options contracts, swaps, and forwards contracts. In this section, we will explain each type of derivative in detail.

Futures Contracts

A futures contract is a standardized agreement between two parties to buy or sell a specified asset at a predetermined price and at a specific time in the future. Futures contracts are traded on organized exchanges, and they are often used by investors to speculate or hedge against the future price movements of commodities, currencies, and financial instruments such as stocks, bonds, and indices.

Futures contracts have several key features, including:

Standardization: Futures contracts are standardized in terms of the quality, quantity, and delivery date of the underlying asset. This ensures that all parties to the contract know exactly what they are buying or selling.

Margin Requirements: Futures contracts require the parties to the contract to put up a margin, which is a percentage of the total contract value, as collateral. This helps to ensure that the parties will fulfill their obligations under the contract.

Marking-to-market: Futures contracts are marked-to-market, which means that the gains and losses on the contract are settled on a daily basis.

Options Contracts

An options contract is a derivative contract that gives the holder the right, but not the obligation, to buy or sell an underlying asset at a predetermined price and within a specified time period. There are two types of options: call options and put options.

A call option gives the holder the right to buy the underlying asset at the predetermined price, while a put option gives the holder the right to sell the underlying asset at the predetermined price. Options contracts are traded on organized exchanges and over-the-counter (OTC) markets.

Options contracts have several key features, including:

Premium: The holder of an options contract pays a premium to the seller of the contract for the right to buy or sell the underlying asset at the predetermined price.

Strike price: The predetermined price at which the underlying asset can be bought or sold is known as the strike price.

Expiration date: The expiration date is the date by which the options contract must be exercised or it will expire worthless.

Swaps

A swap is a derivative contract in which two parties agree to exchange cash flows based on a notional amount. Swaps are often used by investors to hedge against interest rate risks, foreign exchange rate risks, and credit risks.

There are several types of swaps, including interest rate swaps, currency swaps, and credit default swaps.

Interest rate swaps involve exchanging a fixed interest rate for a floating interest rate. Currency swaps involve exchanging one currency for another at an agreed exchange rate. Credit default swaps involve exchanging the risk of default on a particular bond or loan.

Forwards Contracts

A forward contract is a customized agreement between two parties to buy or sell an underlying asset at a predetermined price and at a specific time in the future. Unlike futures contracts, forwards contracts are not traded on organized exchanges, and they are often used to hedge against specific risks in a portfolio.

Forwards contracts have several key features, including:

Customization: Forwards contracts can be customized to fit the specific needs of the parties involved, including the quantity, quality, and delivery date of the underlying asset.

Margin requirements: Forwards contracts may or may not require the parties to the contract to put up a margin deposit. If a margin is required, it is typically only a small percentage of the total value of the contract.

Credit risk: Since forwards contracts are not traded on exchanges and are not guaranteed by a clearinghouse, there is a risk that one of the parties involved in the contract may default on their obligations.

Examples of forwards contracts can be found in a variety of markets, including commodities, currencies, and interest rates. For instance, a coffee grower may enter into a forwards contract to sell a certain amount of coffee beans at a fixed price to a coffee roaster at a specified date in the future. This protects the grower from fluctuations in the price of coffee and allows them to lock in a price for their product ahead of time.

Similarly, a company that needs to purchase a large amount of a certain commodity, such as steel, may enter into a forwards contract with a supplier to buy a specific quantity of steel at a predetermined price and delivery date in the future. This allows the company to budget for its expenses and protects against unexpected price fluctuations.

Conclusion

In conclusion, futures contracts, options contracts, swaps, and forwards contracts are important tools used in the world of finance to manage risk, speculate on price movements, and hedge against specific risks in a portfolio. Each of these derivatives has its unique features and risks, and it is important for investors to understand how they work before using them. When used correctly, derivatives can be powerful instruments to help investors achieve their financial objectives. However, they can also be complex and risky, and investors should carefully consider their risk tolerance and financial goals before investing in them.

Risk Management and Derivatives

In today's fast-paced and unpredictable financial markets, risk management has become a crucial component of financial decision making. One of the key tools used in risk management is derivatives. Derivatives are financial instruments that derive their value from an underlying asset or group of assets. They are widely used in financial markets to manage risk and to speculate on price movements. In this section, we will discuss how derivatives are used in risk management and how they can be used to hedge against various types of risk.

How Derivatives are Used in Risk Management:

Derivatives are widely used in risk management to reduce or eliminate exposure to various types of risk. Some of the most common types of risk that derivatives are used to manage include:

Market Risk: Market risk refers to the risk of loss due to changes in market prices. This type of risk can be managed using derivatives such as futures, options, and swaps.

Credit Risk: Credit risk refers to the risk of loss due to the default of a counterparty. Credit risk can be managed using derivatives such as credit default swaps.

Currency Risk: Currency risk refers to the risk of loss due to changes in exchange rates. This type of risk can be managed using derivatives such as currency forwards and options.

Interest Rate Risk: Interest rate risk refers to the risk of loss due to changes in interest rates. This type of risk can be managed using derivatives such as interest rate swaps and options.

Liquidity Risk: Liquidity risk refers to the risk of loss due to the inability to sell an asset at a reasonable price. This type of risk can be managed using derivatives such as futures and options.

How Derivatives can be Used to Hedge Against Various Types of Risk:

Derivatives can be used to hedge against various types of risk. The use of derivatives to hedge against risk involves taking a position in a derivative instrument that is opposite to an existing position in an underlying asset. The objective is to reduce or eliminate the risk associated with the underlying asset.

Futures Contracts: Futures contracts are often used to hedge against market risk. For example, a farmer who is growing corn may enter into a futures contract to sell a certain amount of corn at a predetermined price on a future date. By doing so, the farmer has locked in a price for the corn and has reduced the risk of a decline in market prices.

Options Contracts: Options contracts can be used to hedge against both market risk and currency risk. For example, an importer who needs to pay for goods in a foreign currency may purchase a currency option to hedge against the risk of a decline in the value of the currency.

Swaps: Swaps are often used to hedge against interest rate risk. For example, a company with a variable-rate loan may enter into an interest rate swap to convert the loan to a fixed-rate loan. By doing so, the company has reduced the risk of an increase in interest rates.

Forwards Contracts: Forwards contracts can be used to hedge against various types of risk, including currency risk and commodity price risk. For example, a company that imports oil may enter into a forward contract to buy a certain amount of oil at a predetermined price on a future date. By doing so, the company has reduced the risk of a price increase in the future.

Conclusion:

In conclusion, derivatives play an important role in risk management. They are widely used in financial markets to manage various types of risk, including market risk, credit risk, currency risk, interest rate risk, and liquidity risk. Derivatives can be used to hedge against these types of risk by taking positions in derivative instruments that are opposite to existing positions in underlying assets. The use of derivatives in risk management requires careful analysis and understanding of the risks involved. By using derivatives effectively, financial institutions and other market participants can minimize their exposure to risk and improve their overall financial stability.

However, it is important to note that derivatives can also be used for speculative purposes, which can lead to excessive risk-taking and contribute to financial instability. Therefore, it is essential that the use of derivatives be subject to appropriate regulatory oversight to ensure their proper use and prevent excessive risk-taking.

Finally, it is worth noting that while derivatives can be powerful tools for risk management, they are not a panacea. They cannot eliminate all risk, and their use requires a clear understanding of the risks involved. As with any financial instrument, there are potential downsides and risks associated with the use of derivatives. Nevertheless, when used appropriately and with proper risk management techniques, derivatives can be an effective means of mitigating risk in financial markets.

Benefits and Drawbacks of Derivatives

Derivatives have become increasingly popular in recent years due to the various benefits they offer. However, there are also drawbacks associated with their use. This section will discuss the benefits and drawbacks of using derivatives in more detail.

Benefits of Using Derivatives

Increased Liquidity

One of the primary benefits of using derivatives is increased liquidity. Derivatives allow investors to buy or sell assets without actually owning them. This means that investors can quickly and easily enter or exit positions, making it easier to manage their portfolio. This increased liquidity can lead to lower transaction costs, as investors can easily buy and sell derivative instruments without having to deal with the underlying assets themselves.

Reduced Transaction Costs

Derivatives also offer reduced transaction costs compared to buying or selling the underlying asset directly. For example, buying or selling a futures contract typically involves lower transaction costs than buying or selling the underlying asset. This is because futures contracts are traded on organized exchanges, which offer standardized contracts and centralized clearing. This makes it easier to match buyers and sellers, reducing transaction costs and improving market liquidity.

Greater Flexibility

Derivatives also offer greater flexibility compared to traditional investments. Investors can use derivatives to take positions on various market factors, such as interest rates, currencies, and commodities, without having to invest directly in these assets. This flexibility can be particularly useful for investors who want to diversify their portfolio or manage risk in a more targeted way.

Drawbacks of Using Derivatives

High Levels of Complexity

One of the primary drawbacks of using derivatives is their high levels of complexity. Derivatives can be difficult to understand and analyze, especially for investors who are not familiar with financial markets. This complexity can make it difficult for investors to assess the risks and potential rewards associated with derivative instruments, increasing the likelihood of making poor investment decisions.

Risk of Large Losses if not Used Correctly

Another major drawback of using derivatives is the risk of large losses if they are not used correctly. Derivatives are highly leveraged instruments, which means that investors can potentially lose more than their initial investment. For example, if an investor buys a futures contract and the price of the underlying asset falls, the investor may be required to provide additional margin to cover the losses. If the investor is unable to provide the required margin, they may be forced to close their position at a loss. This risk of large losses can make derivatives unsuitable for inexperienced investors or those who are not willing to take on higher levels of risk.

Potential for Market Manipulation

Finally, derivatives have the potential for market manipulation. Because derivatives are highly leveraged and often traded in large volumes, they can have a significant impact on market prices. This means that large investors or institutions may be able to manipulate prices by taking large positions in derivative instruments. This can lead to market distortions and increase volatility, making it difficult for other investors to make informed investment decisions.

Conclusion

Derivatives offer various benefits, including increased liquidity, reduced transaction costs, and greater flexibility. However, they also have drawbacks, such as high levels of complexity, the risk of large losses if not used correctly, and the potential for market manipulation. Investors should carefully consider the benefits and drawbacks of using derivative instruments and seek professional advice if they are unsure about their suitability for their investment objectives and risk tolerance.

Criticisms of Derivatives

Derivatives have been criticized for their role in the 2008 financial crisis, concerns over speculative trading, and ethics concerns over their use in certain industries. In this section, we will discuss these criticisms in more detail.

Role in the 2008 Financial Crisis

One of the most significant criticisms of derivatives is their role in the 2008 financial crisis. Derivatives played a significant role in the crisis as many financial institutions held complex derivative positions that they did not fully understand. When the housing market collapsed, these positions resulted in significant losses for many institutions, leading to a widespread financial crisis.

The use of derivatives, particularly credit default swaps (CDS), was one of the factors that contributed to the crisis. CDS are derivatives that provide insurance against default on bonds and other types of debt. They were heavily used by financial institutions to hedge against the risk of default on mortgage-backed securities (MBS) and other structured products. However, these instruments were often sold without adequate collateral and in excessive amounts, leading to the potential for systemic risk.

Concerns over Speculative Trading

Another criticism of derivatives is the concern over speculative trading. Derivatives are often used by investors to speculate on future market movements. While this can provide liquidity to markets and increase efficiency, it can also lead to volatility and market instability.

Speculative trading can lead to a situation where a large number of investors are betting on the same outcome, creating a self-fulfilling prophecy. For example, if a large number of investors are betting that the price of a commodity will increase, they may buy up large quantities of that commodity, driving up the price and making their bets more profitable. This can create a bubble that eventually bursts, resulting in significant losses for many investors.

Ethics Concerns over their Use in Certain Industries

Derivatives have also been criticized for their use in certain industries, particularly the energy and food industries. In these industries, derivatives are often used to hedge against the risk of price fluctuations. For example, a food company may use derivatives to hedge against the risk of a rise in the price of wheat, which is a key ingredient in their products.

However, critics argue that this use of derivatives can lead to market manipulation and price volatility. In the energy industry, derivatives have been used to manipulate the price of oil and gas. In the food industry, derivatives have been used to manipulate the price of agricultural commodities.

Conclusion

Derivatives have been subject to a number of criticisms, including their role in the 2008 financial crisis, concerns over speculative trading, and ethics concerns over their use in certain industries. While derivatives can provide many benefits, such as increased liquidity, reduced transaction costs, and greater flexibility, it is important to be aware of these criticisms and to use derivatives in a responsible and ethical manner.

Regulation of Derivatives

Derivatives are financial instruments whose values are derived from underlying assets. They are widely used in financial markets to manage risk, enhance liquidity, and provide investment opportunities. However, derivatives can also pose significant risks to financial stability and investor protection. As a result, regulators around the world have implemented a range of regulations to oversee the use of derivatives in financial markets.

Overview of current regulations surrounding derivatives

Derivative regulations vary across jurisdictions, but they generally fall into two categories: market-based and entity-based regulations.

Market-based regulations are designed to promote transparency, improve price discovery, and reduce counterparty risk in derivatives markets. Some examples of market-based regulations include:

Mandatory reporting: Financial firms are required to report their derivative transactions to a trade repository, which allows regulators to monitor and analyze derivatives activity.

Central clearing: Many jurisdictions require standardized derivatives contracts to be cleared through a central counterparty clearinghouse (CCP). This helps to reduce counterparty risk by ensuring that both parties to a trade have sufficient collateral to cover potential losses.

Margin requirements: Margin requirements are the amount of collateral that financial firms must post to cover potential losses on their derivative positions. Margin requirements help to ensure that market participants have sufficient financial resources to meet their obligations.

Entity-based regulations focus on the activities of specific financial institutions, such as banks and investment firms, and aim to reduce systemic risk in the financial system. Some examples of entity-based regulations include:

Capital requirements: Banks and other financial institutions are required to hold sufficient capital to absorb potential losses on their derivative positions.

Stress testing: Financial institutions are required to conduct stress tests to assess their ability to withstand adverse market conditions.

Volcker Rule: The Volcker Rule, which is part of the Dodd-Frank Wall Street Reform and Consumer Protection Act in the US, prohibits banks from engaging in proprietary trading and limits their investments in hedge funds and private equity funds.

Discussion of potential future regulations and their impact on the use of derivatives

There are ongoing debates about the appropriate level of regulation for derivatives markets. Some argue that current regulations do not go far enough to address the potential risks posed by derivatives, while others argue that excessive regulation could stifle innovation and liquidity in financial markets.

Some potential future regulations that have been proposed include:

Transaction taxes: Transaction taxes, which are taxes on financial transactions, have been proposed as a way to reduce speculative trading and generate revenue for governments. However, critics argue that transaction taxes could increase transaction costs and reduce liquidity in financial markets.

Position limits: Position limits are caps on the size of derivative positions that market participants can hold. Position limits are intended to prevent market manipulation and reduce systemic risk. However, critics argue that position limits could reduce liquidity and hinder risk management strategies.

Clearinghouse resilience: Clearinghouses play a crucial role in reducing counterparty risk in derivatives markets. However, if a clearinghouse were to fail, it could have significant repercussions for financial stability. Some experts have called for increased regulation of clearinghouses to ensure their resilience.

The impact of these potential regulations on the use of derivatives is difficult to predict. Some regulations, such as transaction taxes and position limits, could reduce the use of derivatives by increasing costs and reducing liquidity. Other regulations, such as increased oversight of clearinghouses, could improve market stability and increase confidence in derivatives markets.

Conclusion

Regulation of derivatives is a complex and ongoing process. While regulations can help to mitigate the risks posed by derivatives, they can also have unintended consequences, such as reducing liquidity and hindering risk management strategies. As such, regulators must strike a balance between protecting investors and promoting market efficiency. The future of derivative regulation is likely to be shaped by ongoing debates and discussions about the appropriate level of oversight for financial markets

Conclusion

In this chapter, we have explored the complex world of derivatives and their role in finance. We have examined the various types of derivatives, their functions, and their uses in risk management and speculation. We have also discussed the benefits and drawbacks of derivatives, as well as the criticisms and regulatory issues surrounding their use.

Key points from this chapter include:

Derivatives are financial instruments whose value is derived from an underlying asset or reference rate.
The main types of derivatives are futures, options, swaps, and forwards.
Derivatives are used for risk management, speculation, and arbitrage.
The benefits of derivatives include increased liquidity, reduced transaction costs, and greater flexibility.

The drawbacks of derivatives include their high levels of complexity, the risk of large losses if not used correctly, and the potential for market manipulation.

Derivatives have been criticized for their role in the 2008 financial crisis, concerns over speculative trading, and ethics concerns over their use in certain industries.

Derivatives are regulated by various governmental bodies, including the SEC and the CFTC, but the regulations surrounding derivatives are complex and constantly evolving.

Final Thoughts

The use of derivatives in finance has grown rapidly over the past few decades, and their importance in financial markets cannot be overstated. While derivatives offer significant benefits in terms of risk management and speculation, they also come with significant drawbacks and criticisms.

Despite the criticisms and regulatory challenges, the future of derivatives is likely to be one of continued growth and evolution. As technology advances and financial markets become increasingly interconnected, derivatives are likely to play an even greater role in finance in the years to come.

However, as the use of derivatives continues to expand, it is important for regulators to ensure that appropriate oversight is in place to protect investors and promote market stability. The ongoing debates and discussions about the appropriate level of oversight for financial markets are likely to shape the future of derivative regulation, and it is important for all stakeholders to remain engaged in these discussions.

Overall, while derivatives are a complex and often misunderstood area of finance, their importance in financial markets is clear. As such, it is essential for all market participants to have a basic understanding of derivatives and their role in finance, in order to make informed investment decisions and to contribute to the ongoing discussions surrounding their use and regulation.

www.ingramcontent.com/pod-product-compliance
Lightning Source LLC
Chambersburg PA
CBHW082003190326
41458CB00010B/3049